Love's Uncertainty

Love's Uncertainty

THE POLITICS AND ETHICS OF CHILD REARING
IN CONTEMPORARY CHINA

Teresa Kuan

UNIVERSITY OF CALIFORNIA PRESS

University of California Press, one of the most distinguished university presses in the United States, enriches lives around the world by advancing scholarship in the humanities, social sciences, and natural sciences. Its activities are supported by the UC Press Foundation and by philanthropic contributions from individuals and institutions. For more information, visit www.ucpress.edu.

University of California Press
Oakland, California

Library of Congress Cataloging-in-Publication Data

Kuan, Teresa.
    Love's Uncertainty : The politics and ethics of child rearing in contemporary China / Teresa Kuan.
        p.   cm.
    Includes bibliographical references and index.
    ISBN 978-0-520-28348-0 (cloth : alk. paper)
    ISBN 978-0-520-28350-3 (pbk. : alk. paper)
    ISBN 978-0-520-95936-1 (ebook)
    1. Child rearing—China—History—21st century.   2. Child rearing—China.   3. Parenting—China.   4. Education—Parent participation—China.   5. Homebound instruction—China.   I. Title.
    HQ792.C5.K83   2015
    649'.109510905—dc23   2014029031

Manufactured in the United States of America

24   23   22   21   20   19   18   17   16   15
10   9   8   7   6   5   4   3   2   1

In keeping with a commitment to support environmentally responsible and sustainable printing practices, UC Press has printed this book on Natures Natural, a fiber that contains 30% post-consumer waste and meets the minimum requirements of ANSI/NISO Z39.48–1992 (R 1997) (*Permanence of Paper*).

To my parents, who are nothing short of exemplary

The character of brickwork is such that its charm derives from the effects of aging, irregularity, and even imperfections.

ANDREW PLUMRIDGE AND WIM MEULENKAMP
Brickwork: Architecture and Design

CONTENTS

Acknowledgments xi

Introduction 1

1 · The Politics of Childhood 30

2 · The Horrific and the Exemplary 62

3 · "The Heart Says One Thing but the Hand Does Another" 85

4 · Creating *Tiaojian,* or, The Art of Disposition 110

5 · The Defeat of Maternal Logic in Televisual Space 140

6 · Investing in Human Capital, Conserving Life Energies 162

7 · Banking in Affects 186

Conclusion 208

Notes 213
Bibliography 229
Index 245

ACKNOWLEDGMENTS

This book began as a dissertation project funded by a US Department of Education Title VI Foreign Language and Area Studies Fellowship Award, administered through the University of Southern California East Asian Studies Center. A Hunt Postdoctoral Fellowship, provided by the Wenner-Gren Foundation for Anthropological Research, supported the bulk of the dissertation to book revision. I am especially grateful to the latter for their support of young scholars and the development of anthropological theory. I began to formulate some of the ideas presented in this book when I was an Andrew W. Mellon Postdoctoral Fellow at Whittier College. I am indebted to Ann Kakaliouras, my faculty mentor at Whittier, and to Sealing Cheng, an unofficial mentor at the Chinese University of Hong Kong, for their efforts in protecting my space for writing.

I am especially lucky to have had the opportunity to work with Cheryl Mattingly, my dissertation supervisor. Her way of thinking—about narrative reasoning, the vulnerability of human action, and ethical predicaments—has been a tremendous source of inspiration. I have learned not only how to understand people but also how to understand for myself this thing called life. Gene Cooper's demand for clear, jargon-free arguments, his encouragement that I familiarize myself with the "primeval slime," made me a better scholar and writer. Charlotte Furth got me thinking more historically. Her feedback encouraged me to be more conversant with the research coming out of Asian studies, thereby broadening my view. Thanks to Stan Rosen for always answering, in great detail, my many questions. All errors are my own.

A brief encounter with Hugh Raffles, who recommended Jullien's *The Propensity of Things,* led me to much-needed clarity on how to formulate a coherent theoretical framework. I am also grateful to Jie Yang for many stimulating conversations and helpful recommendations. I benefited tremendously from my time with the Mind, Medicine, and Culture group at the University of California, Los Angeles. Thanks to Doug Hollan for sponsoring me as a visiting scholar, to Carole Browner for making me feel so welcome, and to the rest of the MMAC community for helpful feedback and inspiring conversations. Linda Garro's and Elinor Ochs's comments at an MMAC presentation led to some of the comparative observations made in this book.

My interest in China began in 1999, many thanks to Jean Hung, who introduced me to the late Professor Wang Zhusheng. He kindly gave an inexperienced college graduate the opportunity to teach a visual anthropology class at Yunnan University. Through Professor Wang I met Yang Hui, who sponsored my research a few years later. She made important introductions, gave helpful advice, and embraced me like a daughter. Her kindness is immeasurable. Thanks also to Jay Brown, He Jiangyu, Stefan and Sylvia Kratz, Mike Xu, Yang Yuyu, and Yu Ming—friends in Kunming—for their insights, hospitality, and introductions.

Many former teachers, classmates, and colleagues have animated this journey: Ann Anagnost, Erica Angert, Tami Blumenfield, Joe Bosco, Susanne Bregnbæk, Ju-chen Chen, Sealing Cheng, Sidney Cheung, Jenny Chio, Jenny Cool, Arianne Gaetano, Tricia Gilson, Kathy Hon, Janet Hoskins, Lanita Jacobs, Danny Jauregui, Matthew Kohrman, Anita Kumar, Nancy Lutkehaus, Veronica Mak, Hanna Mantila, Gordon Mathews, Steven Rousso-Schindler, Zhifang Song, Danning Wang, Kaming Wu, Lorin Yochim, and Huang Yu. My dearly remembered dissertation writing group— Jason Ingersoll, Lili Lai, and John Osburg—read earlier versions. Arianne Gaetano especially helped with chapter 5. My "sisters" Melissa Park and Lone Grøn have been there since the very beginning. MPhil supervisees cheered me on at the end. And a shout out to the homeys.

Andrew Gura gave me my first lessons in good writing. Jin Lu gave important practical advice. Kate Fung and Stacy Eisenstark helped with the cover image. The many students who have passed through the MA program in the Department of Anthropology at the Chinese University of Hong Kong have given me a clearer sense of purpose. A thousand thanks to Reed Malcolm for his support of this project, to the anonymous reviewers, and to Vanessa Fong and Andrew Kipnis, reviewers who revealed their identity. Thanks to Elisabeth Magnus for her meticulous editorial work.

Finally, I am thankful to the various people who spoke to me—the teachers, administrators, psychiatrists, and psychological counselors who took time out of their busy schedules, and especially Zhou Ting, for allowing me to follow her so closely. My deepest gratitude goes to the families—they opened their homes and their hearts. I wish you all happiness and prosperity; may every day of your life be cheerful and bright.

I dedicate this book to my own family, and to our parents especially, who have taught us so much about ethics and the art of living.

Introduction

CHEN JIALING HAD NOTHING BUT GOOD INTENTIONS when it came to her daughter Precious, but she could be a little heavy-handed. Like the time she reached for a little notebook of mine, where Precious, who had invited me to visit her third-grade classroom, had just finished writing the name of her school, along with her room number. Mom just wanted to make sure the writing was acceptably legible. She probably also figured she could divine the child's propensity for conscientiousness in the handwriting while she was at it. This of course was extremely irritating to Precious, who pulled the notebook close to her chest.

Embarrassed, Chen Jialing turned to me and explained, "Precious doesn't like it when we check her homework."

For Chen Jialing, there was a delicate balance to be struck between raising a child who could compete in an intensely rigorous education system and respecting her child as an autonomous subject. The former required small acts of governance, like inspecting a casual exchange of information as if it were a homework assignment. The latter, an idea produced by a global discourse on good parenting, went against the intuition of the former. It was a discourse that carried serious and actual weight for this mother. After all, I had met this family in the psychiatric ward of a major hospital, where Precious was being treated for having "too much pressure"—as she herself told me.

The event had caused Mrs. Chen to reconsider her determination to fill her daughter's schedule with as many educational experiences as possible. Before the hospitalization, she, like so many of the parents around her, had packed Precious's life with learning activities, worried that if she failed to do so Precious would be outcompeted. After a week of school, the weekends would start with English from 8:30 to 12:00. After 12:00, mother and daughter would have lunch. Then it was off to violin class at 1:30 until 2:30, then drawing class from 3:00 until 6:00. Sundays were for bathing and completing school assignments to be handed in the next day.

Since Chen herself did not feel tired from all the shuttling back and forth, she figured Precious, being young and therefore more energetic, shouldn't have any problems either. But she was wrong. One night during the Spring Festival holiday in 2004, she got a call from her mother-in-law, with whom Precious had been staying. It came a couple hours past midnight. Precious had been throwing a fit of some kind. She was crying uncontrollably: about not being able to sleep, about a discomfort somewhere, something that didn't feel right. Both Chen and Precious's father arrived, and the family eventually decided to take the girl to the hospital. They could not figure out what was wrong. Was it the chocolate she had eaten that afternoon? Had that kept her up? What was the nature of her discomfort?

They went to the pediatrics department first and got sent up to psychiatry, where the doctor made a tentative conclusion and wrote a prescription for Deanxit and a sedative. Later, close to dawn, Chen Jialing was completely dismayed when Precious's "symptoms" began to flare up again. She started to throw the same fit, crying about a terrible itch under her skin, thudding the ground with her foot. Only when the sedative started to take effect did Precious finally doze off in her mother's arms.

In the weeks to follow, the mysterious and unbearable itch continued. It began to manifest even when Precious was at school. At home, her temper grew "weird." She would get frustrated easily, even angry, and continued to have trouble sleeping. Another hospital visit to gynecology, still another to neurology, a CT scan that turned up nothing, a second psychiatric opinion on the first diagnosis, a prescription change from Deanxit to Prozac, and still the symptoms not only persisted but became more frequent at home and in class. Precious's temper continued to worsen, and she demanded to play games she had long grown out of, such as hide-and-seek and guessing colors. An otherwise serious student, Precious became careless with her homework assignments.

Another visit to the doctor followed, along with a prescription change from Prozac to Seroxat, which was supposed to stabilize her emotions, and a certain psychotropic drug named Biwusuanna, because Precious had become physically aggressive toward her parents. Still, after a couple of weeks, there was no improvement. So during yet another hospital visit it was suggested that Precious participate in psychotherapy as an inpatient, where, according to the doctor, things would be more "systematic." It was at this point that I first met Precious and her parents.

By the time I sat Chen Jialing down for an interview, the situation had improved. But it wasn't because of anything the hospital had done. She told me, "My feeling is that we didn't really get anything out of it. And I don't know if it was any good for her." Moments later, she said the same thing again, only with more conviction: "Nothing came of it, I'm telling you." The "systematic psychotherapy" she had expected never materialized.[1] But there was this unexpected surprise: Precious was happy at the hospital. She got along with everybody—the doctors, the nurses, even the stark raving mad teenager who would go around reciting famous texts, claiming to be the original author. When I visited the ward, it was Precious who approached me and chatted me up, turning the nurses' station into a social gathering place.

If anything, Chen felt, Precious's improvement had more to do with a decision she and Precious's father made to move back into the old neighborhood, where they had lived since the day Precious was born. The old neighborhood was full of neighborly intimacy because all the families used to work for the same work unit—a holdover from the socialist years. In the new residential community, located in a newly developed area of Kunming, they knew no one, not even the household across from their flat. In the old neighborhood there had been at least six other children also born in the Year of the Pig, but in the new neighborhood children did not play outside. At the time, Chen saw this as an additional boon to more upscale living, thinking, "*Aiya*, having no friends is the best! You have more time to study." But she came to see this as a mistake, as having "ignored the child's nature." Precious was actually very lonely.

What is more, maybe Chen had *added* pressure to the pressure teachers were already giving. In the first grade, Precious had a teacher who would keep talking even after the bell rang, until the start of the next class period. Even if Precious had to use the restroom, she would not dare to raise her hand, so she would hold it for so long she eventually went in her pants. Already a very "self-aware" and "earnest" kind of person, Precious would even wake up in the middle of the night to check that her backpack was packed for the next day. She would set her alarm for 5:30 in the morning, worried she might be late—because the teacher would scold and publicly shame students for all sorts of reasons: for tardiness, for incomplete or missing homework assignments, for forgetting books, and for daydreaming.

The whole course of events got Chen thinking about "respect"—especially the importance of respecting a child's opinion—a notion that had become quite popular among middle-class parents thanks to mass-mediated popular advice. She decided she would no longer "force" any interests on Precious and that she would enroll her daughter only in the classes that she herself expressed interest in. Before the illness incident she had arranged extracurricular learning with great determination, thinking, "The competition will be so fierce later, if you don't have a specialty, you won't be able to adapt to society." When Precious protested having to practice her violin, she would get a scolding. "*Aiya*, she would cry, she would play holding her tears."

"All that," Chen said, thinking back, "was really a little cruel."

I open this book with Chen Jialing and her daughter's story to evoke the pressures that shape middle-class family life in contemporary China. Although their encounter with psychiatry and pharmaceuticals was unusual, the events surrounding Precious's illness point to a number of shared experiences: the stresses of urban life, the rigor of school discipline, the intensification of social competition, the emergence of a psychological common sense, and the intensification of maternal labor in the face of uncertain futures. I originally began the project that led to this book with the intent of collecting ethnographic material on the medicalization of childhood in China, having been inspired by Margaret Lock's work on the invention of "school refusal syndrome" in Japan—a condition in which a child apparently *wants* to go to school but ends up spending the day in bed. School refusal syndrome was just one of many "diseases of civilization" that also included "apartment neurosis" and "salaryman depression." Together these categories rendered social problems recognizable and amenable to medical management in 1980s' Japan (Lock 1991: 511–12).

I thought I might find something similar in China, since I had seen, in preliminary research, the phrase "psychological health" littered all over popular magazines and professional literature addressed to adults who dealt with children. I wondered if the discourse on psychological health extended to clinical forms of management. As in Japan, there seemed to be a deep concern with the psychological well-being of children, so I presumed that in China as well I might find a medicalization of social issues, similarly focused on the body of the child. But when I began my fieldwork in 2004, I had trouble. The medicalization of childhood was not a pervasive enough phenomenon to study—at least this was the view from Kunming, a smallish city in the southwestern interior. I eventually came to realize that China's response to childhood and adolescent distress was more pedagogical than medical.

While Precious's case is unique, there is in fact a widespread concern with the psychological well-being of children in Chinese society. Granted, mind-body health and well-being is not the *only* concern. The race among parents to raise an outstanding child, the race among teachers to produce outstanding test scores, and the race among schools to achieve outstanding rates of promotion usually trump all other considerations, with "educational desire" being very intense (Kipnis 2011). But the common and pervasive desire for educational achievement is simultaneously accompanied by the specter of psychological unhealthiness. For Chen Jialing, it was her own unsettling personal experience that led her to reconsider her zeal to keep her daughter ahead of the competition. For another parent, it could be the experience of a neighbor or a coworker, a niece or a nephew, or perhaps just the nine-year-old they read about in the newspaper—the one who drank poison in a suicide attempt.

That psychological health has come to matter is partly related to what Yunxiang Yan (2011) has identified as the changing moral landscape and the individualization of what constitutes happiness and life meaning, partly to the very real pressures and stresses of life under market capitalism, and partly to the political instrumentalization of psychological discourse in promoting national revitalization and protecting "social harmony."[2] This emergence has not necessarily extended to the medicalization of childhood. Instead, the problem of psychological health is primarily construed as an educational issue that concerns all of society.[3] Party organizations, schools, communities, and parents—all are to take responsibility for ensuring the psychological health of young people. By the turn of the twenty-first century, the notion of "psychological health" (*xinli jiankang*) had become an official policy-level concern. Schools, from the primary level all the way up to the universities, were to incorporate the promotion of psychological health into curriculum design—with some schools going so far as to offer required courses on psychological health and stress management. Communities were to take more responsibility for ensuring wholesome environments and for offering healthy activities for young people to participate in. And parents, meanwhile, were to learn how to control their urgent wishes and autocratic styles, as guided by the child-rearing experts.

Popular advice for parents is widely disseminated through state and popular channels in China. One may find it in advice manuals, popular television shows and magazines, local newspapers, online discussions, lectures organized by schools, and one's circle of friends and family. When Chen Jialing mentions the importance of respecting a child's opinion, she invokes an increasingly common idea that children ought to be respected as autonomous subjects who have a right to self-determination (Naftali 2009, 2010). When she questions her own assumptions about what an adult may expect of a child, she exercises the kind of self-reflexivity experts hope all parents can learn. Chen Jialing's experience is part of a larger trend toward child-centeredness in Chinese society, one that began with the one-child policy decades ago and later was reinforced by expert definitions of good parenting as parenting that attends to inner life of the child. This is significant, culturally speaking, because Chinese socialization puts a premium on cultivating children's relational sensitivity, so as to rear the kind of person who can coexist in a community of others, adept at reading subtle cues and anticipating needs. Psychological interiority is quite irrelevant in a social system that values relationships rather than individuals. Yet in the context of China's transition to market capitalism the notion of the psychological child with a rich but vulnerable inner life has emerged—or reappeared (see chapter 1).[4] The person who requires socialization in the family is no longer the immature child but rather the problematic parent.

The problematization of parental behavior is not unlike medicalization in that complex social problems are reduced to individual terms—most commonly to the mother who cannot control her hopes and emotions. The proliferation of advice does, however, differ in its aim to create change not merely at the level of the problematic individual but also, more significantly, at the level of culture itself. It is rather common to see statements such as this one in the advice literature, identifying problematic parenting as a cultural phenomenon: "One could say that the care and love that Chinese parents have for their children is number one in the world, but they love their children as if they were property, limiting their freedom, disregarding the child's basic rights" (Chen Shanyuan and Zhang 2003: 248).[5]

According to the popular experts, Chinese parents are too "nagging"; they "pull at sprouts to help them grow," "hate that iron does not become steel," "meddle in the affairs of others," "raise filial sons under the club," and "make mountains out of molehills"; they treat their children like "bonsai trees," "fine porcelain," and pieces of "private property"; and they govern so autocratically that personality, initiative, and creative potential—all qualities essential to scientific advancement and entrepreneurial success, and by extension to the revitalization of China as a great nation—are too easily wiped out. Chen Jialing typifies the kind of parent that would horrify the popular experts. But what is at stake for her? What is being obscured in constructions of the problematic parent? If the task of the cultural anthropologist is to explicate the logic behind seemingly problematic behavior, what can ethnography illuminate about something that on the surface might appear "cruel"— for example, expecting too much of a third grader? What is the experiential context in which her zeal makes sense?

This is a book about child rearing in the context of a major historical transformation—a transformation that has been and continues to be engineered by the state. In this context, engineering is no mere metaphor. The architects behind the one-child policy—implemented at the very beginning of the post-Mao period as the keystone of the government's modernization plan—were predominantly systems control engineers trained in cybernetics (Greenhalgh 2003). Quantitatively oriented, they saw the one-child policy, which would link the intimate lives of individual families to the programs of the state, as the only solution to a demographic crisis that would obstruct China's path toward modernization. At the same time, many of China's technocrats were also concerned with qualitative issues concerning the constitution of the human person, and they proposed plans based on their belief that economic modernization and the modernization of subjectivity went hand in hand. The first decade of the post-Mao period saw much discussion about "human modernization" (Bakken 2000: 60–66), with statist concerns getting translated into the popular domain. It is against this larger historical background of controlled transformation that the everyday lives of families ought to be situated. In China, child rearing is both a private and a political matter.

But this book is not merely about the politics of child rearing. It takes as its central question the problem of moral agency in contemporary life. In a context where so much seems to be determined "from above" and constrained by what's around, is it still possible to theorize human action without reducing lived experience to large-scale historical processes? I begin this book with the story of Chen Jialing and Precious because they represent two key sites of biopolitical knowledge and control in the government of post-Mao society: the "good mother" and the "high-quality child." These are subject positions that belong to a regime of normalization unique to China's population concerns and governmental techniques (Greenhalgh and Winckler 2005). Although this political reality cannot be ignored, it would be an unfortunate mistake, and conceit, to assume that the lives of ordinary people are best explained with reference to a larger social order. Surely it is the job of the social scientist to establish connections between the micro and the macro, but in the case of interpreting contemporary China especially, one must stay very close to the ethnographic material at hand.

Chinese social reality is tremendously contradictory and inconsistent, and this poses constant challenges for actors on the ground—challenges that require the reconciliation of contradictory moral goods and the location of opportunities for exercising personal efficacy. The opening case resonates with the frenetic lives of middle-class families in developed countries such as the United States, but family life in the Chinese context may be much more extreme because China is still a developing country, one challenged by imbalances of various kinds—for example, between population size and available resources, between the overproduction of college graduates and an economy unable to absorb the surplus of white-collar labor, between new norms for good parenting and the realities of social competition. These imbalances pose a great challenge to middle-class aspirations, generating a kind of anxiety and insecurity that is uniquely Chinese. The deep malaise permeating everyday life, in turn, mobilizes scripts for action that are also uniquely Chinese.

This book ultimately aims to soften an enduring tension in anthropological thought—the tension between humanist and antihumanist interpretation—by considering how the practical strategies of ordinary parents propose, rather quietly and unheroically, an alternative theory of power rooted in indigenous Chinese thought. The book will even go so far as to suggest that there exists some correspondence between the power of the state and the power of the person—between governmentality and the actor's concern with worldly efficacy. While conventional anthropological readings tend to slot the techniques of states and institutions into the "power" category, and the "responses" of ordinary people into the "agency" and "resistance" categories, I begin with the simple and perhaps obvious premise that all human activity is enmeshed within relational webs made of various ideas, people, and things. This premise recognizes that all action is preconditioned by circumstances surrounding the situated actor—whether that actor is a human person, an organization, or a state institution. It simultaneously recognizes that all actors participate in vital chains of causality, generating worldly differences—large or small—by virtue of activity itself.[6]

"Causation in a Daoist world is a kind of influence and reaction," one scholar of Chinese philosophy writes. "Whether of a flower, a squirrel, a human being, a forest, or a state, influence and reaction come in patterns that follow naturally from circumstances" (Bruya 2010: 213–14). While this Daoist world understood influence and reaction in relation to the concept of *qi,* a circulatory energy connecting and permeating different forms of life, I will deploy the notion of "affectivity" in interpreting China's population project and middle-class child-rearing projects. Not to be confused with human emotion, *affectivity* refers more broadly to the power and susceptibility humans, things, and circumstances have to influence and be influenced.[7] What differentiates human from nonhuman activity is that human actors have the capacity to manipulate reality by artfully disposing and arranging things in a strategic way (Jullien [1992] 1995). How and when to do so, discerning the relationship between existing constraints and the scope of human agency, is an ethical question.

ENGINEERING NATIONAL REVITALIZATION

In his book *Walk into the Hearts of Children*, Chinese popular expert Wang Xiaochun relates this: "Some parents come to me for advice and say right away: 'Teacher Wang, I came here today to ask for some tricks so I can go home and get my kid under control.'" Wang goes on to describe this kind of thinking as "harmful" and tells such parents that "the problem isn't how to deal with your child, but rather how to understand your child" (2000: 2). Like many other popular experts giving advice in China, Wang promotes the idea that children have psyches full of depth and complexity. Good parenting attends to the inner life of children, cultivating personality, self-confidence, a sense of initiative, creative thinking, and overall "quality" (*suzhi*). Bad parenting, on the other hand, not only fails to nurture subjectivity but can inadvertently lead to tragedy. In defending their assertion that the psychological unhealthiness of children stems from grown-ups, Sun Yunxiao and Bu Wei write, "Grown-ups love children, care about children, want their own child to be physically healthy, but very few parents are able to pay attention to the psychological health of their child, some parents haven't even realized or faced up to their child's psychological issues, some parents are even unknowingly creating new tragedies of the spirit" (1997: 319).

This turn toward inner life is not, as Nikolas Rose teaches us, a private matter. Rather, the intensification of subjectivity is tied up with a mode of government that forges a symmetry between political agendas and "the personal projects of individuals to live a good life" (1990: 10, 51). This is nowhere more evident than in the education reform movement known as *suzhi jiaoyu gaige* ("education for quality reforms")—of which advice for parents is a part, as national agendas and familial hopes converge on the problem of how to raise well-rounded children. In this context, "psy"—which includes not only psychiatry and other psy-disciplines but also less formal techniques of subject formation such as popular advice—enables a "harmonization between the promotion of the family as a locus of private aspirations and the necessity that it become a kind of 'social machine' for the production of adjusted and responsible citizens" (Rose 1996: 163). Rose had in mind liberal societies in the West, yet his insights are helpful for understanding why the psychological interiority of the child has become so central to the construction of good parenting in post-Mao China. Although China is by no means a liberal society, and although the distinction between private and public is not applicable, the economic transition from a planned to a market economy pivots on the art of subject making—one that is expected to produce citizen-subjects fit for the demands of a market society and global economy by endowing them with a spirit for entrepreneurship and innovation.[8]

The *suzhi jiaoyu* reform movement occupies a significant position in post–Mao era goals for modernization; it is situated as the project that will finally bring China to her rightful place among the world's most powerful nations. As a guidebook on curriculum reform put it: "China is an ancient civilization with a long history. It has made an indelible, universally recognized contribution to the development of human civilization. Even so, since the beginning of the Opium War in 1840, the development of our country has fallen behind that of the developed nations everywhere in the world for various kinds of complicated reasons. To a developing nation like ours, this curriculum reform has a profound meaning for the revitalization of the Chinese race" (Zhu 2002: 5–6). Meanwhile, in the advice literature, the puzzling question of why a domestically educated scientist has yet to win the Nobel Prize, even though Chinese high school students win championships in International General Knowledge and Mathematical Olympiad competitions every year, is frequently raised. Experts cast their blame everywhere, from schools to parents to Chinese culture, in answering the question of why China has "fallen behind."

In this context, family life is not a private matter. While revolutionary mobilization, collectivization, and the socialization of housework in the Mao years precluded the formation of a private sphere of domesticity, in the post-

Mao era ordinary families were obliged to collaborate directly with the population project by limiting family size in accordance with the law. Ordinary parents, mothers especially, were also given enormous responsibility for helping, with the guidance of popular expertise, to produce quality persons. Their efforts would contribute to making up for a debilitating lack among the "unwashed masses" (Anagnost 1995).　　　　　优生优育

In the 1980s, advice circulated under the banner of *yousheng youyu*. This advice was preoccupied with "scientific" techniques and the rationalization of child rearing, aimed at producing high intelligence and strong bodies (Champagne 1992; Woronov 2007). Over the 1990s, we see a remarkable shift in the advice literature, one that reflected the logic of deepening economic reforms that began with Deng Xiaoping's Southern Tour in 1992, a shift toward "human-centered" governance at the level of the state, and, most importantly, a shift in economic strategy from a dependence on cheap labor to the building of a knowledge economy (Greenhalgh 2011: 21). The image of the good parent was no longer the technocratic manager engaged in the task of improving and perfecting a child. Instead, the parent was to become a subject of ethics, engaged in the task of governing and improving oneself. Popular experts giving advice under the banner of *suzhi jiaoyu* encourage parents to find within themselves a "natural" attitude. To rediscover the "natural" attitude, the good parent monitors and regulates her own feelings and behavior, while the bad parent obstructs the expression of nation-transforming human potential, maybe even creates "new tragedies of the spirit."

But popular advice is only one component of a much larger population project, one that has contradictory lines of force. To the dismay of everyone—policy makers, educators, and parents—surviving academic competition eventually trumps all other considerations. Beyond the reform policies and the discursive world of popular advice, not only does China's exam-centric education system remain firmly in place, but competition within this system has intensified. Many Chinese insist that measuring students by examination makes the most sense, given the country's population size, and is still the fairest method in a culture where advancement is too commonly attained by currying favor. Meanwhile, historical and economic factors have intensified the demand to compete, as the expansion of higher education following the Asian financial crisis in the late 1990s produced more college graduates than could be absorbed by the economy.[9]

The parents I spoke to in the mid-2000s felt extremely pressured by academic inflation, seeing how competitive entry-level positions in their own industries had become. Depreciation in the value of a college diploma, along with society's preoccupation with educational attainment and status, has contributed to situations such as the one Carolyn Hsu describes in her research in the city of Harbin: employers looked for college degrees even when hiring restaurant waiters, with managers relying on the academic credentials of their workers to impress their foreign colleagues and local customers (2007: 170). While China under Mao valued serving the people and serving the nation, Chinese society has rapidly become a society of striving individuals, and an ethos of *ren shang ren,* "a person above other persons," cuts across the urban-rural divide. Yunxiang Yan has noted that success has become "crucially important for the individual because only a person above persons can have all the power and privileges, which will in turn accord the person dignity and social respect" (2013: 271). It is no wonder that "You don't want to lose at the starting line" has become such a popular saying among middle-class parents in China. In an increasingly stratified education system, situated in—and productive of—an increasingly stratified society, earning educational credentials that mean something starts with attending the right preschool.

While it was primarily economics that motivated the expansion of higher education in the late 1990s (expansion was expected to stimulate the economy through a variety of mechanisms), the policy received the support of scholars who "added that increasing the nation's average educational level would also meet goals of improving population quality" (Kipnis 2011: 86). The government's grand scheme to modernize and strengthen China's position on the global stage seems to be working at the aggregate level. Taking as evidence the United Nations' Human Development Index (HDI), which includes education in its average, Susan Greenhalgh notes that China boosted its HDI from a mere 55.9 in 1980 to 77.7 in 2005, an increase of 21.8, while the United States and Japan experienced only a 6- to 7-point increase (2011: 73). In a national index, Comprehensive National Power or CNP, that rates China against its competitors, dramatic improvements can also be seen, particularly in the area of human capital, which is measured by "the proportion of working age people in the world's total and the average years of schooling" (Greenhalgh 2011: 111). China's CNP rose by 6.4 percent between 1980 and 1998, while that of the United States fell by 3 percent.

As Greenhalgh rightly notes, China's dramatic transformation in the years since Mao's death and the end of high socialism must be attributed to the energy and focus the PRC has invested in not only managing population size but also improving population "quality." This has been a biopolitical project through and through. If in early modern Europe the "entry of life into history" generated new objects of knowledge and subjects of power in the figures of the "the hysterical woman, the masturbating child, the Malthusian couple, and the perverse adult," then in post-Mao China the new objects of knowledge and subjects of power were the "high-quality child" and the "good mother."[10] All the micro-level efforts that parents and children make to maintain health, discipline the self, accumulate cultural capital, and survive academic competition simultaneously contribute to the macro-level project of nation building. The willingness of families to take on financial burdens related to schooling supports the system's mass expansion, as payment of extra fees funds school construction and improvement (Kipnis and Li 2010). The mass expansion of the education system, in turn, serves to raise human capital at the aggregate level, and it may well be the decisive factor in shifting China's economy from one that depends on low-skilled labor to one driven by information, knowledge, and innovation.

LOCATING MORAL EXPERIENCE

The speed and intensity of China's transformation in large part derive from the buzz of micro-level activities, which include the everyday efforts that ordinary parents make to ensure children's academic survival while attending to them as psychological selves. In situating contemporary Chinese parenting in the context of a human engineering project, however, I am in no way suggesting that people have been duped and manipulated into toiling on behalf of the country. In fact, this book is a critique of the ideological mystification argument, commonly found in studies of motherhood under capitalism.

Barbara Katz Rothman argues that when mothers toilet "train" their children, they are invoking the ideology of technology. She also argues that the ideology of capitalism will lead to the proletarianization of motherhood: "Babies, at least healthy white babies, are very precious products these days. Mothers, rather like South African diamond miners, are the cheap, expendable, not-too-trustworthy labor necessary to produce the precious products" (1994: 149). Similarly, motherhood in Japan is a form of labor that ensures continuity between home and work (Field 1995), and the seeming innocence of the lunchbox is shown by way of an Althusserian reading to belie a form of oppression that subjects Japanese mothers and children to the normalizing order of the *gakureki shakai*—the academic-record society (Allison 1996).

The "commonsense acceptance of a particular world is the work of ideology, and it works by concealing the coercive and repressive elements of our everyday routines but also by making those routines of the everyday familiar, desirable, and simply our own" (Allison 1996: 83).[11]

Even though literature on childhood, class, and population politics in the anthropology of China tends to employ theoretical frameworks that emphasize subjectification rather than ideology—that is, the process by which an acting subject takes form rather than the distorting mechanism that serves to reproduce relations of production—there remains a residue of suspicion that the individual subject's experience is one of misrecognition.[12] The picture we get from the literature looks something like this: in a neoliberalizing China where the forms of power that can be found to operate are more insidious than those under previous regimes, Chinese parents, especially mothers—having internalized norms and taken up the subject position of the "good mother"— are excessively ambitious for their children, treat them like projects, and obsess over producing the perfect child.[13] Ann Anagnost's argument in her seminal essay "Children and National Transcendence in China" is nuanced in its sensitivity to uncertainty as an experiential problem, but the central analytical metaphors suggest misrecognition: "Today the (single) child becomes the narcissistic object of desire onto which anxieties about an eroding class position in a society undergoing rapid economic transformation are increasingly displaced" (1997a: 199). Anxious about class position, parents practice a form of fetishism that endows commodities such as nutritional supplements, educational toys, and test-prep materials with magical powers (1997a: 218).[14]

The parents I knew did feel burdened, and they were indeed ambitious and anxious. But they also knew and recognized more than what a critical analysis would give them credit for. In a study on the moral dilemmas of Urapmin Christians in Papua New Guinea, Joel Robbins contends that "people are highly conscious of the cultural materials they work with and the contradictions between them" (2004: 14). While Urapmin Christians are caught in the dilemma of balancing community commitments against their preoccupation over individual salvation, urban middle-class mothers are caught in the dilemma of balancing the demands of a competitive education system against the concern to protect a child's happiness. Contradictions of this nature reveal the limitations of social theories that fail to account for the inconsistent or incoherent quality of a given social order. If a social order is more contradictory than orderly, just how complete are the processes by which subjects are made to conform to the dictates of a particular regime, whether a kinship system, a religious dogma, or modern capitalism? Interpretations that reduce everyday experience to the order of political economy miss not only how people actually experience their lives but also the opportunity to track inconsistencies, multiplicities, ironies, and subtle shifts.

A focus on moral agency and experience provides a remedy for structural or political-economic reductionisms without reverting back to the kind of humanism that assumes a rationally and morally autonomous subject—a worry littered across the history of anthropological theorizing.[15] *Moral experience* refers to the intermediate space between the force of social norms and moral codes, on the one hand, and the capacity of actors to deliberate about their situation and to make the effort to respond accordingly, on the other (Lambek 2010; Robbins 2004: 14, 315–16). When the situations in which actors find themselves are crossed by multiple lines of force of both the historical/cultural and the idiosyncratic variety, their responses will bear a significant degree of singularity. That singularity is an index of the contingent qualities of a given circumstance.

The most exemplary model for such an approach in the literature, perhaps the first of its kind, is Unni Wikan's *Managing Turbulent Hearts* (1990). This ethnography, which was a critique of a regional tradition, argued that the theatrical model used to interpret Balinese life in general, and Geertz's claim in particular that the Balinese were motivated more by aesthetics than by virtue, miss how life is actually lived and experienced. Wikan returns to the personal story of a woman named Suriati throughout the book to evoke the kind of internal struggle involved in maintaining the composure the Balinese are famous for.[16] Her approach is not a celebration of subjective interiority as a site of human authenticity but rather an argument for the kind of *work* involved in living a life. The Balinese, she tells us, are acutely aware of their existential problems and "frequently complain that 'there is so much to care about'" (27). The "coincidence of events and the multiplicity of concerns" require management, "how to steer, move, be with safety in the world, salvaging respect while securing practical ends: making a living, attaining a position, nourishing cherished bonds, preserving mental calm" (108).

In focusing on the ethical and moral domain, anthropologists are not interested in making assertions about what is right and wrong. As Michael Lambek put it in introducing the volume *Ordinary Ethics*, "Our ethics is neither prescriptive nor universalist, in the sense of advocating uniform global rights or straining for a version of the common good" (2010: 6). What anthropologists *are* interested in is the exercise of practical reason as required by the conduct of everyday life, and in the question of "What is the good I want to pursue?" (Mattingly 1998a, 1998b, 2012, 2014).

Of course, anthropologists have long been able to relativize seemingly problematic moral systems by demonstrating their logical consistency. What they have not theorized systematically is how ordinary people negotiate conflicting moral values that coexist in a given society, not to mention the conflict of goods within the life of an individual person. Nor have anthropologists thought to think of ethics as more than just an issue in research methods, that is, not until the emergence of the "new anthropology of morality" about ten years ago, largely stimulated by the impact of Foucault's late career work on ethics in the Greco-Roman world.[17] Those at the helm of this conversation have attributed the discipline's neglect of something as pervasive as morality to Durkheim's conflation of morality with society, the good with the collective, thereby rendering the formulation of ethics a distinct theoretical problem "neither necessary nor possible" (Laidlaw 2002: 312; Zigon 2008: 32–36). But ordinary people contend with ethics all the time. It is an inescapable part of everyday life (Das 2012; Mattingly 2014).

Ironically, the anthropology of morality takes judgment as its central concern, something cultural relativism systematically avoids. But there is a twist here: while cultural relativism avoids the judgment of moral systems that differ from systems found in the West, the anthropology of morality investigates how people judge themselves, their situations, and other members of a shared community. How do people make judgments about how to act? Why do they berate themselves for things they could not have controlled? How do people try to close the gap between who they think they should be and who they take themselves as?[18]

Anthropology of morality

In following moral experience, anthropologists document the work actors do to figure out the boundary between what they can and cannot control, what they are and are not responsible for. How this boundary is drawn differs from culture to culture, society to society. For example, people living in modern secular societies tend to take more blame for consequences they were not entirely responsible for, because there are no witches, ghosts, and unhappy spirits to share in the blame. The moral philosopher Bernard Williams (1981) illustrates this phenomenon poignantly with the hypothetical scenario of two truck drivers who run a red light.

The first truck driver unintentionally runs a red light and kills a child he failed to see. The second truck driver, who also unintentionally runs a red light, is less unfortunate because no child suddenly jumped into the street as he crossed. There only happened to be a policeman nearby. That we might consider driver A to be more blameworthy than driver B, on the basis of the consequences of the same negligent action, is the product of what Williams calls "moral luck." That driver A will feel terrible about his role in causing the child's death, an experience Williams calls "agent-regret," points to the murky boundary between the circumstances that surround human action and the scope of human agency and control. In a situation such as this, driver A would not only feel agent-regret, but might also wonder whether he could have done something different, even though it might be futile to do so. For example, he might think, "If only I had left the house five minutes earlier" or "If only I hadn't been daydreaming."

If ethics is an inescapable part of everyday life, then we may find such predicaments even in conduct as seemingly repugnant as, say, intergenerational heroin use between mothers and daughters, as observed by Angela Garcia in New Mexico's Española Valley. A woman named Lisa mourned her daughter's death by heroin overdose—a mourning that involved not only feelings of loss but also feelings of tremendous guilt for not being able to determine whether the overdose was intentional. Lisa didn't entirely take the blame for her daughter's death, even though an outsider might be quick to blame the immorality of sharing heroin. As Lisa herself saw it, there were causes and agencies well beyond her control, such as former boyfriends and failed social services (2010: 180). Yet even here the actor draws a line in the sand: had she known her daughter was in pain, Lisa thinks, maybe she could have done something differently.

Although the experiences of middle-class Chinese mothers are nowhere as heart-wrenching as those of heroin-addicted mothers in Española Valley, ethical issues pertaining to personal responsibility are just as relevant. At best, the kind of ethical work middle-class Chinese mothers do to think well of themselves could not look more banal. At worst, the effort they make appears to be a kind of blind conformism that contributes to a frightening reality. As one reform advocate put it, "Lenin once said: 'The force of numerous people's habits is the most terrifying kind of force.' We are all a unit of this force of the numerous. Whether consciously or not, we have been accomplices in increasing pressure and increasing burden" (Fu 2005: 33). While the popular experts criticize "Chinese parents" for failing to attend to psychological health, and the anthropologists might see them as operating under a false consciousness, I argue that all the ambition and anxiety obscures a moral dimension, expressed in the exercise of moral agency. When Chen Jialing packed her daughter's schedule with learning activities, she did so out of a concern that if she failed to do so Precious would be outcompeted. Indeed, she invested a certain faith in activities such as learning the violin, thereby endowing the commodity form—a privatized educational good—with magical powers. But this faith was concerned not only with instrumental efficacy but also with making an assertion that was "achieved in the action itself" (Douglas [1966] 1994: 69). "At least I will not regret not having tried," I have heard many mothers say.

Moral agency relates to what I would like to call an "ethics of trying." It is a variety of moral experience that has less to do with conforming to normative moral codes than with a kind of practical philosophy, which takes causation and efficacy, responsibility and blame, as its central concerns. Like the hope Cheryl Mattingly describes in her study of African American families raising children with serious medical needs, the hope of Chinese mothers is more complicated than it seems. In Mattingly's case, hope is much more than wishful thinking—wishing for a medical cure. In my case, hope is much more than a parent's ambition for social status and for reciprocation in the form of family honor. In both cases, hope is a practice that imposes a moral burden and an ethical responsibility: to hope is to make a judgment that a situation requires action (Mattingly 2010). For Mattingly's key informant Andrena, the moral problem consisted of whether she had truly left every stone unturned in pursuing a diagnosis for a sick child (114). For many of my informants, the moral problem consists of whether one has tried everything possible to secure the good life for one's child in the face of intense social competition.

But effort is of course a tricky thing.

While maintaining their child's competitive edge, parents are also asked to take responsibility for helping to cultivate a well-adjusted, creative future innovator who will contribute to national strength. This demand has a reality beyond the level of discourse, not only for those who have sought professional help. The people I knew were genuinely puzzled by the amount of effort students had to make in climbing the ladder of academic success. The popular saying "American children grow up playing, Chinese children grow up suffering" (*Meiguo de haizi shi wan chulai de, zhongguo de haizi shi ku chulai de*) points to the sense of imbalance. Many primary school students have had at least one classmate who has returned from living abroad with the report that American and Canadian children do nothing but play. This gives them a relativistic perspective on childhood—an awareness that childhood might be different in other places—which makes them feel their labor is arbitrary. Why is it that American children get to play, yet their country is strong, while Chinese children are diligent, yet their country is weak?[19]

Parents too are aware that academic demands are often arbitrary. Once Chen Jialing forgot to sign a homework assignment for Precious, a common requirement teachers impose to ensure parental involvement in the daily grind of school. She did not always have the opportunity to check homework, nor was she available during the lunch break to make up for the oversight on this one occasion. This sent Precious into a spiral of negative thoughts: no signature would mean getting detained after class, being scolded by the teacher, and then being scolded at home—thoughts Chen could have protected Precious from having if she had stayed vigilant and on task.

These types of incidents create a predicament: be an easygoing parent who can facilitate the flourishing of a child's potential, not to mention her happiness, to the greatest extent possible? Or be a hypervigilant parent who can stay on top of a child's academic life and protect her from embarrassments? Add to this historically shaped dilemma the various life contingencies that emerge—work-related social obligations that arise, a teacher who has arbitrarily decided that your child is not worth the effort, a husband who goes out of town often, a child who is beginning to act very "strangely"—and we have ethnographic material that demands the kind of theoretical framework that takes the concerns of ordinary people seriously, not only for the sake of avoiding structural reductionism, but also for the sake of understanding the kind of work that goes into living a life that affords some measure of moral comfort—the comfort that comes with knowing one has tried one's best in the face of existing constraints. Given all the factors in play (or at odds), it becomes all the more important to be discerning, to assess when to be vigilant and when to let go, when to act and when to concede.

Experience at the Macro Level

Following moral experience can bring us closer to "on the ground" processes, but it is not only at this level that movement can occur. At the international scale, China the great power also has its vulnerabilities, practical concerns, and even moral striving. From her ethnographic research with policy makers, Susan Greenhalgh discovered that "the one-child project was driven by a profoundly ethical agenda, one they thought would gain worldwide approbation. . . . By taking decisive charge of Chinese population growth, they figured, the PRC could lower the population growth rate of the entire world, benefitting humanity at large" (2011: 100). But a set of historical contingencies in the 1980s led to the use of physical force to impose family planning in rural areas, inviting harsh criticism from the Western world and leaving Chinese population planners "genuinely mystified by the about-face exhibited by the international population community" (2011: 103).

At the national scale, practical concern and moral dilemmas can be found in how the state deals with stigmatized groups such as the HIV-positive and the mentally ill. In one of the chapters of *Deep China*, Guo and Kleinman explain that "the state must deny or ignore certain disadvantaged groups' claims to the protections and benefits that accrue to the status of full, socially sanctioned personhood when meeting those claims would put the state in conflict with mainstream interests and concerns," even though the state risks international legitimacy in doing so (2011: 257). Although marginalization of the weak is hugely problematic from a Western liberal perspective, stigma in China is actually a reflection of a very deep cultural logic that defines personhood in terms of reciprocity. It is a response to that which threatens the social order—namely, persons who do not or cannot reciprocate. Stigma is rooted in a deep cultural need for security, which then gets expressed at the level of the state. The point here is not to justify state-level neglect. Instead, Guo and Kleinman offer an explanation for why it even exists in the first place.

Finally, the privatization of educational funding—which supports school construction and improvement—reveals how striving exists at every level of society. From the families who willingly pay extra fees to send their child to the right school, to the businessmen who make generous donations with an eye toward increasing social capital, to the banks who make loans under political pressure for school-building projects related to a cadre's ambition for political promotion, everyone is in a competition of some kind, at every scale of Chinese society.[20] This includes the nation as a whole vis-à-vis the developed nations of the world, in its "agonizing search for modernity" (H. Kuan 2013). Needless to say, the drive for development has exacted and continues to exact innumerable social and human costs.

THE ART OF DISPOSITION

To argue that subjectivity is constructed, as many anthropologists tend to do these days, myself included, is not saying anything new. Foucault-like "antihumanism" is deeply rooted in indigenous Chinese thought and social practice. State rulers and ordinary parents alike act and govern with the understanding that there is no "beautiful totality of the individual" prior to force relations (Foucault 1977: 217). Both spheres of government—running a country, raising a child—involve something I would like to call the "art of disposition." The art of disposition is a moral practice that simultaneously recognizes the embedment of human activity while locating opportunities for strategic manipulation. This concept will be handy for linking the governmental techniques of rulers with the life management strategies of middle-class parents, and Foucault's midcareer interests in automaticity with early Chinese political thought. I take the "art of disposition" from Foucault's famous 1978 lecture on governmentality, which notes an early European definition of artful government as "the right disposition of things, arranged so as to lead to a convenient end" (1991: 93). Interestingly, this very idea is an enduring theme in Chinese philosophy.

In his book *The Propensity of Things* ([1992] 1995), François Jullien has observed that the notion of (*shi*)—a concept that has received far less attention than *dao* or *li*—points to a culturally distinctive understanding of how reality works. Found in texts as multifarious as early political theory and treatises on how to finger a lute, it can be translated as "propensity," "tendency," or "potential born of disposition." It is a concept that continues to have relevance to this day, with sayings such as "She who discerns timing and situations wisely is a hero" (*Shi shi wu zhe wei junjie*) and "Accord with propensity and all will go well" (*Shun shi zhe chang*) as popular as ever.[21] It can go a long way to explain how contemporary Chinese try to make their way through the world.

[margin handwritten: Shí]

[handwritten: not the same character. 识时务者为俊杰, vs. 顺势者昌]

Disposition in Two Schemes

For authors such as Guillaume de La Perrière, writing in mid-sixteenth-century Europe, the art of government differs from princely rule in many respects. While sovereign power seeks to draw a line between the power of the prince and other forms of power found within a given territory, the art of government seeks to establish continuity among them (Foucault 1991: 91). While the prince is external to his principality, the art of government is immanent (91). While the ultimate end of sovereignty is obedience to the law, the ends of government are plural (91–95). Foucault explains, "With government it is a question not of imposing law on men, but of *disposing things*: that is to say, of employing tactics rather than laws, and even of using laws themselves as tactics—to *arrange things* in such a way that" a plurality of ends may be achieved (95, emphasis added). Artful government does not depend on direct force; it requires instead the creation of circumstances that will spontaneously give rise to desired effects—productivity, health, responsible conduct of the self. Effects are generated by arranging things in a certain way, by empowering multiple centers, and by acting on others' actions. An activity that exists in the plural, *government* in this theoretical context can be defined quite simply as "techniques and procedures for directing human behavior. Government of children, government of souls and consciences, government of household, of a state, or of oneself" (Foucault [1994] 1997: 81).

If this Foucauldian scheme exemplifies a kind of antihumanism that prioritizes circumstance over human subjectivity in attending to dispositional effects, then similar ideas have long existed in Chinese thought. Take the *Sunzi* (fourth century BCE) as an example. A treatise on the art of war, the *Sunzi* asserts that the virtue of an individual soldier, whether he is intrinsically cowardly or brave, is not as consequential as the means by which he is deployed. Courage is a "'product' of an external conditioning." For "if the troops have *shi* [i.e., if they benefit from the potential born of disposition], then the cowardly are brave; if they lose it, then the brave are cowardly" (from a commentary quoted in Jullien [1992] 1995: 30).

Chinese views on the relationship between human subjectivity and historical circumstance are similar. In the Legalist text *Shangjunshu* (fourth century BCE), "Public morality stems entirely from the historical conditions of the era: if, because of a totalitarian regime, the situation is such that it is no longer possible to behave badly, even the worst brigands will become trustworthy. But if the situation is reversed, everyone's morality, even that of paragons of virtue, will be suspect" (Jullien [1992] 1995: 178). Here laws themselves are merely tactics that produce the circumstances in which certain effects become inevitable. For the seventeenth-century writer Wang Fuzhi, who was thinking about history, the transformation from feudalism to centralized bureaucracy had less to do with the personality of the emperor who established the first administration than with the imbalance that had emerged between the ability required of positions and the number of "stupid minds" that inherited them. Working with a coexisting tendency toward unification within the feudal system, namely the enlarging of fiefdoms, the imbalance gave way to change as a matter of course.

Now, one might argue that these ideas concerning dispositional effects contribute nothing to culture theory, as they simply restate the idea that environmental factors are more decisive than subjective ones. I will concede that so much is true. But what Jullien's discussion of dispositional effects brings out, and what Foucault's governmentality lecture downplays, is that the art of disposition constitutes a practical activity. This is crucial for understanding the ethnographic material considered in this book. Although the force generated by the dynamic interaction of factors in play is ontologically more significant than personality, there is always room for human initiative, room for management and manipulation. In the case of warfare, it is up to the good general to discern the propensity of a given circumstance so as to identify opportunities for strategic manipulation. Victory is achieved if appropriate measures are taken in a timely manner. It is not the consequence of a battle heroically fought but the outcome of tactically deployed relations of force.

The famous story "Borrowing Arrows with Straw Boats" from the classic epic *Romance of the Three Kingdoms* is paradigmatic. In this story, the talented military strategist Zhuge Liang tricks an enemy troop into shooting much-needed arrows at boats that are actually made of straw by sending the boats out on a foggy day, accompanied by the sound of war drums. With their vision obscured, the enemy troop falls for the trick. Zhuge Liang, meanwhile, achieves maximum effect with minimal effort simply by deploying relations of force, namely, the contingent force of fog. He acquires more than one hundred thousand arrows at his enemy's expense.

Wang Fuzhi believed that human management was important, despite his understanding of the historical process in terms of tendencies that bore their own logic. For if one wanted to influence a course of events, or to avoid a particular state of affairs, one had to divert a tendency at its incipient stage; otherwise any effort would be insignificant in the face of accumulated force (Jullien [1992] 1995: 191). Key to this understanding is the idea that history is governed by an action/reaction dialectic whereby every excess engenders its opposite over time. Thus, if the logic of a given historical tendency is bound to alternate and eventually exhaust itself, all situations are amenable to manipulation so long as one can wait for opportune moments. Efficacy is best maximized by discerning, waiting, and acting only when an opposing tendency is in a state of decline.[22]

Jullien interprets this as a valorization of "moral constancy," which draws on the "fortitude of the soul" and is coextensive with the process of time ([1992] 1995: 202). In this way, the otherwise insignificant scale of human subjectivity achieves maximization with action that works with rather than against existing circumstances.[23] This mode of agency may be further illustrated by the story of Cook Ding in the Daoist text *Zhuangzi*, in which a common man who is carving an ox achieves cosmic power by following a natural course of action materially determined by ligaments, tendons, and bones (Brindley 2010: 59). The art of disposition may not always involve the deployment of troops; it simply entails a recognition of the force(s) of otherness that determine possible courses of action. As Jullien explains, practical reason in the Chinese scheme "lies in adapting to the propensity at work so as to be carried along by it and exploit it" ([1992] 1995: 263).

All of this may smack of opportunism and conformism, and this can indeed be the effect. Jullien acknowledges this possibility when "praising" the bland personality, that is, the sage who avoids attachment to any one virtue in developing greater powers ([1991] 2004: 59–61). But this is precisely my point: as banal, conformist, and opportunistic as middle-class Chinese parenting may appear to be, maternal effort expresses an ethics of trying and of artful disposition. Like the generals and rulers addressed in the ancient texts, parents work to exercise discernment and to identify opportunities for taking initiative and managing tendencies. They face a formidable extrapersonal force—competition, which possesses the power of elimination. The parents I knew feared that the most minute things might make or break a child's chance for success. It was therefore important to take advantage of opportunities when opportunities presented themselves. "Opportunities" in this context could include those of the "cultural" sort—widely available extracurricular classes that promised to raise the child's *suzhi*, thereby endowing the child with a competitive edge. They could also include opportunities of a situational kind—the chance to divert a negative tendency before it gathered force.

What makes reasoning about courses of possible action for mothers like Chen Jialing a messy affair is the coexistence of contradictory tendencies in contemporary Chinese society. Packing her daughter's schedule with learning activities derived from the discernment of one historical tendency, but this course of action precluded her from seeing another: Precious's unhappiness. This left her with a feeling of agent-regret—*maybe I could have done something different.*

What this shows is that while the art of disposition in early Chinese thought concerned instrumental efficacy, for my informants the art of disposition had a prominent ethical dimension. Because there was little a human agent could do in the face of accumulated force, it was all the more important to try when and where one could.

By orienting the forthcoming discussion around the central image of "arrangement" and "disposition"—a way of managing and manipulating vitality and flow—I hope to establish some degree of correspondence between exercises of power at different scales. This is, essentially, an experiment in reconceptualizing the very notion of power so as to offer a framework that can simultaneously accommodate, on the one hand, the consideration of political rationality, expert knowledge, and economic transition, and on the other hand, the actor's view of power, that is to say, the concern with personal efficacy and the capacity to influence. I realize that suggesting any similarity between what states do and what people do may be preposterous, especially in the context of a country where there are very real and problematic disparities between those who have power and those who do not. I do not deny this reality, but I would like to point out—at the risk of valorizing the "elite" texts of early China—that the idea of scalar correspondence is a rather old one. It is not my invention.

Judith Farquhar and Qicheng Zhang come very close to offering an alternative theory of power, and this book is very much inspired by their essay "Biopolitical Beijing" (2005). Here Farquhar and Zhang consider the *yangsheng* (cultivating-life) practices of elderly Beijingers—*taiji,* sword dancing, ballroom dancing, diet and nutrition, control of emotions—as a form of biopolitics that must be situated in relation to the state's withdrawal of health care provisioning and to historically recent political exercises in the taking of life. Intriguingly, however, they argue that the convergence of life and power in *yangsheng* must be understood in a way that theorists of modern power could not anticipate. Informed by advice books that draw on texts as old as the *Spring and Autumn Annals* (third century BCE), texts that construct the efficacy of a ruler in terms of his ability to cultivate himself in exemplary ways, *yangsheng* practices enact a form of power that is "nonmodern" (2005: 304). For practitioners, achieving sovereignty over one's own life in a way fit for a lord is generative of power and efficacy, even if only in a personal sense. In so doing, *yangsheng* "creates a space apart" even while collaborating with the state (2005: 323).

In laboring to raise a child who is both academically competitive and psychologically healthy, full of personality, and happy, I could argue that urban, middle-class mothers have been duped into serving a state agenda. Indeed, the anxieties that drive parents to push their children must be situated in relation to the fact that individual persons and families are now responsible for their own life security, which is no longer guaranteed by the "iron rice bowl." But reading intense maternal effort solely as the expression of some hidden force or mutation in power would obscure the very real coexistence of multiple lines of force and influence. Some of these lines are related to politics and economics; others are not. In managing their own immediate realities, ordinary mothers too create a space apart even while collaborating with the state. In this space apart, we can find "governmentality." Although political and personal situations call for the arrangement of different things for the achievement of different ends, I argue that we may be able to expand possibilities for thought and interpretation, and maybe even for how to live, if we are willing to redistribute power, vulnerability, and practical concern along the political-personal continuum. Doing so requires abandoning binary categories, once and for all, for the following of process.

The idea contained in the art of disposition is actually quite simple. Consider the dinner party, for instance. The essential subjectivity of the party hostess is less significant than the hostess's skill at disposing and arranging, her ability to put the agencies of multiple heterogeneous elements into interactive play, from the lighting that activates a certain mood, to who ends up sitting next to whom, to where the appetizers are set and whether their arrangement facilitates mingling. These things matter more than whether or not the hostess herself is affable, generous, or funny—a charming hostess can still throw a bad party. In Chen Jialing's case, nothing mattered more to the situation of Precious's illness than rearranging relational elements. Reducing the geographic distance between home and school and the social distance between one's household and surrounding neighbors by moving back to the old neighborhood was experienced as having significantly changed things for the better. Although Chen's subjectivity as a reflective parent played an important role, activating the agencies of the children in the old yard proved to be much more efficacious in mitigating the pressures of a rigorous academic life, even if only for a few more years.

THE RESEARCH

Love's Uncertainty is based on many years of textual research using official state documents pertaining to children and education, as well as popular magazines, television shows, newspapers, and advice books intended for parents. The ethnographic research was conducted primarily in 2004, supplemented by shorter trips taken in the fall of 2006 and in the summer of 2010.

I observed parenting classes and lectures, primary and middle school class-rooms, and family life among the "new middle class" in Kunming, the capital of Yunnan Province. Though the "middle class" is by no means a given entity in China, I put my families in this category on the basis of their consumption power (L. Zhang 2010). The families I knew were all double-income families, many traveled for leisure, some owned private cars and the home they lived in, and all devoted an enormous amount of their energy and income to the education of their only child. Born between the late 1960s and early 1970s, the parents I knew were also themselves educated. They were too young to be members of the "lost generation," and most had college degrees. Of the ten families I followed closely, nine were Han Chinese.

I conducted open-ended interviews with psychological health counselors, popular experts, schoolteachers, and parents themselves. During the research process, I identified linkages between popular advice and parenting by asking informants to name experts who had made an impression on them. I noted the stories and examples they recalled and then looked for them in the advice literature. Sometimes parents simply gave me copies of what they were reading.

An informant recommended the popular television drama I discuss in chapter 5. I analyze the show in great detail so as to understand why the show resonated with her in particular and why it was so popular in general. While anthropologists tend to frown on focusing too much on textual data, I combine ethnographic research with the analysis of popular texts because they are key actors in this story. Popular texts have played a major role in redefining good parenting, thereby giving rise to moral dilemmas. It is important to note that the direction taken does differ from the approach often found in, say, cultural studies. Rather than start with a text and then ask how people respond, I start with people and then figure out what texts their worlds are populated by.

Because I am specifically interested in the interface between popular advice and those who consume this advice, my ethnography primarily focuses on experts and parents—especially mothers. Although a discussion of extended kin relations is beyond the scope of this book, a few words about grandparents are in order because maternal attitudes toward grandparents shed some additional light on the stakes involved. Only one of my case families lived with a grandparent under the same roof, while grandparents in some of my other cases provided support by cooking dinner when schedules got too busy. Precious's paternal grandmother, in the opening vignette, was quite involved in her life—perhaps because she had studied foreign languages and worked as a translator in her youth, positioning her well as a home tutor. But generally speaking, the mothers I knew felt that one must take full responsibility because grandparents were too doting and failed to understand the kind of risks and dangers children ought to be protected from.[24] Moreover, middle-class child rearing is highly rationalized, with scheduled activities taking precedence in the organization of leisure time (cf. Lareau 2011). This is not to say that grandparents are not important: intergenerational intimacy is tucked away in the hidden corners of family life, and it may well be that parents do not fully appreciate the contributions of their own parents (cf. Goh 2011).

Research with busy urban families is extremely difficult, and the field situation was so unlike the one Malinowski first mythologized: pitch your tent in the middle of a village, and watch life go on around you. In the research situation where I found myself, doing ethnography was a lot like keeping up friendships with busy friends in Los Angeles, which was then my home base. I would get invited over for dinner, go on trips, make dates to go to the zoo, sit around and drink Pu'er tea for hours on end, share entertaining text messages, see a movie, discuss a movie, and so on. On the weekends, I would play games with the families' children in an effort to help increase their English vocabulary. In some cases, I found myself in institutional contexts that intersected with the lives of families I was already following, giving me an additional angle from which to understand their lives. Some families were first met in an institutional context.

I used the case study method to gather my material, restricting the sample size to a very small number so as to get to know individuals and families at a more intimate level—as intimate as was possible given my position as a young American woman with limited command of the local Kunming dialect. Because my sample size of ten is extremely small, I do not at all intend for my cases to be representative of urban middle-class Chinese families in general. As is true for any ethnography, the findings presented in this book are representative of particular people at a particular time. Although I have in fact organized many of the discussions around observed patterns, and although I often give examples I see as representative, I would like to remind the reader that attending to the particular is theoretically and philosophically important.

Lives are shaped by context and history. But a life is also composed of innumerable moments in time, moments that involve a coming-together of people and things that could have occurred only once, never to happen again in exactly the same way.[25] Anthropology is a science of context, but it is also and always has been an exercise in the appreciation of variability—variations across space and in time, variations between individuals and events. It is in this anthropological spirit that I have written this book.

ONE

The Politics of Childhood

Why the low productivity of our country's enterprise economy and the situation of the inability of our products to compete have not changed in a long time, why agricultural science and technology have not achieved wide dissemination, why precious resources and the ecological environment have not been fully used and protected, why the increase in population has not been effectively controlled, and why some bad social conduct cannot be stopped despite repeated bans undoubtedly have many reasons, but one important reason is that the *suzhi* of laborers is low.

STATE COUNCIL, PEOPLE'S REPUBLIC OF CHINA,
"Zhongguo jiaoyu gaige he fazhan gangyao" [An outline for the
reform and development of Chinese education], 1993

AT THE TURN OF THE TWENTY-FIRST CENTURY, some books written by somebody named Huang Quanyu describing school and family life in the United States hit the market in China, making this author a household name in Chinese cities. Titled *Education for Quality in America* (1999) and *Family Education in America* (2001), they are filled with vignettes describing Huang's experience of raising a son during his years as a graduate student in the United States, admiringly showcasing American educational practices. Decidedly nontheoretical books aimed at a popular audience, they describe family life, bake sales, and soccer games—mundane middle-class Americana meant to reflect everything Chinese educators are supposedly doing wrong.[1]

To illustrate, the first chapter of *Education for Quality in America* tells a story about how Huang first perceived his son's art class with disapproval and how he eventually understood the logic behind what had first appeared to be a complete lack of structure and purpose. Huang uses this experience to question whether creativity can be taught, linking something as mundane as a child's extracurricular activities to national destiny. The art class story is emblematic of the kind of transformation educators are being asked to make in embracing the ideals of the *suzhi jiaoyu* movement, aimed at improving the human "quality" of China's population by modernizing the human subject. The assertion Huang makes in telling the story could not be more culturally significant: he performs a complete reversal of a deeply rooted logic regarding how to teach.

Once, before his wife and three-year-old son joined him in the United States, Huang got a letter in the mail from his family. It contained a traditional Chinese brush painting, a beautiful drawing of a bamboo "with scattered leaves and bending stalks, balanced composition, fine shading, and perspective" (1999: 12). It was so good Huang could not believe his three-year-old son had produced it. When his wife and son arrived in the United States a couple years later, the couple continued their son's art education and sent him to an art class organized by a university. After no more than five classes, their son began to express discontent with the class and reported that his art teacher did not even teach: "She just gives us a subject and then lets us draw. You just draw however you want to draw, the teacher doesn't even care. When you're done the teacher only knows to say 'Great! Great!'" (16).

At first, the couple did not pay much attention. But when their son continued to complain, Huang decided to investigate the matter for himself. He used having to bring his son something warm to wear as an excuse to visit one day, and he came upon a scene that looked to him like utter chaos. Huang recalls, "The instructors on duty were three art department graduate students. One male student sat on the podium staring at the ceiling with his legs crossed, a female student paced around chewing gum, another stared out the window at the snow absentmindedly" (17). Meanwhile children were drawing while standing, kneeling, and lying prone. The drawings Huang saw lacked in proportion, composition, structure, shape, and discipline. The students, he felt, did not even know how to hold a brush. He subsequently withdrew his son from the class, thinking it was the kind of class that "leads the young astray."

Following a conversation he had with an American primary school art teacher who had lived and taught art in China and who described how her Chinese students were unable to draw something without a model, Huang began to rethink art education. He came to see that his son's artistic competence was merely the product of a "photocopying" process (*fuying de guocheng*). He writes, "I began to carefully observe my son, and I realized that no matter what we gave him to draw, he could pretty much draw it to perfection, or you could say 'copy' it, 'clone' it. But if you wanted him to creatively draw something according to an assigned topic, that was difficult" (1999: 21).

Huang argues that this was because his son had been taught according to a simple transmission process: a teacher draws a model on the blackboard, students look at it and reproduce the drawing on paper by hand. Though his son had the technical skill to produce a traditional painting quite elegant for his age, he was stumped when given free rein. He could reproduce something someone else had already done, but he could not create something of his own.

Huang's story is meant to encapsulate the putative differences between Chinese and American education. The moral is that the seeming chaos of American education is precisely what promotes creativity. Huang came to realize that whether a child's art piece exhibited proportion, composition, and structure was beside the point. By providing little direction, American educators encouraged children to use their imagination. Creativity cannot be taught, but it can be facilitated with a change in educational style that promotes subjectivity in the child.

The *suzhi jiaoyu* movement to which Huang's efforts belong is the most recent iteration of an old debate, going back to the late nineteenth century, over how to modernize education against a historically entrenched tendency to privilege rote learning. Such debate strikes deep at the heart of Chinese conceptions of personhood and the nature of reality. Huang's characterization of traditional art education as a kind of "photocopying" process obscures the indigenous logic that gives copying its meaning. There is a strong cultural belief in the importance of internalizing models of various kinds through imitation—whether the good deeds of a cultural hero or the artistic production of an exemplary teacher. Over time, imitation and repetition—undertaken in the manner of *linmo*, copying in the close presence of great work— gives rise to enlightened understanding and originality (Bakken 2000: 134–37, 145–46). It is in the individual's total submission to external forces that creative spontaneity can arise.

It is significant that Huang Quanyu refers to this process in terms of photocopying (*fuying*), which shares the character for "to repeat" with other phrases related to repetitive learning. Unlike reviewing (*fuxi*) or repeatedly (*fanfu*) trying something, photocopying derogatorily suggests a mechanical process with little meaning and vitality, where doing is of no consequence. Thus Huang articulates the modern liberal view that locates subjectivity in the interior depths of the human person, rather than in the dynamic between influence and response so central to indigenous Chinese thought.

What is the context that has conditioned such a reversal in logic? What made such a critique possible? Cultural transformations that follow the historical experience of grand humiliation can often involve coming to "hate" what one has (Robbins 2004: 9). In the case of China, this humiliation is commonly traced to the nineteenth century, when China lost the Opium War. Why a great civilization found itself in an inferior position on the global stage is a question that has inspired various attempts at modernization since, including redefinitions of a proper childhood. In the early twenty-first century, the mundane details of domestic life have become especially fraught with political significance as China gears itself up for adapting to a global, knowledge- and information-based economy.

CHILDHOOD IN MODERN CHINA

Since the beginning of the economic reforms of the late 1970s, "the child" has been and continues to be linked in thought and practice to the destiny of the nation through the notorious one-child policy. Perceiving population size to be a threat to goals of economic modernization, and perceiving a mismatch between available resources and need, the Party-state implemented the one-child policy as a solution. This policy was positioned to solve, in fact, two problems at once: population size reduction and improvement of overall population quality. In this context, the single child came to embody hope and became a privileged subject of investment and care, in contrast to the "unwashed masses" who were supposedly responsible for China's backwardness (Anagnost 1995).

Concern for and attention to children in the present are part of a longer history of China's struggle for dignity in the face of foreign powers. Late Qing intellectuals looked to the West for ideas, with a Chinese translation of Thomas Huxley's *Evolution and Ethics* serving as a critical lens for thinking about the national situation (Bai 2005: 175). With another defeat in the Sino-Japanese War in 1895, reformers began to argue that the education of children was "critical to China's survival or extinction" (175). The traditional education system was seen as preoccupying the nation's youth with useless studies that did nothing for military strength or scientific invention. A series of reforms was promulgated in 1898 in an attempt to abolish the civil service examination system and establish a modern school system. Liang Qichao, an important reformer in this era, had concluded that the Chinese were not necessarily inferior to Western people; rather, the rote learning required in Chinese education stunted the development of a child's "brain power"

(Bai 2005: 187). Furthermore, Liang felt, Chinese education treated pupils like prisoners, which was harmful to their physical development (195–96). A set of regulations announced in 1904 officially abolished the civil service examination system and stressed the importance of gymnastics in the primary school curriculum.

Not long after the fall of the Qing dynasty, intellectuals of the New Culture Movement (1915–21) located the child—as well as women, workers, and the family—as a site for cultural transformation and national revitalization (Barlow 1994; Glosser 2003). For these intellectuals, modernity could be achieved only by radically breaking with the past, challenging traditional forms of authority, and promoting social democracy. Their project was mainly a literary one. Though they worked to reform writing practices and experimented with realism (Anderson 1990), many New Culture intellectuals also wrote about and for children. They expressed their concerns over national strength and character through the figure of the child, as in the essay "Shanghai Children," where Lu Xun contrasts the Chinese children with their "tattered" clothing and "lackluster expression" to the "splendid, lively foreign children" nearby (quoted in Anagnost 1997a: 201). Some debated proper childhood and embraced the developmental models of child psychology, which categorically separated children from the world of adults. Zhou Zuoren, who created a modern children's literature, argued that Chinese adults were unable to understand children and their age-specific needs, instead "forc[ing] as many of the 'classics of the sages and annals of the worthies' down their throats as possible" (quoted in Jones 2002: 710). Others worked to reform family relations and child-rearing practices, as exemplified by the foreign-trained child psychologist Chen Heqin's *Family Education*, Lu Xun's essay "How Are We to Be Fathers Now?", and Zhang Zonglin's "How to Be a Parent That Conforms to Current Trends." This discovery of modern childhood would go into hiatus in the Maoist era, when the "rural masses displaced the child as the principal object of a revolutionary pedagogy" (Anagnost 1997a: 213).

A focus on the child was revived in the post-Mao period, as was eugenics in the form of a campaign that went hand in hand with the implementation of the family planning policy.[2] Eugenic thinking and practice in this period were relevant not just to intellectuals but also to ordinary people in a way that yoked their intimate and everyday practices to a collective project (Anagnost 1995). The *yousheng youyu*, or "excellent births, excellent rearing" campaign, focused a general concern with population quality on the body and mind of the individual mother and child. Marriage and even one's reproductive cycle were important state business, with the latter monitored by birth-planning cadres who were responsible for dispensing birth control (Rofel 1999: 149).

The "excellent births" campaign involved mass pedagogy: medical knowledge concerning reproductive health was widely disseminated to the public. From advice on timing conception so as to conceive intelligent children, to advice on diet and nutrition during pregnancy, much of this literature gave enormous responsibility to parents, especially mothers, in the production of quality persons.[3] Certain aspects of the "excellent births" campaign aimed to minimize "defective" births in ways that echoed eugenic campaigns in the West decades earlier (Dikötter 1998: 160–75). But much of the campaign in post-Mao China constituted a form of positive eugenics, one that emphasized adding rather than subtracting, educating rather than eliminating. The use of cassette tapes in fetal education provides a clear and material manifestation of the way in which "excellent births" and "excellent rearing" blurred. Developed by a doctor from Beijing Medical College, one set of three tapes playing Western classical music was to be used at different stages of reproduction: before conception, during pregnancy, and during the first years of a child's life. These tapes, the doctor concluded in a follow-up research study, birthed and reared more intelligent children who hit developmental milestones earlier than those in the control group (Milwertz 1997: 131–32).

In the 1980s and early 1990s, there was a strong preoccupation with not only the nutrition and physical constitution of children but their intelligence as well. Susan Champagne found child-rearing manuals from the 1980s to be full of practical advice for producing intelligence in children. The literature provided "charts and tests so that parents can assess their children's intelligence, elaborate etiologies so that the causes of low and high intelligence can be better understood, and explanations of the terminology of intelligence, to better help parents classify their own children" (1992: 5). Though moral education was also important, Champagne argues that the preoccupation with intelligence in the advice literature may be attributed to an idea that intelligence was systematically attainable and measurable. Intelligence education was to be "administered in formalized situations through discrete activities which ideally should be carried out on a regular basis, and according to a fixed schedule" (153).

A factory-style production of the child, which later education reformers criticized, was quite literally undertaken and then described in the best-selling book *Harvard Girl Liu Yiting* (Liu and Zhang [2000] 2004).[4] Liu

Yiting was born in 1981. Her mother, Liu Weihua, who coauthored the book with Yiting's father, had a plan for Yiting's "scientific" child rearing starting at conception. She kept a diary throughout her daughter's development from which she drew in writing the book *Harvard Girl*. Child rearing was a concerted project: "When the baby was only two weeks old, Liu began training her daughter's attention span by using her fingers and stuffed toys to track the child's vision. By the age of nine months, Liu was deliberately putting objects out of Yiting's reach, requiring the baby to work ever harder to grasp what she wanted, in order to teach her persistence and to overcome difficulties" (Woronov 2007: 37). When Yiting was handed over to other caregivers, her mother provided "copies of the manuals she used to implement early child education, requesting that they read these materials, carry out their directions on a daily basis, and write frequent reports to her on the child's development" (38).

A shift in emphasis occurred in the 1990s from "excellent births, excellent rearing" to *suzhi jiaoyu*, in parallel with a number of historical developments: Deng Xiaoping's Southern Tour, renewed market reforms, an economic boom, the privatization of public goods, decentralization of birth planning, a shift from a focus on reducing population quantity to a focus on raising population quality, optimization of government performance, and a general—though not complete—movement toward neoliberal governance and the fostering of population vitality.[5] *Suzhi jiaoyu* first appeared in 1988 but became more generally used after the Ministry of Education promulgated an official policy entitled the "Resolution for Fully Moving *Suzhi Jiaoyu* Forward" (Kipnis 2006: 300; State Council 1999b). *Suzhi jiaoyu* was originally a concept that education researchers used in professional journals such as *Middle School Education, Scientific Education Research,* and *Compulsory Education Research* to describe how to teach competence (Kipnis 2006: 299). It has since become a relatively common phrase for ordinary families, thereby taking on a looser meaning that associates human quality with learning in general.

If the "excellent births, excellent rearing" campaign of the 1980s and the more recent *suzhi jiaoyu* movement have in common a mark of scientific legitimacy, they differ in that the *suzhi* of *suzhi jiaoyu* links many disparate domains of governance, beyond biological reproduction and child rearing. *Suzhi* discourse is found in domains as disparate as rural development, domestic migration, private business, and corporate culture. It constructs the problem of national strength and economic development in terms of human improvement and encourages individuals to be more personally responsible by acting on their desires. Although *suzhi* is often invoked as a potential that one can nurture and cultivate through personal effort, *suzhi* discourse typically serves to justify social and geographic hierarchies and even undue use of force.[6] The child—especially the urban child—serves to sustain *suzhi* hierarchies in being constructed as a "repository of value," an antithesis to those who cannot embody value (Anagnost 1995, 2004). As a recipient of *suzhi jiaoyu,* the child carries the hope for national transformation, while the rural migrant symbolizes the raison d'être for the population improvement project. As such, *suzhi* discourse obscures—through symbolic violence—the tremendous contributions migrants have made to China's breakneck development.[7]

In sum, the history of linking the child to the destiny of the nation is long, and it is against this broader context that efforts to reform education must be situated. The most recent iteration of problematizing Chinese education is connected to the expansion of population governance and China's aim to more fully adapt to a global, knowledge- and information-based economy (Greenhalgh 2011). For a popular expert like Huang Quanyu, modernization can easily be seen in China's many skyscrapers and freeways, but the country has a long way to go before the human subject becomes fully modernized (2001: 4). His concerns are shared by other popular experts in China, and importantly, they are found at the highest level of government. Improving the human quality of China's population by raising *suzhi,* starting with children, has been a concerted project pursued by the state since the implementation of the one-child policy. In this context, the mundane details of everyday life are connected to what is quite literally a social engineering project informed by cybernetics and systems theory (Greenhalgh 2003, 2011) and guided by a series of official policy documents. These documents are a form of political technology, and they demonstrate how the state—like ordinary people in general and parents in particular—is striving and aspiring for a better future to come.

BLUEPRINTS FOR CONSTRUCTION

In an essay on school-based efforts to raise the moral *suzhi* of children, Terry Woronov writes, "A study of how children today are learning to govern themselves using the discursive and material resources at their disposal shows how the state sets the conditions of possibility for raising high-quality children, but also demonstrates the limits of the state's power to fix boundaries around the concept of 'quality'" (2009: 569). Woronov found a large gap between official and adult expectations and the lives young people actually live. One lesson in the morality class that she observed set out to inculcate love of regular exercise, which would require hard work and discipline, but students cited logistical issues such as busy parents as the reason why they rarely exercised. In another example concerning the reception of a news story about junk food–carrying Youth League members on a wilderness trek, adults expressed horror at the inability of its participants to go a few days without luxurious junk food. Yet junk food is part of the larger consumer culture in which the *suzhi jiaoyu* movement is implicated, as officials, teachers, and the media exhort families to consume a variety of commodities—food, books, supplies, and life experiences—commodities that promise to raise other aspects of their overall *suzhi*. For Woronov, these examples indicate that *suzhi jiaoyu* is an "inherently contradictory project, one in which state-led efforts chafe against disciplines of the market economy" (569).

The *suzhi jiaoyu* project is indeed contradictory, and the state does play a crucial role in promoting the reform, since it has prioritized education as a key strategy for national revitalization. But it is important to keep in mind that the state is only one node in a larger network of activity. Putting aside for the moment the intricacies of actual policy implementation, I take official documents related to education reform as literal blueprints for construction in a social engineering project that enacts state striving.

The contradictory nature of the *suzhi jiaoyu* project and the lack of specificity in the 1999 Resolution led Terry Woronov to argue that the reform is less a blueprint than an imaginary (2009: 572–73). She is right to relate this lack to the sweeping breadth of the policy, but I would argue that documents such as the 1999 Resolution are *relatively* specific for what they aim to do and that such documents are themselves contradictory. In other words, official documents are hardly as simple as the Ten Commandments with complexity emerging only in the process of implementation. Tensions are inherent, as the documents are responding to and acting within a complex historical situation: the Party-state's legitimacy rests on economic success, which in turn rests on opening up to the world and increasing the country's store of human capital. To maintain the former while promoting the latter is a tricky matter. For example, official documents related to guiding education reform insist on modernization and facing the world, and they encourage pedagogy that promotes independent thinking and curricula pertinent to the realities of students. Yet the very same documents lay out a program for ensuring, protecting, and promoting the legitimacy of socialism and the Party-state, and they insist on the continued importance of socialist ethics. That such contradictions pervade even official discourses shall serve as a reminder that the state, like human actors, is situated in history.

There is in fact a history to be read from the official documents pertaining to the adoption of the *suzhi jiaoyu* concept by the state. The State Council's "Outline for the Reform and Development of Chinese Education" (1993) is an important document because it was formulated in the wake of a watershed in post-Mao history, namely the establishment of the term *socialist market economy* and official calls for deepening economic reforms. The document attributes a series of social and economic problems to the low *suzhi* of laborers, but it never uses the phrase *suzhi jiaoyu* in proposing a solution to the *suzhi* problem. The phrase first appears in the 1999 "Action Plan for the Vigorous Development of Twenty-First-Century Education" (State Council 1999a), which lists the promotion of *suzhi jiaoyu* as one of its main goals. The 1999 Resolution is a response to this "Action Plan," intended to "accelerate the implementation of the strategy of national revitalization through science and education."

Starting in 1999, the cause of advancing *suzhi jiaoyu* begins to appear in various other documents concerning other aspects of education, children, and youth. In August 1999, the Ministry of Education issued the document "Recommendations for Strengthening Psychological Health Education in Primary and Middle Schools." The opening paragraph relates psychological health education to the *suzhi jiaoyu* reform and quotes from the 1999 Resolution: "[We] must cultivate dauntless will in students, a spirit for working diligently in the face of difficulty, and strengthen the ability of youth to adapt to social life." A "Guiding Outline" for psychological health education published by the Ministry of Education in 2002 reiterates that psychological health education is an important aspect of *suzhi jiaoyu,* combining a concern for mental health issues with the promotion of socialist virtues such as the ability to endure in the face of difficulty.

Promoting *suzhi jiaoyu* and the holistic development of students, as well as their "consciousness for innovation, practical ability, and scientific spirit," is one of the items under a section on education in a ten-year development plan titled "Outline for the Development of Children in China, 2001–2010." But *suzhi jiaoyu* was not mentioned in the State Council's "1990s Program Outline for the Development of Children in China," issued approximately ten years earlier in 1992. *Suzhi* itself does, however, appear a number of times, as in the first sentence of the document: "The children of today are the subjects of the twenty-first century, and the survival, protection, and development of children are the foundation for raising population *suzhi*." There is also an item devoted to highlighting the importance of "whole development" (i.e., moral, intellectual, and physical). But otherwise these two "outlines" for the development of children devote space primarily to issues such as lowering infant and maternal mortality, combating malnutrition, universalizing compulsory education, eradicating illiteracy, and constructing healthy social environments for children.

Two important policy documents concerning "family education work" (*jiating jiaoyu gongzuo*), which includes the education of parents, reflect a similar development. The tenth five-year plan for family education work (National Women's Federation and Ministry of Education 2002) directs that such work should be implemented in the spirit of the 1999 Resolution. But the ninth five-year plan for family education work makes no mention of *suzhi jiaoyu* (National Women's Federation and State Education Commission 1996). *Suzhi* itself, however, is mentioned, as in a sentence found under a discussion of main goals: "Guide parents in establishing a correct orientation toward child rearing, and raise the *suzhi* of parents through their mastery of scientific education methods" (National Women's Federation and State Education Commission 1996).

This short history of how the concept of *suzhi jiaoyu* entered the official language is important because it reminds us that the state is just as subject to the dynamic of influence and response as any kind of actor in a web of causality. Of course the state is a significant center of power, but it too participates in an even larger world crossed by multitudinous lines of force, affecting the world that has affected it. Education reform is directed at a changing world in which China is eager to be a major competitor, and the relationship between education policy and modernization is deliberately made. The gradual entry of the *suzhi jiaoyu* concept into official discourse reveals how the official discourse has been influenced by what first started out as the concern of a globalizing education profession. In turn, the state—namely the State Council, the Ministry of Education, and the National Women's Federation—acts back upon the world by issuing directives and guidelines explaining why and how education reform will transform national destiny.

As a socialist state, the Chinese government has always taken an active role in the engineering of society, using political technologies that have existed since the formation of the People's Republic in 1949. Various genres of policy making issue directives and guidelines for action, including "notices" (*tongzhi*), "suggestions" (*yijian*), "outlines" (*gangyao*), "resolutions" (*jueding*), and "action plans" (*xingdong jihua*). Some documents are promulgated to set concrete goals to be reached within five-year or ten-year periods. Such plans may be understood as tools of strategic design, a bastion of central planning in an era of political decentralization (H. Kuan 2013: 19).

"Socialist construction" is a key concept in post-Mao governance, and social engineering is no mere metaphor. China's ruling elite is largely composed of technocrats who very earnestly believe in the promise of science in designing and planning an orderly society. In the first decade of reforms especially, the technocratic elite took great interest in the small details of human conduct and in the development of new fields of study that would generate knowledge about human improvement. Such knowledge, they hoped, would then be implemented to form modern individuals. The technocratic elites strongly believed that modernization and human development went hand in hand, and they applied their engineering backgrounds to formulating solutions to social problems. For example, the aerospace engineer Qian Xuesen proposed a system for engineering culture that would involve the development of "education, science, literature and art, press and publication, radio and TV, public health and physical culture, libraries, museums, and recreation and other activities and institutions for raising the educational level of people" (Bakken 2000: 58). Qian's plan demonstrates that the notion of "human technology" is not simply the theoretical invention of governmentality theorists, a dispassionate instrument for piercing beneath the surface. Human technologies are consciously planned out for the practical management of the empirical world.

Although the spirit behind the *suzhi jiaoyu* movement reflects the humanism of the 1990s rather than the technocratic logic of the 1980s, the official documents that endorse its importance are themselves technological, as policy documents in general are meant to provide building plans. Like "engineering," "technology" is not a metaphor—if understood as any human-invented means for channeling energy and attention in a certain direction. Prayer is a form of technology that focuses a devotee's energy and attention inward toward the self. A midterm exam is a form of technology that directs the concerted attention of a class to a particular subject. Irrigation is a form of technology that channels the flow of water in a certain direction. A survey of frequently occurring active verbs in PRC government policies indicates that these documents channel energy and attention by orienting its readers to a set of priorities. Frequently occurring verbs include to implement (*guanche*) policies, to establish (*jianli*) systems, to lay a foundation (*dianji*), to create (*chuangzao*) conditions, to concentrate (*jizhong*) resources, to persist (*jianchi*) in a priority, to prioritize (*zhongshi*), to further (*jin yi bu*), to push on (*tuijin*), to promote (*cujin*), to put into effect (*luoshi, shishi*), to optimize (*youhua*), to launch (*kaizhan*), to develop (*fazhan*), to broaden (*tuokuan*) the scope, to deepen (*shenhua*) reform, to popularize (*puji*) knowledge, and of course, to raise (*tigao*) *suzhi*. Interestingly, many of these verbs encourage an intensification of existing effort, which suggests that national projects are given their "steely quality" with the encouragement of sustained actions over time.[8]

The *suzhi jiaoyu* project does not begin and end with the state—state projects themselves are embedded within affective relations, and the official documents indicate that policy usage of this phrase begins ten years after its first appearance in professional education journals. Moreover, textual analysis demonstrates that the contradictory nature of the *suzhi jiaoyu* project can be traced to the official documents themselves, setting guidelines for both facing the world and ensuring the continued legitimacy of socialism and the existing Party-state. Contradictions pervade the entire education field in China. They are not found only in the ambivalence of ordinary parents, in classroom pedagogy, and in the process of policy implementation. The agendas set by the state are themselves contradictory and as such render the task of constructing "socialist modernization" contingent and unpredictable. In a surprising case I once came across, a city government tried to engineer innovation by making a detailed official plan: in 2011, Ningbo invested 50,000,000 RMB in a project that would "forge" ten Steve Jobs within a five-year period.[9]

Disseminating Child-Rearing Knowledge

If China's nation-building project links macro-level agendas with the micro-level efforts of self-improvement among ordinary people, what is the actual material that activates this link? What mediates the coming together of political ambitions and personal aspirations?

One crucial link can be found in popular advice for good parenting, widely available in urban China. The one-child policy, rapid social transformation, and intense competition have created a situation in which young urban parents are eager to consult expert advice. "You have never been a parent before and you definitely cannot use the methods your parents used on you," is a sentiment I often heard. Meanwhile, the publishing industry is eager to exploit the market demand for titles related to child rearing. Publishing houses have only recently (relative to their counterparts in capitalist countries) become financially independent with the withdrawal of government support, so that what gets published in China is determined less by Party interests and ideological agendas than by popular interest and market demand (Kong 2005).

When Huang Quanyu's book *Education for Quality in America* became a best seller in 2000, sharing the list with the wildly successful Harry Potter series, publishing houses noted the commercial appeal of *suzhi jiaoyu*, and Huang's book was studied for the making of future best sellers. Huang himself reports in the sequel *Family Education in America* that his first book was reprinted eighteen times in a single year. If both legitimate and pirated copies are counted, there were—in 2001—seven hundred thousand to eight hundred thousand copies in circulation (2001: 1–2).

Books bearing the slogan of *suzhi jiaoyu* provided relief to a publishing industry that had been negatively affected by the "reducing burden" policy of 2000, which specified restrictions against the organization of book purchasing at schools (Ministry of Education 2000), ordinarily a channel for selling children's books. One president of a publishing house noted with hope that the "hotness" of *suzhi jiaoyu* provided a solution to the challenges posed by government restrictions on book selling in schools and an already competitive book market (Li Yuanjun 2003).

I felt the market demand for books related to child rearing and education most keenly when shopping at Kunming's book-cities, multistory superstores. These establishments dedicated a substantial amount of space to books related not only to child rearing and education but also to the related genres of popular psychology and self-help. Some offered free lectures given by authors of new books. I once attended a lecture on "social transition and psychological adjustment" by a local psychologist at a Xinhua Bookstore. It was a highly engaging standing-room-only event that ended with a book signing and the opportunity to purchase the speaker's works. The current popularity of psychology contrasts starkly with its former status as a capitalist evil.

Beyond the books are also the Internet; the serialization of best sellers in daily newspapers; popular magazines such as *Must-Read for Parents, Family Education,* and *Child Psychology;* and CCTV programs that sometimes address parenting issues, such as "Psychological Interviews" and "Tell It Like It Is." Local governments and public schools also play an important role in disseminating popular advice. Parents of school-age children attend lectures that are organized by their schools, with content that resonates with commercially channeled advice—namely how to understand and promote a child's subjectivity. I once attended a lecture for parents of first-year students at one of Kunming's key-point middle schools. The title was "Helping Children Pass through Adolescence," and the speaker lectured on the psychological needs of adolescents and the unique social pressures they face, the changes in self-awareness they undergo, and of course, how to help them sort out academic difficulties.

In Kunming, parents of children preparing to enter the first grade are required to attend "preschool training classes."[10] Speakers vary in what they concentrate on and have covered topics such as managing expectations, the importance of showing affection, and how to work with the school, as well as practical advice for academic survival (e.g., how to make the transition from reading pinyin to reading Chinese characters). These training classes are organized by the Women's Federation of a local district and are held a month or two before a child enters school. They grant a certificate, which then allows a parent to proceed with primary school registration. Once a child is in primary school, he or she brings home a paper called *Family Education Digest,* a division of Kunming Daily. Like *Population and Family,* an advice-giving newspaper distributed by birth-planning offices until its termination in the early 2000s, *Family Education Digest* is free of charge.

That parenting advice flows through so many channels is largely a result of the state's investment in what it calls "family education work," a throwback to socialist era mass mobilization. Discussed in the "1990s Program Outline for the Development of Children in China" (State Council 1992) and a series of subsequent documents principally authored by the National Women's Federation (National Women's Federation and State Education Commission 1996; National Women's Federation and Ministry of Education 2002, 2004), family education work aims to raise the "proficiency" of parents by using multiple channels for the dissemination of "scientific methods" of education, to provide "correct" knowledge and methods to parents.[11] The "National Plan for Family Education Work in the Ninth Five-Year Period" is especially worth noting (National Women's Federation and State Education Commission 1996). It gives further directions for running "parent schools" and calls for strengthening theoretical research and "fully utilizing modern communication media to disseminate family education knowledge." The document specifically names television stations and periodicals as having to take responsibility. As discussed in the previous section, these documents—depending on their publication date—situate the importance of their agendas in relation to *suzhi jiaoyu*.

If improving population quality by cultivating a cohort of well-rounded, entrepreneurial human talents has become a major political preoccupation in the post-Mao era, then popular expertise serves as the mediating technology that harmonizes state agendas with private aspirations. In sponsoring and endorsing the circulation of child-rearing expertise, the state—as embodied in official documents concerning family education work—exercises a modality of power that is expressed in acting on the actions of others. But this mode of power is nothing new in the history of Chinese statecraft, as widely circulated texts for guiding human conduct in general, and the conduct of educators in particular, have been around since the Han dynasty (206 BCE–AD 220).[12]

Creating a pedagogical environment rather than imposing force from above generates effects spontaneously by acting upon the human capacity to act upon oneself. In the case of contemporary popular advice, sheer exposure to its aesthetic properties can generate transformation, even if minute and ephemeral. If raising population quality is said to be a foundation-laying engineering project, one that—I would add—assembles persons (readers) and things (texts), then popular expertise constitutes a mediating technology that channels the energy and attention of parents in a certain direction. The next two chapters explain how this actually takes place—that is, how the advice generates change as well as new dilemmas. The next section considers the function of ambiguity in the *suzhi jiaoyu* movement.

Effecting the Affective Subject

China anthropologists have noted the ambiguity and flexibility of *suzhi jiaoyu*, pointing to the concept and program's lack of definition and specificity. It is true that what gets stuffed into the *suzhi jiaoyu* frame can often be surprising, a reflection of the official status of *suzhi jiaoyu* and the legitimacy it confers on those who invoke its language.[13] But ambiguity is not only a contingent accident, nor does it necessarily point to the limits or inconsistency of discourse. Reform advocates and even parents themselves insist on leaving the definition of suzhi jiaoyu ambiguous. Thus the question I would like to raise is whether this ambiguity might be the logical consequence of a broader historical tendency.

For popular writers such as Huang Quanyu, *suzhi jiaoyu* is an attitude, an orientation, and a way of thinking. Following the success of *Education for Quality in America,* Huang Quanyu was pressed by reporters, parents, and educators to give more concrete instructions for how *suzhi jiaoyu* might be carried out. But Huang refused to comply just as strongly as his interlocutors pressed him. Everyone wanted "a reduction of complexity" and "invariably concrete plans or measures" (2001: 8–10). Huang insisted that *suzhi jiaoyu* could not be summarized and operationalized. That he met with so much pressure to come up with a list, he argued, revealed the "utilitarianism and impetuousness of Chinese society" (2001: 10). In such an environment, *suzhi jiaoyu* would lose not only its meaning but also its vitality (10). If creativity, understood to mean the breaking of rules and routines (92), was at the heart of *suzhi jiaoyu*, then what *suzhi jiaoyu* ought to entail had to remain an open question because creativity was really nothing more than a potentiality.

I believe Huang Quanyu is genuinely concerned with the well-being of children and feels troubled when his audiences demand a prescription that would yield quick results, or, as he put it, a "golden touch prescription" (9). For writers such as Huang, advocating education reform can provide a means of critiquing the problems of Chinese society at large, in this case a widespread gain-seeking mentality. At the same time, however, the correspondences between the style of parenting he encourages and shifts in political reason at the highest level of government are undeniable. Reforms are intended to release the human and economic potentialities that have supposedly been suppressed for too long. Given this, governors of all kinds must rethink their approaches and remake themselves as facilitators rather than direct rulers.

Starting in the 1980s, Chinese intellectuals, officials, businesses, and ordinary people began to critique administrative intervention—rewards, punishments, quotas, and commands—as "overly heavy-handed," producing passive objects of instrumental reason (Sigley 2006: 499). The 1992 introduction of the term *socialist market economy* into official policy represented a significant conceptual shift that embraced the market as "conducive to creating superior subjectivities" (500). Just as intellectuals and officials argued that a planned economy restricted economic development and productivity, education reformers argue that hierarchical authority limits human development. Just as the market came to be understood as "conducive to forging superior citizens and enterprises" in contrast to the passive subjects of the planned economy, education reformers understand *suzhi jiaoyu* as doing the same in contrast to the passive subjects of education for exam taking (500). Just as the planned economy came to be seen as overlooking "the importance of economic levers such as price, monetary [*sic*], and taxation to shape and guide the economy" (501), education reformers argue that the importance of the child's subjectivity has been overlooked. Both levels of reform share an emphasis on nonintervention, so as to enable and promote the internal mechanisms of a given object of government (T. Kuan 2012: 1098–99).

If economic development has to come from technological breakthroughs, as Deng Xiaoping theorized, then the ambiguity of the *suzhi jiaoyu* project is functionally related to the nature of the breakthrough: it is unforeseeable. A major theme in the *suzhi jiaoyu* movement is a broadening of the definition of success, which is related to the movement's emphasis on facilitating the expression of potentialities to the greatest extent possible. In an important speech given at a meeting of the Standing Committee of the Politburo in February 2000, Jiang Zemin stated, "One does not necessarily have to go to college in order to succeed. Society needs multiple kinds of human talent. 'Three-hundred and sixty occupations, every occupation has a *zhuangyuan* [top scorer, or the very best in the field]'" (2001: 5). Then President Jiang was alarmed by a series of new stories about youth violence, but the idea that society needs "multiple kinds of human talent" had already been a policy concern. Diversifying the education system through the development of vocational and technical schools was positioned as a strategy for meeting the needs of economic diversification, and there have been attempts on the part of central officials as well as local governments to improve the appeal of vocational and technical training.[14]

Huang Quanyu also seeks to widen the definition of success. In the opening pages of *Family Education in America,* he clarifies: "This book is not merely for the cultivation of a Harvard genius or an Oxford talent; my own child will not necessarily be able to attend these schools, so I really do not dare to speak irresponsibly. This book is for the proletariat masses; it is written for the *suzhi jiaoyu* of the children of tens of thousands of ordinary families" (2001: 13). To make the idea of ordinariness compelling, Huang draws comparisons between Chinese and American education. Whereas Chinese family education, under the prompting of the exam-centric system, aims to cultivate "geniuses," American family education puts more emphasis on cultivating "real-life successes" (23).

Although the *suzhi jiaoyu* movement is often situated in relation to the puzzle of why Chinese education has failed to produce a Nobel Prize winner, popular writers like Huang Quanyu commonly stress the value of ordinariness. The following statement is illustrative: "The purpose of *suzhi jiaoyu* is to tap a person's potential to the greatest limit, so as to let a person's *suzhi* fully develop. Therefore, we should tell our children with the assumption that justice is on our side: 'As long as your potential has been expressed to its greatest limit, and your *suzhi* has been able to develop fully, then you have succeeded!'" (2001: 14). Education experts in China commonly insist that simply having the right attitude is both enough and crucial for facilitating the full expression of human potential, and they repudiate offering something more concrete and defined. This fuzzy logic, if you will, is expressed even by ordinary parents. A father I knew, in explaining how he understood the meaning of being "outstanding," said that in Chinese society today one does not necessarily have to become the best in a field to be an outstanding person. "As long as you have an acquired specialty," he told me, "and then you find a position that suits you, something you find interesting, something you are willing to do, and something that allows you to contribute to society, then you are a successful person. That is good enough." Another parent expressed her understanding of the phrase "become useful," what she hopes for with respect to her daughter, in similar terms: "Becoming useful is, actually, I think becoming useful does not necessarily have to accord with something I have designed for her. Rather, whatever she is interested in, I want to let her freely express it."

This notion of potentiality generates moral and financial responsibilities of a new kind. If a person will find his or her appropriate place in society as long as that person's unique potential is expressed, and as long as that person has had a chance to explore his or her interests, then parents are to take responsibility for doing "excavation" work (*wajue*). They have to excavate their child's potential by providing as many chances to explore and develop personal interests as possible. The more opportunities given, the more likely it is that a given person's potential will find expression. The cultural logic here is less a technocratic one that presumes a manufacturing system with quantifiable inputs and outputs than an affective logic that follows environmental feedback loops. Citing Howard Gardner Wang Lingling, a popular expert in Kunming, optimistically claims that "there is surely a special talent that suits your child" because every child is intelligent (2004: 71).[15] In a chapter titled "Establishing a Market Economy Child-Rearing Mentality," taken from a manual intended to help her readers adapt to the times, Wang argues that parents have no right to make decisions on behalf of their children. "Parents may only research their abilities and interests, so as to create the conditions that would foster and make real their abilities and interests" (112).

The notion that parents ought to do research expresses a historical tendency some would identify as "post-Fordism" or "Toyotism," in which the relationship between the producer and consumer becomes a rapid feedback loop. Under Toyotism, communications between the factory and the market are constant and immediate. While the Fordist mode of production manufactured goods to sell, the Toyotist mode of production maintains "zero stock," producing goods only after a market demand has been communicated (Hardt 1999: 93–94). Not dissimilarly, parents are to maintain a "zero stock" in terms of their expectations, creating conditions only after the child's wishes have been communicated. An open-ended approach to working with a child's interests thus corresponds to the open-endedness required by information-, knowledge-, and innovation-driven economies. Exercising flexibility, understanding, and tolerance as a parent facilitates the diversification and specialization such economies depend on. To diversify—economically, educationally, or individually—is to create layers of intensity from which something unexpected might emerge: a special talent, a competitive advantage, maybe even a Steve Jobs.

A story the famous expert Sun Yunxiao tells ties some of these themes together. It concerns a vibrant teenager he once knew named Autumn, who was exceptionally talented in many things, including choreography and songwriting. So when Autumn committed suicide in her second year in senior middle school, Sun was shocked. In the process of co-writing a report inspired by her passing, he discovered that she had some academic weaknesses in junior middle school and that, understanding her own limits as well as interests, she had decided she would attend a normal school for kindergarten teaching. Her parents were strongly opposed, however, and pushed her onto the college prep path toward university. So when she failed two of her subjects in her second year of senior middle school, which led to some disappointments in a relationship with a boy, she took her own life without a second thought.

At the end of the story Sun gives parents this advice: "Ask children what they think," and pay careful attention to what their emotions communicate about their feelings without demanding to know their every thought (2006: 150). For the tragedy of unresponsive parents, in Sun's eyes, is the failure to notice potential. Sun tells us that at Autumn's funeral her classmates lamented that "Autumn could have lived a happy life given any one of her special talents. That she kept failing in her weak areas was forced by her parents" (149).

The parents I knew commonly claimed to respect their child's interests and would choose classes according to their wishes. "Like piano," my friend Zhang Xin told me with regard to her son, "he would come home and practice and practice and practice. And then he didn't want to practice anymore. He thought it was very monotonous. So I said, if you can't do it, forget it, who cares." But they are staying with Olympic math "because he is still willing to learn it. And there is no burden. It's not like he has to do something when he comes home. They just take care of business right then and there."

Developing a child's special talent does not usually require much more than accommodating a child's request or expression of interest, but I have encountered instances where parents debated more supernatural techniques. I once observed a group of mothers engage in a passionate discussion about a palm-reading test that could divine a child's potential and identify eight major skills as early as the first year of life. One mother explained, "It could help decide which aspects of the child you should foster." One thought it made a lot of sense considering that fingerprints never change, and another attributed the test to "someone from Harvard." Still another wondered about the test's relationship to the *Book of Changes*, an ancient manual for divination. An exchange of public stories about geniuses who were born with disabilities concluded the conversation, to demonstrate that everyone had hidden potential. It was the job of adults to excavate it.

The parents I knew would send their child to as many "special-talent classes" (*techang ban, tese ban*) as possible, as many as a child could tolerate. These would include badminton, Chinese calligraphy, Chinese chess, the study of Chinese classics, composition, dance, drawing/art, electric keyboard, English, Go, Olympic math, piano, ping-pong, the Chinese lute, swimming, and violin. Since the Hongta Sports Center opened in 2000, middle-class children in Kunming could also learn ice-skating, and some parents would enlist private coaches to teach a particular sport. Parents felt that pursuing as many learning opportunities as possible would fulfill their responsibility for helping the child to develop an interest. The more information children received, the more abundant they might become. Parents also commonly insisted that the point of these various classes was not to raise, say, a professional artist or a professional pianist—these were utilitarian aims. The point of special-talent classes was to help the child become well rounded, a goal that corresponded to official agendas and to the hopes of reform advocates.[16]

A logic of potentiality resonates throughout the whole of the education field, demonstrating a certain cohesion to the reform project. To liberate human and economic potential, administrators and educators are to provide as many channels for diversification as possible, whether this means expanding educational options and opportunities or building as many capacities into the child as possible. The more variations layered into the field, the more possibilities for the expression of potential. The more potential expressed, the higher likelihood that something unexpected might emerge. In the hands of the popular experts, *suzhi jiaoyu* is anything but technocratic. But these experts share with the technocratic elite a vision of a glorious future to come.

Importantly, however, the logic of potentiality in the context of family life is blended with the struggle for social recognition (Anagnost 2004: 194). The arrangement of special-talent education may carry an intention of facilitating the expression of potential and of fostering a child's interests, but parents are also motivated by middle-class concerns and the acquisition of cultural capital. Importantly, such competition is less an expression of rational calculations made in the pursuit of self-gain and class status as ends in themselves than an expression of the will to survive what Allison Pugh has called the "economy of dignity," where social visibility and recognition are most at stake (2009). In this context, special-talent education is seen as having the potential to confer not only a competitive edge but also confidence—the lack of which may generate psychological discomfort in the future. "When she goes off to college and meets people of various classes, she won't feel bad," one mother explained. "She won't feel inferior."

Indeed, one could say that middle-class parents in urban China, like those in the United States, practice what the sociologist Annette Lareau (2011) has called "concerted cultivation," as they elicit children's opinions, develop interests, try to foster potential, and organize family life around scheduled activities expected to confer benefits in later life—practices that conform to expert definitions of good parenting and middle-class norms that reproduce socioeconomic inequalities. But the experience of middle-class Chinese parents differs from the experience of middle-class American parents in significant ways—largely because of factors that are unique to China's social and economic context. Special-talent classes eventually take a backseat by the time children get to lower middle school, when they begin to prepare for one of two key entrance exams, which serves to decide the fate of each individual test taker.

THE EXAMINATION REGIME

Every other Saturday, I offered English classes to some of the children in my study. I had two separate groups over at different times of the day, and I worked hard to create lesson plans that would involve more game playing than formal instruction. The last thing I wanted to be was yet another learning burden, so I tried to make our time together fun.

One nine-year-old named Abby liked my activities so much she came to both groups. Because she seemed to always come so eagerly, I was surprised when she arrived in a bad mood one Saturday in July. She started to complain about how tired she was as soon as she arrived, how she had two other English classes in addition to mine, as well as a pile of summer homework to do. I tried to cheer her up by saying, "Well if you finish it now maybe you can play when August comes." She retorted, "I will have more to do in August!"

A few months later, while visiting with Abby and her mom and dad one weekend after a Mid-Autumn Festival dinner, I learned more about why she was complaining. Abby's parents had been explaining that they do disagree about special-talent classes in what is otherwise a very collaborative parenting relationship. Abby's mom explained, "Her dad feels that with special-talent classes there's no need to go to so many. But *I* feel like the reason why the kid turned out as great as she has today has to do with going to special-talent classes."

Abby estimated that in the nine years of her life she must have attended at least twelve different kinds of classes. She tried to list them for me and then threw her arms into the air. "I can't even keep track anymore!"

Then Abby's father spoke up, "The reason why I have this point of view is, I think with learning special talents, it's like what the experts say, go according to the kid's interest, don't force more burden on them. It's like they say, the kid's naiveté is still really important. Maybe it's good enough to create an easygoing environment that's beneficial to her body-mind health. Maybe she can't even absorb everything you're trying to teach her with so many special-talent classes so suddenly."

But they *were* chosen according to interest now, Abby's mom said to her own defense, prompting me to ask Abby about that one weekend. As it turned out she still remembered—she knew which weekend I was talking about.

"What happened with you?" her mom demanded to know.

"Well the night before was Friday, right? I had gone to an English class. And then in the morning I went to a calligraphy class! And then in the afternoon I went to your class!"

Surprised, her mom asked her, "You see going to Teacher Kuan's as going to class?"

"Right. I do see it as going to a class!"

"But didn't you say you really liked what Teacher Kuan was doing?"

"Right! But the vocabulary words that Teacher Kuan taught, I have to remember all of them! And then you *test* me when I get home! When I can't answer you *scold* me! You say," Abby began to impersonate her mom, "'*Aiya!* She doesn't even take money, and you don't take it seriously! I'm not letting you go anymore.'"

Naturally, this caused embarrassment to Abby's mom, creating tension in the room. But this moment was also highly revelatory. I had always felt guilty about being complicit in the overscheduling of children, but I did sneak in a little vocabulary here and there to please the parents. I had no idea Abby was getting tested at home.

Abby's mom, Zhao Haihua, was a well-educated professional woman who believed in the importance of maintaining a friendship with her daughter. She tried to promote her daughter's subjectivity in a way that accorded with expert advice. For example, she once told me a story about taking her daughter out of her "little lunch table" group—one of the supervised lunch groups that schoolteachers arrange for busy parents who are willing and able to pay the extra fee. The "little lunch table" teacher had been complaining that the other children imitated whatever Abby did. If she ate two bowls of rice, they would eat two bowls of rice. According to Zhao Haihua, Abby's teachers generally had a problem with her having a personality, and although there was not much she could do to prevent the conflict between the culture of school and her daughter's individuality, she could at least take Abby out of the lunch group to protect her from being "flattened."

Zhao Haihua always spoke proudly of the closeness and mutual affection she shared with her daughter, but the logic of China's examination regime compromised her efforts to be a friendly parent. It is always a tricky matter to balance the demands imposed by a rigorous education system with the provision of "warmth" in the home, as Zhao Haihua once put it.

As much as reform advocates and policy makers strive to change an educational system that measures primarily according to test scores, exams remain firmly entrenched, with individual futures hinging upon how well a test taker performs on the ultimate college entrance exam (*gaokao*) and the penultimate senior middle school entrance exam (*zhongkao*). The centrality of exams in the lives of Chinese children and families cannot be overestimated. While middle-class Chinese parents *want* to do what the experts advise, the pressure to ensure academic survival becomes more and more intense as a child grows older and as that child comes closer to confronting key entrance exams.

The *zhongkao*—a citywide test—determines whether one goes on to senior middle school past the state-mandated nine years of compulsory education and what kind of high school one will attend (college prep or vocational). The national *gaokao* determines not only the kind of college or university a student will end up at (academic versus vocational, elite "211" versus non-211) but also one's major. Because so much hinges upon these two exams, parents feel that it is extremely important to gain admission to the right junior middle school, the stage that prepares students for the *zhongkao,* which then sets the stage for how well a student is prepared for the *gaokao.* Seeking admission into a reputable school expresses not merely an empty obsession with status but more importantly a practical concern with efficacious teaching methods and, for some, the securing of some modicum of life quality for one's child. Students take the same standardized entrance exams, so the schools that are overly dependent upon review classes and assigning large amounts of homework without producing high rates of promotion are avoided. Meanwhile, reputable schools mitigate the intensity of studying for these exams with talented teachers who use clever methods.

In Kunming, most of the families I knew had their sights set on the junior middle school affiliated with Yunnan University because it had been ranked number one for promoting their students to senior middle school year after year. This junior high has such a strong reputation that people now joke that the university is an affiliate of the junior high. As a private institution (*minban*), it charges families who are not affiliated with the university 7,000 RMB a year, totaling 21,000 RMB for three years of schooling. And they hold an entrance exam consisting of two subjects—Chinese and math—to select their student body.[17] According to the Compulsory Education Law, all children have the right to a free education, free of entrance examinations for the first nine years of their academic life at a school within their neighborhood district. But many Kunming parents are willing to "school-select" (*zexiao*), to seek a school outside of their assigned district and to try for admission at this junior high even though the 21,000 RMB price tag is an enormous expenditure for the average double-income family. One of the families I followed decided not to send their daughter to this school even though she got in because it would have been too much of a commute. They ended up regretting this decision because their daughter is now drowning in homework, and passing the entrance exam was not an easy achievement.

The standardized entrance exams for which schooling prepares students are intense because they test three years of cumulative knowledge in multiple subjects over the course of three days. The amount of material students have to learn and memorize by rote—whether thousands of years of historical facts and figures or the infinite varieties of math problems that may or may not appear on a test—is simply unimaginable to anyone who did not come of age in this system. It is common for schools to spend an entire semester simply reviewing rather than teaching new material, because there is so much to stuff into the brain.

The contemporary system is rooted in the imperial civil service examination system that originated in the Tang dynasty: *keju*. This was a standardized, merit-based, empirewide mechanism by which governmental officials were selected—and there was no greater glory than to succeed and secure gentry status through *keju*. Candidates had to memorize over four hundred thousand characters to master a curriculum that included classic Confucian texts, while making appeals to deities and using mantic devices to cope with the pressure (Elman 1991: 16; 2000). That superstitions remain commonplace to this day points to the sense of anxiety and uncertainty that surrounds the standardized exam: parents will propitiate at local temples and cook with ingredients homonymous with words like *smart* and *calculate* (i.e., green onions and garlic). Students meanwhile, will avoid ingesting any food or drink inauspiciously homonymous, and they even avoid getting haircuts, lest one "start from the beginning" (*congtou kaishi*). One young woman I knew wore matching red undergarments for good luck. It was her mother's idea.

The *gaokao* is infamously torturous and constitutes a system that pushes students to the limits of human endurance (Kipnis 2011). But the *zhongkao* is just as generative of anxiety because unlike the *gaokao*—which one can theoretically take multiple times until a satisfactory score is achieved—students may take the *zhongkao* only once. In 2007, to give a sample year, the *zhongkao* tested six subjects: Chinese, physics, math, politics/moral education, English, and chemistry. The total score was 660 points, with the cutoff lines of Kunming's key-point high schools predicted to fall somewhere around 600 points. Students were to register their preferences of high schools after they took the test without knowing their scores, on the basis of estimates derived from the results of practice tests as well as the different cutoff lines of different high schools from previous years, which change from year to year depending on the total number of applicants and how well they perform on average. For this reason, entrance exams have this additional layer of work, as the registration of preferences requires the ability to weigh factors and predict outcomes. Ideally, indicated preferences should correspond to performances on mock exams, because a school that you may have tested into but that ranked low in your preferences will not look kindly upon you.

For the *zhongkao*, a student who tests above a given school's cutoff may attend as a publicly funded student (*gongfei sheng*). Meanwhile students who fall 10 points below the cutoff of a given school have the option to try for admission as a "school-selecting student" (*zexiao sheng*), with actual places limited by permitted quotas. Like attending a junior high outside one's residential district, attending high school as a school-selecting student is expensive. (Such students are sometimes also referred to as self-funded students—*zifei*.) I was never able to verify exact fees in any concrete way, but I repeatedly heard and read that school-selecting students had to pay 10,000 RMB for every point below the cutoff.

School selection is widespread, first, because the desire for a good education is strong, with good schools setting high admission score thresholds and requiring nonpassing students to pay extra fees; and second, because the disparities in pedagogical quality between schools even within the same city create a situation in which everyone is scrambling to get into the better schools despite the exorbitant fees associated with going outside one's district. This second factor has less to do with the existence of high-income and low-income neighborhoods than with the specifics of educational policy in China.[18] Good schools are able to reproduce their popularity and status by investing the revenue that school-selecting families bring into institutional development—alongside other sources of revenue—to improve infrastructure and compete for top-notch teaching personnel. Institutional development in turn strengthens a school's educational resources, justifying high fees and selectivity.

Supporters of school selection see the phenomenon as a much-needed market mechanism that diversifies funding channels while benefiting the public as well as the individual. They argue that school selection simply reflects a desire for good schooling on the part of the masses, a desire that is met through the rational disposal of resources through the market system, while at the same time making up for deficiencies in state funding (Working Committee 2005). Critics, meanwhile, argue that school selection violates the principle of educational equality, deepens existing disparities between schools, facilitates corruption, and puts too much of a financial burden on the masses (Working Committee 2005; Yang Dongping [2004] 2006, 2006). Because sending one's child to a desirable school often involves paying school selection fees, families feel the pressure of having to cobble together whatever resources they have. Because performing well on an entrance exam could make the difference between paying or not paying tens of thousands of RMB in extra fees, students feel intense psychological pressure to study hard. Because teachers and schools are evaluated on the exam-based success rates of their students, the delivery of education becomes a narrow project in "teaching to the test."

An inadvertent consequence of a system oriented around test taking is the tendency of schools and teachers to focus on promising students while "discriminating" against others in the form of treating them unfairly, holding them back, suspending them, and expelling them (Man [1996] 1997). Such discrimination is more prominent at elite key-point middle schools that have reputations to protect, but it can begin as early as primary school. I often heard stories about children who were either pressured or asked to leave a school, or parents who transferred a child to a different school because of a conflict that had arisen with a teacher in a primary subject. One of the worst things that can happen to a student is a teacher who no longer cares, a phenomenon rooted in the pressures teachers are under and the competitions they are engaged in. Classrooms in Kunming, from primary to middle school, are quite large. With fifty to seventy students to shepherd toward success, teachers too feel a tremendous burden and have little patience for deviance.

I emphasize school selection because it is this manifestation of China's exam-centric education system that parents experience as *the* most pressing moral and practical issue. They want their child to live a good life, which means ensuring that the child will become a respectable person someday by finding a "good job." For their child to find a good job, they have to ensure that they set him or her on a path toward the kind of university that will confer a recognizable degree. To set their child on the right path, they have to sharpen the child's test preparedness with cram classes and daily monitoring and find ways to pay for admission into the right schools. If conflicts or misunderstandings with a teacher arise, they have to either help the child get back into the teacher's good graces or find a new school, because in the view of ordinary parents a good or bad relationship can make or break an academic career.

From a global perspective, anxiety is an intrinsic part of being middle class, a status that must be secured in each and every generation through educational achievement (Kremer-Sadlik and Gutiérrez 2013: 137–38). Like American middle-class mothers, Chinese middle-class mothers actively intervene in unfavorable situations related to school (although classroom situations do differ) (Lareau 2011). The craze for testing into the right school in China also resonates with something Allison Pugh calls "pathway consumption," found among families from both upper- and lower-income brackets in the Bay Area of California. Pathway consumption aims to create opportunities that shape life trajectories and to ensure "comfortable" environments for learning (2009: 177–214). Thus, from a comparative perspective, the intense anxiety of middle-class Chinese parents is not entirely unique. The global economy encourages individuals to "regard themselves as a portfolio of human capital assets that they can manage and develop" (Anagnost 2013: 13). Individuals, and individual families, are the ones expected to absorb "shocks" stemming from systemic contradictions (15). Job markets are precarious, and the specter of graduate unemployment haunts many countries the world over. Investing in human capital by investing financially and energetically in education does not guarantee a return, but it is something a middle-class family can control.

In China, the factors contributing to competition and uncertainty are rather unique to recent history. I began my fieldwork in early 2004, not long after the graduating class of 2003 hit the job market. This was a significant year in the history of higher education in China because this cohort enrolled in 1999, the year the central government decided on an expansion of the higher education system that included a dramatic expansion in enrollment. Between 1998 and 2004, nationwide enrollment into colleges and universities jumped from 9.8 percent to 19 percent. From the perspective of the Ministry of Education, this was an achievement because the goal had been set at 15 percent with a target date of 2010.[19] From the perspective of job seekers, however, this meant nearly 50 percent more competition in a job market where opportunities were constrained not only by the sheer number of competitors but also by their own aspirations for high-paying, high-status work (concentrated in coastal cities), by the country's rigid household registration system, by the preference for locally registered graduates among employers, by a strong bias in favor of graduates from key-point or even elite "211" universities (which themselves have preferences for local applicants),[20] and by the structural mismatch between the number of educated laborers and an economy still predominantly oriented toward construction and manufacturing rather than knowledge and services.[21] As one professor at Peking University's School of Management has pointed out, "High-end jobs that should have been produced by industrialization, including research, marketing and accounting etc., have been left in the West."[22]

Originally a decision that was made in the interest of stimulating domestic consumption, the expansion of higher education has led to academic inflation. In the context of oversupply, relatively arbitrary processes—alongside or even in place of the rational mechanisms assumed by human capital theory—serve to divide the winners from the losers. One researcher has explained this situation with the help of screening theory: "When the number of applicants with the same level of education increased significantly, it correspondingly increased employers' screening costs" (Chan 2012: 35). In such a context, an applicant is hired not necessarily because he or she is the most employable but rather because the applicant's diploma sent a stronger "signal" to the employer. For this reason, students in elite universities "can start celebrating the moment they begin their studies" (35). Meanwhile, parents raising primary school–age children are already thinking about what they need to do to ensure a child's competitiveness in the long term, because not all roads lead to Rome.

TWO MONKS AND A WELL

When I visited Kunming in 2010, I caught up with a group of mothers that had been friends with one another since their children were in the second and third grades. Their children had just finished their first and second years of junior middle school. It was mid-July, and everyone had just gotten out for the summer.

Yet the children going into their third year of junior high were already enrolled in cram classes in anticipation of the *zhongkao*, which would take place the following summer. The third year of junior middle school is a critical year. "*Xiaoyan miman!*" (A cloud of smoke hangs over the battle-field!), a school official might announce to start off an academic year at a parents' meeting.

One day I followed Wu Linlin and Phoebe to a one-week intensive Chinese cram class, where I watched a charismatic teacher lead a discussion and critique of essays students had written the night before. Students shared their essays by reading from them aloud, and the teacher used them as examples in illustrating *zhongkao* expectations for composition writing, which elements would earn you a certain score, and what you would get marked down for. She reminded them on at least two occasions that "you're writing your compositions for hamburger-brain teachers," using Kunming slang (*hanbao*) to make a point about the importance of clarity and organization and fitting oneself to the standard.

Hanging out with this group of mothers, who now faced the pressures of coaching and preparing their children for their first standardized entrance exam, I got a very strong sense of the at-stakeness of the moment. They used all sorts of vivid metaphors for describing the significance of hard work at this stage of life—"plowing and weeding" (*gengyun*), "spreading a cushion" (*pudian*), and "laying in stock" (*chubei*). One mother told me a story to further explain what they meant by some of these terms. It concerned two monks who ran into each other every day, fetching water from a well. They did this for many years, hiking up and down to and from their monasteries for water, until one day one of the monks stopped showing up. The other monk wondered where his buddy could have disappeared to and worried that he had gotten sick. Out of concern, he visited his friend's monastery and, to his surprise, found him sitting cross-legged, meditating peacefully. He asked his friend why he wasn't going down to draw water anymore, and his friend answered, "I don't have to anymore. I have spent many years digging my way to the water source. I don't have to go to the well anymore."

Class tension and anxiety were expressed in these conversations, with one mother explaining that the *zhongkao* will determine what school you go to, whether you will meet good teachers, and what kind of people you will surround yourself with, and another stating more bluntly that a good high school determines "which level [*cengci*] you will live at."

Later chapters in this book will further contextualize these classist expressions in the context of ethics. For now, I should note that, unlike the ideological subjects imagined by anthropologists inspired by Althusser, parents are quite aware that the whole system is arbitrary. Yet they feel there is no other choice but to "adapt" (*shiying*), since they see no alternative and have no luxury to permit the kind of chaos Huang Quanyu admires so greatly about American educational practices. I want to argue that parental intensity expresses a kind of moral agency that takes timely and situationally appropriate effort as a crucial element of being efficacious in this world. It is a kind of agency derived in conformity rather than resistance, offering a folk philosophy of practical action that speaks back to debates in anthropology over the positioning of the subject versus the experience of the person, and to Western assumptions concerning authenticity and identity. While child-centered popular advice for parents reverses deeply rooted cultural logics concerning personhood and the nature of reality, the practical wisdom of parents—mothers especially—continues to assert a different way of being-in-the-world. The story about the two monks and the notion of "plowing and weeding" or "laying in stock" invoke the logic of *shi*—potential born of disposition. Small actions will gather force over time, and the incipient will give way to the actual.[23]

TWO

———

The Horrific and the Exemplary

IF THE *SUZHI JIAOYU* MOVEMENT HAS HELPED attune parents to a child's psychological interiority, this efficacy derives in large part from the experts' knack for seductive storytelling. In providing personal illustrations of the issues at hand, stories can achieve what simple injunctions cannot. This chapter presents two stories in particular—one a positive model that presents virtues to emulate, and the other a negative model that presents errors to avoid—as told by well-known child-rearing experts publishing under the banner of *suzhi jiaoyu*. Popular experts play a pivotal role in rendering the ideals of *suzhi jiaoyu* self-evident and commonsensical, and their use of storytelling as a technique in the context of China's population improvement project expresses the art of disposition. If the art of disposition concerns itself with the generation of spontaneous effects by virtue of a certain arrangement of things, then providing models fits into this category in assembling exemplars together with learners. And if the art of disposition is related to the manipulation of affectivity for human ends, then the use of models is dispositional in playing upon the power of the model to affect and the capacity of the learner to be affected.

Sheer exposure to what François Jullien calls the "inspirational force of virtue" has a spontaneous effect ([1992] 1995: 66). Like the tendency generated by relations of force, whether in history or the art of war, the exemplary lesson creates a situation where the presentation of a model gives rise to its "copy." Although modeling has long been deployed as a political instrument in Chinese statecraft, I would say that the reason why modeling works in the first place has something to do with the natural dynamic of influence and response.[1] To be exposed to something is to enter into a new relation, which inevitably engenders a transformation of some kind. The exposure of plant life to the vagaries of sunlight and rain gets registered in leaves, stems, and branches. The mutual exertion of force in the contact between a rush of water and a riverbank affects the quality of the water and reshapes the contours of the bank. Assembling together a couple of toddlers with opposing proclivities will alter their personalities, even if only temporarily. This is the rule of affectivity: things change by virtue of exposure and recombination.

The famous story about Mencius's mother moving three times offers an instance of affectivity narrativized. When Mencius and his mother lived near a cemetery, Mencius learned to wail and bury things; when they moved into town, Mencius learned to buy and sell things; when they moved near a school, Mencius learned proper manners and thirsted for knowledge. This story points to the Chinese belief that learning and environmental exposure are intertwined, and to the belief that environmental influence—imperceptible and slow acting—is the deepest and most enduring. Modeling has long been a preferred method in educating the young and governing society for this reason. Models are understood as "carriers" of influence (Bakken 2000: 157). Their use plays upon nature to create second nature (Taussig 1993), operating somewhere between the preconceptual level and the level of conscious moral evaluation.

Amy Olberding argues in her discussion of the *Analects* as an exemplarist virtue ethics that exemplarism does not so much illustrate ethical concepts as generate the examples from which an elaboration of moral goods is sourced. In other words, it is in and through the model that conceptual schemes arise in the first place. Olberding explains, "When we employ direct reference in identifying exemplars, we do not yet know what features of their behavior, comportment, or character are salient for the evaluative claim. We must query our responses to exemplars in order to formulate these" (2008: 632). There is an aesthetic response that involves a sense "that virtue is *that*" (633)—something like enchantment—before conceptualization. This initial experience resists articulation because the text, containing seemingly trivial details about all sorts of human figures—as in the case of the *Analects*—is still "pregnant" with possibilities (632). Olberding's theory of theory development may help to explain why modeling has endured as a technique in Chinese statecraft: it is efficacious in affecting people even "in the absence of understanding" (630).

The experts giving child-rearing advice under the banner of *suzhi jiaoyu* in contemporary China are frequently telling stories. Their stories, like the *Analects,* point to a *that,* which usually precedes the formulation of take-away advice. I came to take storytelling seriously because my interlocutors so often invoked horror stories—negative models—in expressing support for my research project.[2] Both in interviews and in casual chats, I heard tales about gambling, bullying, Internet addiction, cruelty to animals, suicide by hanging, the drinking of pesticides, student-on-student murder, and suicides faked with iodine. These tales were presented as full of indication. Just minutes into a conversation, complete strangers would commend me for taking on a major social issue, and their hearty approval would coincide with the telling of stories, as if to point to the source that had given rise to thought in the first place. Horror stories suggest that the young have psychological problems, but their interpretation usually leads to questions about the state of education in China, and subsequently to the formulation of normative guidelines.

The horror story I heard most often concerned a teenager named Xu Li who had beaten his mother to death with a hammer. It had happened in the winter of 2000, in Jinhua City, Zhejiang Province. The event was not at all premeditated—it just happened.

Of course, what shocked the public about this news story was the murder itself: a mother died at the hands of her own son. But what was even more shocking, and therefore deeply puzzling, was the fact that this teenager was a high-achieving, morally upright student. Typically referred to as the "good student kills mother" story, the case stimulated a flurry of questions: What would drive a child to do this? Was Xu Li the one to blame? What is wrong with our education system?

In this chapter, I will explain how the collective interpretation of a horror story such as the "good student kills mother" case provides a moral arena in which truths about how to raise and educate children are produced and naturalized.[3] I will juxtapose this case with an exemplary case concerning a woman named Zhou Tingting. Born deaf, Zhou Tingting was destined to live a life of social exclusion. But because of her father's painstaking efforts to educate her despite an unpromising future, Zhou Tingting defied both fate and social expectations. She came to be known as a genius, skipped two grades at an ordinary primary school, won a national *shijia shaonian* (Top Ten Youth) title, and went on to study at an American graduate school. Zhou Tingting's success catapulted her father, Zhou Hong, into stardom: he has published a number of books describing his method, he goes on national lecture tours, and he is acting principal at a school for deaf children in Nanjing.

While starkly opposite in content, with one displaying errors to avoid and the other wisdom to emulate, horror and exemplary stories render the ideals of *suzhi jiaoyu* self-evident and commonsensical. In the context of popular advice, they provide negative and positive models for "good" and "bad" parenting, operating somewhere between the aesthetic and the moral. While horror stories give rise to shock and exemplary stories give rise to awe, both combine incongruous qualities into single figures—the good student who commits a cold-blooded murder and the disabled child genius. Narrative sequencing, meanwhile, constructs moral arguments in implicating certain causes with certain effects. Horrific and exemplary stories make moral arguments for attending to the inner subjectivity of children and generate new categories to be discovered and understood: psychological health and human potential.

Embedded in the popular advice, stories about good and bad parenting play a critical role in mediating between the grand project of national revitalization and the mundane details of everyday life. They model how parents ought to conduct themselves in a way that does not threaten a child's psychological health or obstruct the development of potential. Although there is in China a large repository of narratives and proverbs about great learners who achieve despite having every reason to give up, the positive model focuses not on the learner's personal attributes but on a particular style of parental love. By attending to the inner life of his daughter, Zhou Hong allowed her potential to flourish. Mother Xu on the other hand, is depicted as having had a one-track mind, caring only about her son's academic performance and very little about his interests and feelings. Since China wants to shift its economic strategy from a dependence on cheap labor to the building of a knowledge economy, how children are raised matters a great deal. Under the banner of *suzhi jiaoyu*, which emerged with a major political shift toward "human-centered" governance, parenting is less a technocratic project of improving and perfecting the child than an agricultural endeavor of optimizing a nurturing environment. In this context, parents are the ones who require socialization, because they—along with schools and teachers, other major targets of reform—can either facilitate or obstruct the nation-transforming potential thought to reside in the subjectivity of the child. The moral dilemmas experienced by readers of the popular advice—that is, ordinary middle-class mothers trying to strike a balance between raising a competitive child and raising a psychologically healthy child—have to be situated against this larger discursive background.

Xu Li's case is very unusual because the crime he committed is so incomprehensible. But there is another reason for its extraordinariness. Whereas in the case of consummated suicide, it is usually not possible to know much about the young person's thoughts and feelings that led up to the act, in the case of "good students kills mother" the suffering child driven to violence has told his side of the story in his own words.

One of the most well-known child-rearing experts in China is Lu Qin, who also goes by the name Intimate Sister (*Zhixin Jiejie*). Lu Qin started her career as a journalist and in recent years has published a number of advice books. She established a periodical for children and their parents, also named *Intimate Sister*, and she tours the country giving talks to both adults and schoolchildren. Lu Qin had the opportunity to interview Xu Li after the murder, and she has spoken about this interview both on television and in print. To analyze this case, I will use her presentation of the interview in a book titled *The Call of Education for Quality*, a collection of discussions, speeches, and essays published by Xinhua Press (2001). To what extent Lu has accurately represented their exchange is not at issue here, for I am equally if not more interested in how she frames his story for the public.

Lu divides her chapter into sections, each establishing a principle of her conception of *suzhi jiaoyu*. These include "giving children room to grow," "cultivating realistic hopes," "allowing positive life experiences," "opening channels of respectful communication," and "rearing through affirmation." The chapter begins with her arrival in the city of Jinhua. Accompanied by two reporters, Lu Qin sets out to hear Xu Li's story, "to find the root cause of Jinhua's tragedy" (2001: 221). Prefiguring the tragedy she is about to investigate, she describes the heaviness of the clouds and the drizzle in the air. After walking down a stone-slab road, she arrives at a drafty detention house.

She meets Xu Li for the first time in a dark room. He wears a blue sweater and a knit yellow cap. She is surprised to see "that this skinny, lanky, fair-skinned boy with a nice, peaceful expression is actually someone who murdered his own mother" (221). She sits across from him. Noticing his nervousness, she reveals that she is Intimate Sister to break the ice. Xu Li immediately warms up and agrees to talk about his family and his mother.

He begins by describing what adds up to be an oppressive world—a household in which he couldn't keep any secrets and in which phone calls from his friends were intercepted. He tells her,

My mother would ask in detail before turning the phone over to me. I had talked to her about this before, but she said: "You befriended some bad influences out there—my words don't get through to you at all anymore." After that, my friends didn't dare to call me anymore. They even laughed and said: "Xu Li, who dares to call your house? Your mom's too much [*lihai*]." Sometimes I felt lonely and wanted to call a classmate, but my mom would say: "If you have something to talk about, finish it at school, what else is there? Call about what?" (223)

Lu' thinks to herself, only hatred could cause a child to kill a parent, so she asks Xu Li if he hated his mom for intercepting his calls. He tells her that he didn't feel hate but felt increasingly stifled. He continues to describe his mother as someone who cared only about his studies. In recalling an instance when he came home ten minutes late from playing ball, he claims that his mother hit him with a club, a belt, and a broom. "When it came to my studies, my parents stood on the front line. Their expectations of me were very high—they hoped I would earn a high enough test score to enter Peking University, Tsinghua University, or at least Zhejiang University. Given my abilities, this wasn't realistic" (224).

Sometime around the beginning of high school, a "raging animosity" slowly began to grow. Doing well in a key-point class that Xu Li had tested into only sustained and elevated his mother's expectations. If less than desirable test scores came back, Xu Li's mother would scold and hit him. "I felt like I had already grown up so much, yet she was still treating me like a primary student. It was really hard to bear—I felt very stifled. I liked to play soccer, read, watch television, but Mother felt that these would affect my studies and always tried to stop me. When classmates at school were discussing current events and television shows, I didn't know anything and there was nothing I could say. I wanted to read the newspaper, but mother would say that college examinations weren't going to test what was in the papers" (224). Xu Li continues to describe his daily life as monotonous, unhappy, and devoid of meaning.

Eager to know what led up to the homicide, Lu Qin carefully asks: "How did the contradiction between yourself and your mother become more intense?" (225). Xu Li answers by describing the day of the murder. It was just after lunch; Mother Xu was sitting in her bedroom, knitting a sweater in front of the television. He wanted to join her, catch a few minutes of television, but she began to say the usual things: "I'm telling you, if you can't get into university, I won't give you a second opportunity. If you don't test into the top ten on your finals, I'll break your legs. I'm the one who gave birth to you anyway—it doesn't matter if I beat you to death" (225). Deeply hurt, Xu Li grabbed his backpack and headed toward the front door of the apartment without a word. On his way out he saw a metal hammer on the shoe cabinet, then burst back into the bedroom with it.

Lu Qin does not ask how he committed the murder, but her question about what he did afterward elicits disturbing details. After aimlessly wandering the streets for a couple hours, Xu Li suddenly realized that he should do something to save his mother. But she had bled profusely and it was already too late to bring her back to life. So . . . he stuffed her body into a suitcase.

PERSPECTIVE BY INCONGRUITY

Incongruity, a theme that emerges again and again in this and numerous other publicly circulated horror stories, produces both an aesthetic and a moral effect on the reader. It has been a popular theme in various literary genres in China for centuries. According to Perry Link, "All sources point to strong popular interest in the unusual, the marvelous, and the unexpected. Apparently opposite features are combined in one character, as in a beggar with a grotesque face but a heart of gold, or an alluring young woman who is also a martial artist who can fling you twenty feet" (2000: 222). Opposing qualities produce a sense of the strange and marvelous (*qi*), "important in Chinese storytelling for centuries, [and] depend[ing] for its allure on the natural tension between presentations that are too strange to seem true and the implicit claim that, nevertheless, they *are* true" (226).

Incongruity serves to dramatize issues. How does this work? Victor Turner's ideas about ritual aesthetics may be instructive here. In his essay on liminality, the interstructural stage within a ritual initiation, Turner identifies three parallel processes in how ritual objects communicate (1967). The first two, disproportion and monstrousness, are relevant here. The first process refers to the disproportionate representation of, say, a nose in relation to other facial features on a mask, or of one bodily extremity in relation to another on a ritual figurine. In explaining why one feature may get exaggerated to the diminution of another, Turner argues that "to enlarge or diminish or discolor in this way is a primordial mode of abstraction. The outstandingly exaggerated feature is made into an object of reflection" (103).

Monstrosity serves a similar thought-provoking purpose in the ritual process. Borrowing from William James, Turner argues that monsters "teach neophytes to distinguish clearly between the different factors of reality" by the law of dissociation. That is to say, the presence of two elements that do not belong together in a unity produces a dissociation of one thing from another at the same moment it evokes horror. The response arises by virtue of a recognition that *a* and *b* do not belong together. Both "grow into an object of abstract contemplation" (105). Turner explains: "Monsters startle neophytes into thinking about objects, persons, relationships, and features of their environment they have hitherto taken for granted" (105).

While there are certainly differences to be noted between the function of ritual in small societies like that of the Ndembu and the function of media in a late socialist state, in both contexts ritual or narrative aesthetics offer symbols for reflection that abstract taken-for-granted cultural elements from their context. In ritual, aesthetics serve to move a group of initiates from one social category to another; in mass-mediated parenting advice, aesthetics serve to change deeply entrenched educational attitudes and practices. Kenneth Burke, who gives us the phrase "perspective by incongruity," ✱ observes that "any new way of putting the characters of events together is an attempt to convert people. . . . It is impious . . . insofar as it attacks the kinds of linkage already established. It attempts . . . to alter the nature of our responses" ([1935] 1954: 86–87).

Xu Li's story is embedded within a book aimed at disseminating the argument that the "old way" is no longer the "right way." It begins with archetypal personas—the hopeful parent and the youthful teenager—as well as a familiar situation, in which extracurricular activities such as playing ball and making friends become secondary to studying. But the story that unfolds is anything but quotidian. Besides the obvious shock of the murder, a catastrophic breach in routine, the power of the story lies in the aesthetic of incongruity. By combining the common and idealized figure of the curious, youthful, and hard-working student with that of a cold-blooded criminal, the story raises the interpretive problem of where to locate the reason for the crime. Who is to blame for what happened? Xu Li's personal narrative gives the reader a sense that he is a "good kid." It provides plenty of evidence for Xu Li's being both a high achiever with considerable academic potential and a morally upstanding youth.[4] In answering Lu Qin's question of whether he has ever done anything that gave him a sense of pride, Xu Li describes his membership in a "Learning to Be Like Lei Feng" group. Explaining his motivations, he says, "I thought, there will be a day when I have to live on my own, so I can't not know how to cook. Learning to help the old lady, I could also improve my own skills" (Lu 2001: 230).

This figure of the good socialist youth contrasts with the scene that takes place after the murder. After Xu Li stuffs his mother into a suitcase, he is on the run. He sleeps in a local swimming hall, just scared out of his wits. To preserve a sense of status quo, he does, however, return on the weekend, when his father comes home from doing business. Xu Li tells his father that Mom has gone out of town, when in reality "Mother's corpse was right next door to my room. I felt extremely tense" (226). At the end of the weekend, he escapes to a hotel in another city, where he is finally caught. This narrative configuration of the fugitive lends monstrosity to the protagonist.

But it is the less obvious incongruity in the Xu Li story that reflects the real horror: his mother's disproportionate parenting style. At first glance, she seems rather ordinary. Between the one-child policy and a competitive education system that measures academic achievement with test scores, parents are full of anxiety. Because securing the good life for children means keeping them on the academic track that will eventually lead to admission into a decent university, which in turn supposedly leads to good jobs, it is quite common for parents to "stand on the front line." But, the reform advocates argue, parenting narrowly focused on exam success fails to correspond to the needs of the new economy—namely the cultivation of self-awareness and a spirit for innovation and enterprise among China's youth. In Intimate Sister's narrative reframing, Mother Xu is simultaneously a familiar figure and an obstruction to Xu Li's development. Her constant interception of phone calls leaves Xu Li feeling increasingly stifled. Her obsession with top-flight universities is pursued to the neglect of locating and nurturing other possible talents. And perhaps the most startling incongruity, one that metonymically links human development and national development, is Mother Xu's refusal to allow Xu Li to read the newspaper or watch TV. Just as the Iron Curtain was responsible for China's lagging development, Mother Xu's restrictions put Xu Li in the situation of having "nothing to say" in the company of friends. He doesn't know anything about current events or public culture, so he can't participate in social exchange.

If disproportion and monstrosity serve to startle Ndembu neophytes into reflection, then it comes as no surprise that public horror stories have startled the Chinese public into a discussion about the problems with the entire education system. The "good student kills mother" case helped inspire a short-lived policy in 2000 known as *jianfu*, or reducing the burden. The prohibition of Saturday classes and the weighing of backpacks at school gates were just two of the many measures instituted to reduce academic pressure on students.[5] Alarmed by the Xu Li case, then president Jiang Zemin even stated at a meeting of the Standing Committee of the Politburo that all responsible parties—from schools to Party organizations—must work to guide the urgent wishes of parents in the right direction (2001: 4). Unwavering diligence did have a purpose, but "we must not confine our youth in rooms and in books all day" (4). Jiang's speech began with a list of horror stories, as if to bring his audience back to the scene of his initial shock. This scene of original shock, the *that,* provided the foundation for the rest of his talk.

Moral Coding and Diagnosing

The rhetorical power of narrative has long been demonstrated by philosophers, literary critics, and anthropologists. In choosing to narrate some events and not others, in assembling disparate moments together in a single plot, stories make moral arguments. In research with North American occupational therapists, Cheryl Mattingly found that the stories clinicians told in team meetings not only recounted "the facts" but also inadvertently constructed a "good" in morally complex situations. Mattingly writes, "The good is never explicitly discussed. Rather, it is naturalized in the very process of the telling itself" (1998b: 289). Similarly, the Illongot hunting stories Renato Rosaldo collected have a way of rendering the evaluation of particular experiences incontestable. "Rather than saying that events were terrifying, dangerous, and extraordinary, storytellers often embed their evaluations in the narrative itself" (1986: 116).

In modern China, we see an explicit recognition of the rhetorical power of narrative, actively deployed in different ways and in different periods for grand social purposes. In the early twentieth century literary culture came to be recognized as a powerful tool for social reform. According to Marston Anderson, Chinese intellectuals "reasoned that literature could reach a deeper level of cultural response than political manipulation had succeeded in doing; a new literature, by altering the very worldview of its readers, would, they hoped, pave the way for a complete transformation of Chinese society" (1990: 3). Initially, Western realism offered promise and embodied many of the ideals that attracted Chinese intellectuals, such as scientism and horizontal social relationships. But they struggled to indigenize the form in a series of debates that unfolded over a number of years, until Mao Zedong's "Talks at the Yan'an Forum" in 1942 established a single orthodoxy for art and literary practice (Anderson 1990: 73; Link 2000: 21). Socialist realism, the dominant genre of the Maoist era, held that a literary work should both reflect reality and serve as an inspired mirror that puts ideals on display. As Anderson puts it, socialist realism was to "reflect and describe reality but also to direct and propel reality" (1990: 57). For our purposes, we may take the instrumentalization of narrative as an expression of artful disposition, because narrative can activate the kind of response that gathers a force of its own—one potentially propulsive of social transformation.

Lu Qin's retelling of Xu Li's story has the qualities of a socialist realist text. At one point, Lu asks the morally loaded question "Do you know how you were brought up?" Xu Li responds by recalling his mother's hard work and sacrifice, which prompts Lu Qin to remind him of the fact that there are many children much more unfortunate than he. Xu Li begins to sob and says, "I am a beast, I used my own two hands to 'send away' my mother. I regret it so much" (2001: 226). Xu Li in this story traverses the opposition from a teen unable to control his anger to a teen capable of gratitude, deep remorse, and the desire to transform his mistake into a lesson for all.[6] At the end of her chapter, Lu Qin includes a handwritten letter from Xu Li to his classmates in which he warns his peers against making the same mistake he has and to appreciate what they already have. "I hope that you will treasure the opportunity to learn, don't wait until it is gone to appreciate it," he wrote, "Classmates, I think of you. If I am free one day, I hope that I will see that you have all succeeded, you have all become oak beams of the nation" (232).

But the "good student kills mother" case also does more than put correct moral positions on display. By presenting a shocking act of unspeakable violence committed by a nonviolent person, Xu Li's story reveals a symptom of a social ill. So unspeakable is the murder that the actual act is hidden from narrative view, with Xu Li's voice trailing off before he finishes his account of it: "I burst into the bedroom, and . . ." (225). We return to his internal landscape after the consummation of the act. He recalls, "After I did what I did, I ran on the street for two hours, I couldn't understand how I could do something so cruel. My mind was a blank, my head very dizzy. I was running and running. Then I suddenly realized, that is my mother! I have to go save her!" (225). Ruled by the passion of anger, Xu Li has a lapse in consciousness during the act. This moment of absence, sandwiched between symmetrical states of moral propriety (a member of the "Learning to Be Like Lei Feng" group before the crime, expressing deep remorse after the crime), appears like a symptom, indicting his mother's parenting as traumatic.

The Xu Li case and others like it simultaneously signify errors in parenting and retroactively constitute a distinct phenomenon to be discovered and understood: the psychological health of children, which is threatened by parenting that does not adhere to the principles of *suzhi jiaoyu*. If incongruity activates an aesthetic response that leads to reflection and discussion, then the symptom constructs and naturalizes a truth concerning trauma and deviance from an ideal state of health. One commentator wrote: "Actually, it might on the surface seem as if the child couldn't handle the burden of his studies, so he killed his own mother. But if you look at it from the perspective of psychology and education, this precisely reflects a serious psychological problem in the child. This has already been acknowledged by many psychologists in the analysis of this case. People also feel that this precisely reflects that psychological health is ignored in the home" (Wang Weiguo 2001: 136).

In Lacanian psychoanalysis, an event must be put into words (a patient's story) for the event to be recognized as being the cause of a symptom. This determines "the lifting of the symptom" (Lacan 1977: 46). But the analysis of the symptom does not reveal a hidden truth about a traumatic past. Rather, the truth lies in the form in which the symptom appears, namely the discourse produced in the psychoanalytic transaction in which a patient's entire speech is symptomatic. Slavoj Žižek explains, "Symptoms are meaningless traces, their meaning is not discovered, excavated from the hidden depth of the past, but constructed retroactively—the analysis produces the truth: that is, the signifying frame which gives the symptoms their symbolic place and meaning" (1989: 56).

Public interpretation of the Xu Li story gives the symptom its symbolic place and meaning. That a good student is driven to commit such violence is symptomatic of bad parenting, uninformed by expert knowledge and principles of *suzhi jiaoyu*. This diagnosis depends heavily on the narrative form. If aesthetics help to dramatize issues, the "lifting of symptoms" in narrative naturalizes connections between cause and effect. Narratives turn "the noise and incidentalness of everyday life into a compacted causal argument (a plot)," so that one thing after another becomes one thing *because* of another (Mattingly 1998a: 45).

Thus the mystery of how a child could be driven to murder is resolved in the sequencing of events that emerges in Lu Qin's retelling. Xu Li was driven to murder *because* his mother's hopes were too high, *because* she gave him little room for growth, and *because* she failed to allow positive life experiences, cultivate realistic ideals, communicate with him on equal terms, and affirm him for his achievements, violating Lu Qin's principles of education. The example gives rise to an incontestable moral evaluation: Xu Li was killed first.

INVERTING DISABILITY

If the "good student kills mother" case offers a negative model that presents parenting errors to avoid, then Zhou Hong's recollection of how he raised his daughter Zhou Tingting, entitled *Appreciate Your Child* (2003), constitutes an exemplary model that offers wisdom to emulate. While Mother Xu is portrayed as constantly criticizing her son, Zhou Hong portrays himself as a wellspring of love. For Zhou Hong, parents ought to constantly give positive affirmations, even in times of failure. He uses his upright thumb, ubiquitous in public photographs of him, to symbolize his version of parental love. He argues, "Different fingers have different meanings. In raising their children, some parents constantly use their index finger to jab their child's head: you dunce, how can you be so stupid?" (39). The thumb muscles of Chinese parents, according to Zhou Hong, are in a state of atrophy.

But good parenting for Zhou Hong does not simply involve encouragement and praise. In fact, he laments that parents often misunderstand him. Appreciating one's child, the phrase that encapsulates his approach, involves attending to their inner life. Once Zhou determined to educate his deaf daughter as if she were perfectly ordinary, he decided that his first "move" (*zhao*)—a verb often used in chess, martial arts, and military strategy—was to help his daughter find a kind of "good-child-feeling."

Zhou Hong recounts the time when Zhou Tingting was just learning to use the abacus. She was the slowest in her whole entire class, something she herself knew. "The child already thinks she's slow," he writes. "It's useless if you criticize her. She will most definitely think, 'If even Mom and Dad think I'm slow, then I must really be inadequate.' I wanted to help her find the feeling for abacus, let her believe that she could do it" (45). So Zhou told his daughter he was convinced that she was fast, entering into a little disagreement with her, and then disproving her with an experiment. He took out his watch to time her, and Zhou Tingting began calculating. He commended her when she got it right and exclaimed he simply didn't have her skill level when he was her age. Over a period of forty days, Tingting's abacus ability improved by leaps and bounds. Zhou Hong confesses that in the process of this experiment he actually repeatedly lied to his daughter. If she took thirteen minutes to finish a calculation, he would look at his watch and then tell her that she had finished in twelve minutes and fifty seconds.

In his books and lectures, Zhou Hong argues it was concrete methods such as this that contributed to Zhou Tingting's success. Born deaf, Tingting not only avoided going to a deaf school but also managed to skip two grades, won a *shijia shaonian* title, and went abroad for a master's degree in the United States. What is so compelling about this story? There is certainly the obvious attraction of a good success story, but what makes a good success story? Why did Zhou Hong become a household name among the families I knew?

In the remainder of this chapter, I will read Zhou Hong's narrative in light of the arguments developed from the "good student kills mother" case. I specifically analyze the manual *Appreciate Your Child*. While "good student kills mother" and Zhou Hong's story occupy opposite poles, they employ similar narrative aesthetics and make a convergent moral argument about what constitutes good parenting.

Battling Fate

Like the "good student kills mother" story, Zhou Hong's features the narrative aesthetic of incongruity in offering characters that combine opposing qualities: the disabled but genius child, the education expert with no formal training. Like the "good student kills mother" story, this narrative offers abstractions that provoke thought. If the former prompts the question of who and what to blame for Xu Li's crime, the latter prompts the question of how to explain Zhou Tingting's and Zhou Hong's achievements.

Zhou Hong begins *Appreciate Your Child* with an illness story, one that recounts the cause of Tingting's deafness, the search for a medical cure, and the experience of social exclusion and stigma. Within this story is a rather tear-jerking episode. When Tingting was in preschool, she often peed in her pants because she did not know how to express herself to the teacher. This was not a problem during the spring, summer, and fall. But as soon as winter arrived, Zhou Hong would burst out of factory gates "burning with anxiety" at the end of a workday. He recalls, "The first thing I would do when I saw her was feel her pants. If her pants were wet, my heart felt dampened. Riding home, my tears gushed forth as winter wind blew on my daughter's trembling, twisting body. It was as if my heart had been pierced by ten thousand arrows" (2003: 3–4).

Zhou proceeds to narrate the time he lost control of his bicycle while wiping tears from his eyes. Tingting fell off the bike and hit her head on the muddy ground. Her wailing attracted the attention of onlookers. Back at home, Zhou washed Tingting's body from head to toe. He recalls, "We didn't have heat, so I used my body to keep her warm. Miserable tears fell drop by drop onto my daughter's delicate little face as she looked at me with puzzlement" (4). The prominence of bodily excretions in this story, in the form of urine and tears (later mixing with mud), derives meaning and intelligibility from the "speaking bitterness" genre.

Highly dramatic and emotional, "speaking bitterness" was a narrative technique deployed during the land reform era. As a part of justifying the redistribution of land and wealth, revolutionary cadres encouraged peasants to narrate their sufferings and to recognize their anguish as a product of exploitation. The presence of the body in the form of blood and tears, the latter of which was both narrated and performatively wept, contributed to the rhetorical power of the "speaking bitterness" narratives. This "spontaneous truth of the body" linked immediate experience with unequal systems of economic exchange (Anagnost 1997b: 23).

But while the goal of "speaking bitterness" narratives was to get peasants to see their suffering in terms of class exploitation rather than ill fortune, Zhou refers to "bad fate" in telling Tingting's illness story.[7] "There is nothing you can do," one doctor in Shanghai told him. "No rehabilitation in the world can help children who are deaf in both ears. Her only way out from now on is to go to deaf school" (3). This doctor's declaration in a single stroke seemed to condemn Tingting to a life of social exclusion, ushering in a dark period of life. Zhou Hong recalls, "Because a parent's circumstances are decided by fate, my daughter's life before three years of age was steeped in loneliness and tears" (3).

It was a Japanese television series, titled *Xue Yi* in Chinese, that sparked a moment of transformation for Zhou Hong. "At the moment when all hope was lost, when we arrived where mountains and rivers end," Zhou found inspiration in the character Dadaomao, whose "endless fatherly love" helped give the life and death of his terminally ill daughter meaning and satisfaction. "From then on," Zhou recalls, "My daughter and I battled with destiny" (5).

Between "surrendering to the design of fate" and engaging in a "battle with destiny" that ultimately leads to success, Zhou Hong's story traverses a dramatic arc between despair and hope. Zhou Hong undergoes a transformation too. In reflecting on his daughter's accomplishments and his own life trajectory, he wonders how he, "a *laosanjie* graduate, a factory technician, a father who had nothing to do with special education, became the principal of Nanjing Deaf School. The change of destiny for this father-daughter pair surely was dramatic!" (16).

By repeatedly marking himself as belonging to the *laosanjie* generation, Zhou Hong intensifies the irony of his life story. The term *laosanjie* refers to the junior high and high school graduating classes of 1967 through 1969, the generation of urban youths who sacrificed formal schooling to go down to the countryside in the spirit of socialist modernization. Though many found success upon return to the cities, most were hired for manual labor on shop floors; Zhou himself was a factory technician. Deep resentment and high rates of hidden unemployment can be found among the *laosanjie* generation, many of whom were rendered "redundant" during the market reforms.[8] Thus, when Zhou Hong invokes his *laosanjie* identity, he marks how far he has come and how his life could have easily turned out otherwise: "A '*laosanjie*' like me, many of us are now unemployed. I'm still considered lucky" (170).

The transformation of a disabled child into a genius, and a blue-collar worker into a self-taught expert, combines incongruous qualities in single characters, not unlike the beggar with a heart of gold or the good student that kills. Zhou Tingting and Zhou Hong's unexpected success prompts questions just as the "good student kills mother" story does: How did this father and daughter achieve success despite their respective social and physical constraints? Zhou Hong's narrative is not unlike the "rags to riches" stories Americans are familiar with. This is not a coincidence. In foregrounding his determination and effort in battling destiny, Zhou makes a moral argument for the potency of human effort. Indeed, his popularity extends well beyond the education reform movement and can be linked to the genre of "studying for success" (*chenggongxue*), which includes the stories of successful entrepreneurs like Bill Gates and Sam Walton of Walmart.[9] Such stories promote the neoliberal notion that rising from one social category into another is possible through sheer effort, a kind of "neoliberal fable of self-making" that links personal development with economic development.[10]

But the heroism in Zhou Hong's story suggests that success stories continue to draw upon a narrative practice long familiar to Chinese storytelling:

offering exemplary models to emulate. They "recycle the traditional Chinese genre of 'tales of famous men'" (Anagnost 2004: 195). Interestingly enough, many of the models in the market reform era have been disabled people or parents or teachers of disabled children. These figures include Zhang Haidi, Deng Pufang, Annie Sullivan, Helen Keller, and the nineteenth-century German Karl Weter—who was born an "idiot" but defied expectations and eventually became a legal scholar in adulthood thanks to his father's parenting methods.[11] That these teachers and learners overcame great obstacles exemplifies a long-held belief in the malleability of the human person, but their stories also serve to construct a new category, to which I now turn.

Naturalizing Potential

Zhou Hong's *Appreciate Your Child* looks much like other popular books such as *Harvard Girl Liu Yiting* and *The Education of Karl Weter*. They all demonstrate how intensive parental labor and investment can build value into a child, value that can be exchanged in a knowledge-based economy. The children featured in these success manuals all go on to prestigious universities and/or professions requiring mental labor.

Zhou Hong's style is quite different from that of the other parents in this group, however. Though he too invests great effort in teaching specific capacities, such as using the abacus, *Appreciate Your Child* is less about how to govern the child than how to govern oneself. In emphasizing that he had no expectations, an attitude he attributes to emotional labor he conducted upon himself, Zhou Hong's advice encourages parents to become a subject of ethics. A manual like *Harvard Girl Liu Yiting*, on the other hand, is much more product oriented.

Both Zhou Hong's narrative and Intimate Sister's retelling of the Xu Li story emphasize not the product and rational means of production but the interior depths of a child's subjectivity. In the "good student kills mother" story, categories such as psychological health and psychological quality are retroactively constituted in the public interpretation of the case. Xu Li was, in a sense, killed before his mother was killed *because* Chinese parents do not attend to the psychological health of their child. Similarly, Zhou Hong's account of how he raised Tingting retroactively constitutes, and thereby naturalizes, a different but related category: potential. If the expert reading of "good student kills mother" reveals a hidden symptom, then Zhou Tingting's dramatic transformation reveals a hidden potential. Psychological health and human potential become categories to be discovered and understood.

In response to queries about how he did it, Zhou Hong insists that his method is accessible to everybody. To discover and excavate a child's hidden potential, a parent must simply rediscover something "natural" to parenting. He maintains that "this method is the most mysterious, and the most common. The freshest, and also the most ancient. Something we already have as parents, yet have not realized. We have used it before, but have unintentionally forgotten it" (17). This something is a state of mind uncorrupted by the social competition fostered by an exam system that ranks students with points. For Zhou Hong this natural attitude can be encapsulated by the word *xing* or "being okay with everything."[12] Parents have this attitude during early socialization, when a young child is just learning to walk and talk. In these early years, parents naturally have no expectations, Zhou argues, as *all* children will be able to walk and talk *some* day. Zhou writes, "Because they firmly believe the child is okay, when the child is learning how to walk, they are able to fully permit failure. . . . When the child is learning how to walk, parents will always encourage their child after ten falls, a hundred falls, even after a thousand falls" (58).

Speaking to the high ambitions that parents have for school-age children, as exhibited in Mother Xu's behavior, Zhou encourages parents to manage and control their expectations by finding the natural attitude, one that permits failure and unceasingly gives encouragement. There is no such thing as a bad child, only bad parenting methods—a point Zhou makes by likening parenting to farming. He writes, "I feel that there is no such thing as a bad crop, only farmers who do not know how to farm. If a crop is not growing well, we never see a farmer with arms akimbo, raging at the side of a field: 'I work from dawn to dusk, all night and day, all the bitterness I have eaten, all the sweat I have exuded, haven't I fulfilled my moral obligations? Why won't you grow taller?'" (37). If there are only bad parenting methods, then parents should criticize not the child but themselves. Zhou maintains that whenever his daughter had problems he reflected on himself and asked *himself* what he had done wrong. This attitude strongly contrasts with the way Mother Xu is portrayed.

In turning attention back upon themselves, parents are better equipped to appreciate their child. For Zhou Hong, good parenting requires the cultivation of optimism through concrete, daily exercises. He claims, "I have a habit of facing myself every morning, reminding myself to live each day with an appreciative state of mind, to welcome each day with gratitude" (174). More than advice for good parenting, Zhou offers a life formula that invokes Confucian virtue ethics, which takes self-cultivation as a precondition for the harmonization of human relations. This logic can be traced back to a famous passage from the Confucian classic *Great Learning*, which posits spontaneous correspondences between different scales of human phenomena—that is to say, between bringing order to states and families on the one hand and rectifying one's heart, making intentions sincere, and investigating the nature of reality on the other (Wan 2004).

Many China anthropologists have pointed to the way in which post-Mao governmentality or biopolitics invokes much older traditions of self-cultivation. Zhou Hong is no exception in his emphasis on finding the natural attitude. At the same time, Zhou Hong's advice undeniably reflects a contemporary logic, not to mention the cheerful optimism of commercial self-help. In situating his style in opposition to what most Chinese parents supposedly do, in raising an academically successful daughter who was destined for a life on the margins, Zhou Hong effectively suggests that potential exists in all children but remains hidden from view. If he can raise an academically successful child, why do parents of ordinary children have so much trouble? Zhou Hong reasons that because most parents "use the carrot and stick judiciously," treat their children like "private property," and become greedy and "pull at sprouts to make them grow," children are disheartened and their potential to flourish is stifled. These attitudes are deeply rooted for Zhou: "From ancient times until now, China's hierarchically determined ethical relationships have led to the stifling of human nature" (2003: 160).

Zhou Hong, like many other reform advocates, is concerned with the fate of the nation. The kind of parenting that suppresses potential and ignores the subjectivity of children cannot produce a self-motivated subject. The way in which Zhou's advice links human development to national development is most clear when he says, "The key is to let children understand the meaning of competition, let the desire to compete come from their inner heart-minds, cultivate a good state of mind and a healthy personality. We must help children start their 'engines,' not push them to move" (71). The interesting thing here is that parents' production of the high-quality subject seems to depend less on building value into a child by investing in educational commodities than on laboring upon oneself, so as to not threaten or obstruct a child's human potential. By becoming the kind of parent that understands a child's subjective needs, one can ensure that latent resources in a child may be better cultivated, enabled, and made accessible upon maturity. Human potential, Zhou suggests, is a natural resource.

In the context of China's shifting economic priorities, now focused on building a knowledge economy, human potential has become an especially salient concept. Out of immediate reach, yet accessible and capable of being developed with intersubjective work, its discovery and cultivation requires anyone involved in human development, whether parent or teacher or company manager, to assume new responsibilities. Child-rearing experts' stories make a moral argument for how children ought to be treated—as active, thinking, feeling subjects whose potential can be actualized only by parents who are able to actively, consciously, and feelingly reflect upon themselves. It is through the intensification of both the child's and the parent's subjectivity that national strength and arrival at modernity are to be secured. A well-told story modeling a certain *that* to be emulated has been influential among not only government officials and educators but parents themselves.

AS WIND MOVES THROUGH THE GRASS

Børge Bakken has observed a "crisis of faith" in the post-Mao period with respect to the state's efforts to promote exemplary models. Self-sacrificing, good deed–performing socialist heroes have lost their appeal, and there have even been cases in which living persons awarded with model status have suffered ridicule and physical attacks (2000: 186–94). Be that as it may, Bakken is correct in saying that the "general approach towards modelling seems to have kept much of its original educational effect," despite the unpopularity of official models (181).

It is unlikely that popular experts tell stories because they have been directed to do so by the state organs with which they are associated. Instead, the tendency toward storytelling reflects an underlying cultural logic, probably sustained by each author's own experience of being exposed to models time and again. Even if the stories of experts have a normalizing effect, they do not generate the kind of suspicion that Bakken describes. Readers and hearers of stories about good and bad parenting are interested and potentially receptive because the narrative content is directly related to their own concerns and dilemmas. In other words, while Bakken has observed a great distance between official models and Chinese youth, there is relatively more proximity between child-rearing experts and middle-class parents.

Moreover, experts' stories do not appear normative because they are often contiguous with parenting stories that ordinary people circulate among themselves. They are often retold and further circulated beyond the sphere of mass media. As such, they appear less like models (tending toward the mythic) and more like ordinary gossip (tending toward "things such as might happen"), thereby opening the text to wider interpretation and personalization.[13] In a context where the definition of good parenting is being debated, the parading of life contingencies rather than virtues can be especially productive of thought—even temporary changes in conduct. Because life in a society undergoing rapid change can feel so unmoored, stories about the lives of others can offer guidance for negotiating uncharted waters. For this reason, the expert's story carries the power to affect.

I provide evidence for this in the next chapter, in documenting how Tingting's and Xu Li's stories have been received by ordinary parents. But before we conclude this one, one piece of ordinary gossip deserves special mention.

One afternoon, my teenage friend Grace started telling her mother and me a story about a mother-son relationship gone awry. It was a story she had heard from a friend of hers who happened to live next door to the family in question. Let's call the mother Mrs. Lan and the son Mu Guang.

Mu Guang and Mrs. Lan got into an argument one morning that ended with the son's disappearance. It started when Mrs. Lan tried to get Mu Guang out of bed for the day: "Mu Guang, wake up!" "Let me sleep for another five minutes." "Mu Guang, wake up!" "Leave me alone." "Mu Guang, wake up!" "I'm not getting up." "Mu Guang, wake up!" "I'm just not getting up." "Mu Guang, wake up!" "I'm just not getting up, what do you want to do about it?" Mrs. Lan gave up and stepped outside to bring some groceries in. Mu Guang locked his mother out of the house.[14] The two went back and forth again, only this time Mu Guang refused to open the door. "Mu Guang, open the door!" "I'm not opening it." "Mu Guang, open the door!" "I'm just not opening it."

Mrs. Lan climbed through an open window to get back in, and the two had an argument that ended with Mrs. Lan telling her son to get the hell out of the house. She proceeded to throw his clothing out on the porch, and Mu Guang left.

Hours passed, and Mrs. Lan began to worry as her anger cooled. She called her son's cell phone to tell him to come back home immediately. He didn't.

In the meanwhile, Mrs. Lan, feeling very distressed, sought the counsel of her neighbor, the mother of the teenager who had told my friend Grace this story. She cried as she lamented, "I just don't know what to do about this kid of mine anymore." The neighbor did what she could to provide some comfort.

As my friend Grace related this story to her mother and me, she was in stitches. After all, the events in the story did border on the absurd. Her mother, Song Hua, meanwhile remained silent, listening very attentively. The newspaper she was reading to lull herself to sleep for an afternoon nap was laid down on her lap. She chuckled here and there, as did I, mostly because Grace's impersonations were so lively and exaggerated—complete with reenactments of grunting, pouting, and Chinese opera–style weeping.

Song Hua and I were struck by the story, gossip really, because Mrs. Lan happened to be a well-respected member of the local literati—one who had strong opinions about interpersonal ethics and how to conduct oneself in China's new world. When we remarked on this irony, Song Hua did a little impersonating of her own, mimicking the kind of authority she had seen Mrs. Lan speak with in local television appearances. I sympathized with Mrs. Lan and said, "It must be so heartbreaking for her, of all people, to have such a conflict with her son." Song Hua agreed and added, "It's a tragedy."

The next morning, when Song Hua went into her daughter's room to wake her up for breakfast, she was full of tender affection! Not that she started mornings in her household with exclamatory wake-up calls, but she did usually give Grace a hard time for always being the last person to wake up in a household that included extended family members. Grace had recently taken the college entrance exam, so Song Hua wanted to let her daughter catch up on all the sleep she had missed. But she was ambivalent: seeing her daughter sleep in did not sit well with her. "People who sleep in are losers [*shibai zhe*]," she once said. On other occasions, she would use guilt as a tactic. As the steam rising from a prepared breakfast began to dissipate, she would call to her daughter, "Everybody is waiting for you!"

That same day, Song Hua and I had an intimate chat about parenting. As a single parent who had lost her husband to illness many years ago, Song Hua felt it incumbent on her to play the roles of both the "strict father" and the "compassionate mother," invoking the traditional division of gendered parental labor encapsulated in the popular saying *yanfu cimu*. "Sometimes I am very mean to her," she admitted, "but if you don't teach and guide this kid, she'll blame you in the future." What remained unsaid in our conversation was that *that* could happen too.

If the "virtuous ruler inspires his subordinates to good conduct as wind moves the grass" (Olberding 2008: 630), then Song Hua's ambivalence reflects the temporary imprint left by the movement of town gossip, acting in this instance as a negative model. That such conflict could arise between a respected public figure and her teenage son suggested to Song Hua that things could always turn out otherwise. Parent-child relationships do go awry. The story inspired a loving appreciation for her less troublesome daughter—an appreciation that had the quality of being out-of-time, standing out from daily routine. Unlike Xu Li and Mu Guang however, Grace harbored no resentment against her mother. Her mother's nagging just sounded like a bunch of *gugeli gugeli gugeli* as far as she was concerned.

THREE

"The Heart Says One Thing but the Hand Does Another"

ONE RAINY DAY IN THE FALL OF 2006, Hu Qiuli's apartment was abuzz with activity. A laid-off worker who had taken a keen interest in child education, Hu Qiuli had converted the covered balcony of her home into a classroom of sorts. As she led activities with her afternoon group, I visited with her friend Wang Yan, who brought her daughter Wu Linlin over to see me. But Wu Linlin, an energetic ten-year-old, was less interested in me than in everything else that was going on. There were children at play everywhere.

When Wu Linlin started up a Chinese checkers game with two other girls, I was gently encouraged to play too. Wang Yan, meanwhile, still wearing her long black raincoat, stood against a kitchen counter not more than a couple feet away, pretending to read a newspaper. She was watching us, of course, and she scolded her daughter many times for simultaneously watching an ongoing computer game nearby. "How are you ever going to get anything done when you are always dividing your mind?" her mother chided.

Wang Yan disliked her daughter's lack of focus, but something else was bothering her as well. Eventually, they got into a spat over Wu Linlin's lack of interest in interacting with me. "I didn't bring you over here to play!! Hurry up!" They exchanged sharp verbal jabs with one another.

Wu Linlin humored her mother for a moment, and the two of us strained to make some conversation. But before long she made herself scarce once again, to watch another video game being played by a group of boys.

Then, in what felt to me like a Jekyll and Hyde moment, Wang Yan turned to me and said with her toothy grin, "I'm too anxious, aren't I?"

The entire afternoon was for me a condensed display of Wang Yan's self-professed "contradictoriness" (*maodun*). Just before the scolding that led to the spat, we had been chatting about how parents increasingly felt the need to restrain themselves in dealing with increasingly defiant tweens. In numerous other conversations, Wang Yan admitted to having a hot temper, which she tried to control in a continual, reflexive effort to become a better parent. She was an avid reader of popular parenting advice dished out by experts who repeatedly urged parents to cultivate more patience. She was eager to consume this advice because Wu Linlin was, after all, her only child. More importantly, Wang Yan saw a dramatic difference between the kind of society for which her parents had socialized her and the kind of society Wu Linlin would have to face one day. She worked to control her hot temper because she believed it might not be so good for her daughter. But because there were always other more pressing concerns beyond psychological needs, Wang Yan found herself in a constant state of ambivalence.

This chapter describes "emotion work" among middle-class mothers, situating their experience of self-doubt in the context of changing ideas about good parenting. On the basis of her study of American flight attendants, Hochschild defined emotion work as labor that "requires one to induce or suppress feeling in order to sustain the outward countenance that produces the proper state of mind in others" (1983: 7). While Hochschild's flight attendants work to suppress their anger in order to produce customer satisfaction, Chinese mothers work to suppress their anger so as to cultivate the child's inner subjectivity.

Popular experts argue that when parents pressure a child too much and get angry over small things they not only obstruct the development of hidden potential but also threaten the child's psychological health. Because the experts so often couch their formulations in storytelling, producing aesthetic and moral effects in readers and listeners, popular advice has been influential among ordinary parents. At the same time, however, expert advice competes with the realities of a high-pressure education system that demands a kind of vigilant parenting that contradicts the ideals of the *suzhi jiaoyu* movement. While ordinary parents are receptive to the advice of experts, they find themselves having to balance two incommensurable goods: protect the child's happiness or ensure survival? These are incompatible values that generate intrapersonal conflicts.

While the mothers I got to know expressed a lot of mixed feelings about appropriate child-rearing styles and methods, taking individual responsibility for their sense of failure, I understand mothers' anger and ambivalence as taking form at the intersection between the regulatory discourse of popular advice, the gendering of parental responsibilities, and the pressures of a competitive education system.[1] The emotion is, as Richard Shweder puts it, "the whole story" (2003: 155). While the experts see excessive emotion as problematic, the experience of problematic emotions can be alternatively seen as constitutive of ethical subjectivity. They constitute a mode of judgment about external circumstances, and they make the assertion that responsiveness and responsibility are inextricably intertwined.

THE GENDERING OF ADVICE AND PARENTAL RESPONSIBILITY

Good parenting as defined by the discourse of popular advice essentially asks parents to undertake a project in self-government and self-improvement, to be guided by the images experts provide. This is a gendered project that makes two implicit assumptions: (1) mothers are the primary caretakers and (2) mothers especially have difficulty with self-control. Experts commonly attribute inability to attend to the inner life of a child to both fathers and mothers, but being "too emotional" is a problem for mothers in particular. Jiang Xuelan, author of a child-rearing manual titled *Decoding the Password to Your Child's Heart-Spirit*, writes, "When guiding and normalizing a child's speech and behavior, we mothers are easily given to anger" (2006: 6).

Decoding the Password is filled with fictional anecdotes intended to unlock a secret to a puzzling aspect of children's behavior, and each of them is followed by a commentary. Jiang speaks to her reader in a soothing tone, commentary after commentary: "Good mother, don't worry, take it easy!" Losing one's temper, she argues, obstructs channels of communication between parent and child, which can ultimately lead to problematic behavior and undesirable outcomes. To keep communicative channels open, to access the child's "password"-protected interiority, mothers must conduct emotion work. Consider lesson 12 in particular, "Why Does the Child Cut Holes in the Blanket Cover?", which argues for the importance of tolerance and restraint.

> It's time that the wool blanket on Bao Bao's bed be removed for a washing. Maybe time to switch the thick cotton blanket out for a thinner one too. All the winter clothes in the closet should be washed clean and stored away.

The washing machine spins from the early morning well into the afternoon. Mom hasn't stopped moving either. The blanket in her hand with little purple flowers all over it has already become soft with age.

Suddenly, mom is stunned. She discovers little holes randomly cut all over it, the work of little scissors.

Mom thinks, who else but naughty Bao Bao would do something like this? Anger fills her, and she rushes into Bao Bao's room shouting. Bao Bao is sitting cross-legged on the floor, calmly assembling a "Super Police Station" toy.

"Bao Bao!" she shouts.

"What?" Bao Bao doesn't even look up. His casual attitude provokes his mom to the point that anger fumes from the seven orifices in her head [*qiqiao shengyan*].

"How did your blanket cover grow so many eyes?" Mom asks. But because her eyes are bulging like lightbulbs, Bao Bao goes right back to what he's doing after he shoots her a look.

Refusing to let Bao Bao off the hook, Mom asks, "What exactly did you think you were doing?" She feels like if she doesn't punish him a little this time, he may bring the building down next time.

Bao Bao can detect the rage in his mom's voice, and says timidly: "I wanted to see how sharp my craft scissors were."

"Then why are there so many holes all of a sudden?"

"I wanted to see if there were any sleepy bugs inside."

"What?" Mom can't believe her ears, her son's idea is just too novel. She can't stop laughing.

The mother's emotions are mentioned four times in this story: anger fills her, then she fumes from the seven orifices in her head, her eyes bulge like lightbulbs, and her rage is detected by her son. Although the story is too brief to depict any "emotion work," it demonstrates a transformation of anger into laughter. In doing so, it offers an exemplary model for emotional restraint, and—with the help of the commentary that follows—persuades mothers to see naughty behavior as the seed of scientific discovery. According to "customary ways of thinking," punishment would be justified as preemptive action, as Bao Bao may do something more serious the next time around. This way of thinking is rooted in the logic of propensity, expressed in proverbs such as "The child who steals needles is the adult who steals gold." But Jiang, contrarily, wants her readers to understand that Bao Bao was simply acting out an innocent curiosity, so that the mother's anger is not an appropriate response to his behavior.

The assumption that mothers have a special responsibility to control their emotions rests on a conception of gender as a biological phenomenon—a conception that has been instrumental to economic development and state building since the early days of the People's Republic. The entry of women into the workforce was accompanied by the dissemination of knowledge concerning maternal hygiene and reproductive health, which rested on notions of biological complementarity and gender-defining reproductive function (Manning 2006). This period also witnessed prescriptions for emotional regulation. Harking back to premodern prescriptions, experts from the 1950s warned menstruating women against getting angry and advised pregnant women to control their appetites and their emotions (Evans 1995: 380).

Although gender difference is still conceived in terms of biology in China, Maoist and post-Maoist understandings of gender difference diverge significantly. In the Maoist context, gender difference was discussed in the context of reproductive concerns, but otherwise the official discourse on gender "did not reduce personality to physiological terms." As Tani Barlow has observed, "The realm of feeling and character remained until recently bound to conventions of Maoism that emphasized social class, not sex anatomy or 'gender'" (1994: 277). The post-Mao period, in contrast, witnessed an expansion of characteristics attributed to the female gender.[2] In the 1980s and 1990s, women were said to have a rich, logic-transcending perception, the ability to appreciate hidden details, and a capacity to care and feel that set them apart from men (Croll 1995: 150–55).

According to these representations, women have special access to the sphere of emotions. But this privilege can also be a liability, particularly in the eyes of child-rearing experts. This turn of argument is not unique to China. In postwar Canada, mothers were commonly seen as a threat, even blamed as a source of pathology in children in their "natural" tendency to "over-mother" or show too much affection (Gleason 1999). The behaviorist John B. Watson, who believed that behavior was something a parent could program like a technician, felt that mother love was an obstacle to scientific child rearing (Grant 1998). In Japan, the fervor of the "education mama" (kyōiku mama) could, the medical experts opined, easily turn into "childrearing neurosis" (Lock 1993: 10; White 2002: 108). These disparate examples show how the attribution of emotional capacity to women can expose mothers to blame, thereby creating a space for the experts to intervene.

Long-standing conceptions about gender difference, and the recent expansion of gender characteristics, allow the notion of emotional mothers to go unquestioned in post-Mao China. But there is another layer to the gendering of advice, which has to do with the double burden that women have had to carry since the founding of the People's Republic. In Maoist China, women's liberation was understood to mean paid employment outside the home, and the socialization of housework freed women from their domestic duties to a degree.[3] But the expectation that women ought to take responsibility for the remainder went unquestioned. The Party "failed to address the production of gender hierarchy as a cultural as well as a class and economic issue" (Evans 2008: 104). Notably, preexisting divisions of labor were reiterated when in 1957 Cai Chang, the chair of the Women's Federation, "pronounced that women should accept 'their chief responsibility for the home' until the state was in a position to 'resolve the contradiction between domestic chores and work'" (107).

During the Maoist period, men were frequently enjoined to help women in the domestic sphere.[4] For example, in the 1950s, husbands who did some of the housework were depicted in "glowing descriptions" of model marriages (Davin 1976: 183). In both town and countryside, men were told that their assistance helped to support working wives, but this encouragement never stressed equal responsibility. In reform era advice for child rearing, authors commonly address parents rather than mothers. But the assumption that women should take primary responsibility, or already are primarily responsible, always bubbles back to the surface. In the 1980s, the press on scientific child rearing addresses both parents, even though advice mostly appears in women's magazines (Honig and Hershatter 1988: 180). More recently, magazine articles idealizing parent-child communication have invoked fathers and mothers, while the examples describe mothers and daughters (Evans 2008: 95). Both parents are commonly the implied audience when Chinese parenting is problematized, but mothers are usually the ones depicted as emotional, too devoted or temperamental, and therefore in need of expert guidance. The manual *Decoding the Password* makes this assumption explicit.

Middle-class fathers in Kunming do in fact have a very important voice in matters of child rearing. But among my informants the double burden that women in the PRC have long carried was manifested in a rather unexpected way. Most of the fathers I knew disapproved of putting unnecessary pressure on a child when he or she already had so much pressure at school, reversing the old saying "strict father and compassionate mother" (*yanfu cimu*). If a child wanted to get out of going to an extracurricular activity class, he or she would have a better chance asking for permission from Dad. Some of the mothers I knew characterized their husband as too "casual" (*suiyi*), willing to simply "go with the flow" (*shunqi ziran*) as long as school assignments were completed. With respect to contributing to the familial pursuit of a child's "quality" in the form of extracurricular learning, fathers I knew contributed by serving, for example, as a chauffeur, a fishing or badminton partner, or a coach. Their hunger simply was not the same, however. Meanwhile, the mothers I knew, all of whom worked full-time jobs, not only contributed to the household income but also took on the responsibility of ensuring a child's competitiveness. They ruled the domestic sphere with the tick-tock of a metronome, while constantly modulating the strength, pitch, and tone of their demands, for fear of antagonizing their child. The "strict mother and compassionate father" phenomenon I observed is best encapsulated in the following statement, expressed by a friend who shared with me how she imagined her son's perception of her: "My father is the best. Mom is a meanie, doesn't let me do this and doesn't let me do that. And then she makes me learn this and makes me learn that. It's so annoying." As this quote shows, gender inequality plays out in the casualness that fathers enjoy in their relationship with a child.

This inequality is not unique to China.[5] The study conducted by the UCLA Sloan Center on Everyday Lives of Families (CELF), focusing on ethnically diverse middle-class families in Southern California, found that mothers especially were "prone to self-reflection." They felt frustrated and guilty about "the corners they had to cut to get through the day" and the strain that daily supervision of homework caused between themselves and their children. Because fathers arrived home later than mothers did, on average, mothers bore most of the responsibility for supervising homework, putting them in the awkward position of being the "bossy, nagging" parent rather than the kind of parent who takes interest in how the day has gone (Ochs and Kremer-Sadlik 2013: 235). It may well be that the gendered division of emotional labor between parents is a global phenomenon, found in competitive societies stratified by the accumulation of human capital.[6]

CASE 1: THE HEART SAYS ONE THING BUT THE HAND DOES ANOTHER

I first met Wang Yan in a local, privately organized mothering class. She worked in an administrative office and her husband was a civil servant. They spent lavishly on the education of their daughter, who was eight years old when we first met. Wang Yan impressed me with her dedication and was, in many ways, the typical middle-class mother who sends her daughter off to all sorts of classes on the weekends: dance, art, English, Olympic math, and ping-pong. She was the one with the toothy grin.

The first time Wang Yan spoke to me about her emotion work was in response to a question I asked about whether she found parenting advice helpful. She told me about Zhou Hong, the *laosanjie* turned deaf school principal discussed in chapter 2. Zhou Hong turned his deaf-mute daughter into a prodigy by undertaking an affirmative style of child rearing he calls "appreciation education," which advocates patience, understanding, and frequent expressions of love. Wang Yan explained that after reading Zhou Hong she stopped measuring her daughter according to scores and claimed that this had allowed her daughter to approach exams without pressure. She pointed out, however, that how much you can apply something like "appreciation education" depends on your "personality." I asked her to explain.

WANG YAN. Because after taking care of her for a while, I don't have such good patience. I'm telling you! Sometimes I even feel, *aiya, tsk,* if only my patience was better, this kid could be even more excellent, even better. But I don't have patience. Ooooh, if she doesn't listen—

(*She raises a hand up as if about to slap somebody.*)

TK. (*Giggles*) *I really like your description.*

WY. That's how it is. My heart says, "Don't spank. It's not good to spank." But that hand still wants to go across. And then I start roaring. *Aiya, tsk,* sometimes I don't even know what the matter is exactly. Sometimes, what I'm thinking in my heart is not the same as what I end up doing. I'm *not* that kind of person actually. I'm usually the kind of person who knows what I'm supposed to be doing at *that* moment. Humans are already emotional to begin with. I also think I . . . I can absolutely admit that this is my weakness. I'm *very* emotional, I tell you. *Aiya,* when I'm really patient, *I* even admire myself. If my patience isn't good, *ai,* two wrong words, and I—, I—, I—, I can't restrain myself.

In her circle of friends, Wang Yan was a person to envy. Her daughter Wu Linlin was remarkably bright. Extracurricular classes had yet to make her weary; in fact, Wu Linlin truly enjoyed them. She not only went with zeal but excelled. Wu Linlin also loved to read, which Wang Yan's friends attributed to her efforts in carrying out "early education" (*qimeng jiaoyu*). When Wu Linlin was a toddler, Wang Yan taught her how to read by turning character acquisition into a game, scattering flashcards face down on the floor and challenging Wu Linlin with finding certain words. Given that Wang Yan managed to cultivate a bright girl with a thirst for learning, I was puzzled by something she once said to her daughter in front of me.

Coming back from dinner one night, Wang Yan tried to make an example out of me: "See Teacher Kuan, see how happy she is? How she does things happily? You should learn from Teacher Kuan and happily learn!" This surprised me because I had been under the impression that everything came so naturally to her and her daughter. A person to envy with a daughter who excelled, why did she have to remind her daughter to take a happy attitude? When I asked Wang Yan about this later, she explained that Wu Linlin did not take criticism well and that maybe her own hopes were too high.

WY. She doesn't know how to manage her time. She . . . at home we've installed one of those swings, so she loves to loaf around on that. "You can loaf on that when you're done with your homework," so I say, "Wu Linlin, you should go and play some piano now. You should go and, do this or that." So this must irritate her. You're telling her, so it must irritate her. Then she ignores you. So then you have to roar at her. So there's this problem. And I don't know how I should solve this problem.

I want her to cultivate the kind of habit where she, she goes and plays piano on her own. That would be good, for her to manage her time on her own. "I should do this, this and this." This is what I hope. But maybe this hope is really . . . Adults can't even do this, how can we expect children to do it? It's really contradictory, parents are really contradictory [*maodun*].

Maodun was a term I commonly heard in my conversations with mothers. Wang Yan represents her experience of contradiction in bodily terms: while she knows what she's supposed to do in her heart, that hand does something else. Though she would like to exercise more patience, and solve the problem of having to "roar" at her daughter, Wang Yan also feels that her personality does not allow for it. She blames herself for not having enough patience and wonders if Wu Linlin might be even more excellent were she able to restrain herself.

CASE 2: IT'S CLEARLY A SITUATION YOU SHOULD BE ANGRY ABOUT

Wen Hui was good friends with Wang Yan. Their children were the same age and attended the same primary school and extracurricular English class.

When I first met her, she often jokingly spoke of her son Li Shengchun as being too obedient and too thoughtful—as if it were something to complain about. She told me a story once about her son picking up a purse she had absentmindedly left behind. She wondered if a boy should be so attentive, so she said to him, "It's a piece of junk anyway, just leave it there!"

When Li Shengchun entered the third grade, the nature of her concerns changed. Li Shengchun was having tremendous difficulty in his Chinese class, as his teachers were no longer using the romanized spelling of Chinese. Li Shengchun was starting to act up. A shy, introverted, and thoughtful boy suddenly began to rebel, act wildly, and say hurtful things to his mother. So one night Wen Hui consulted the teacher of the mothering class where I met Wang Yan about this problem.

Curious to know whether she remembered this meeting, I asked her two years later if she had ever found any expert's advice for parenting helpful. She too mentioned Zhou Hong right away—not to affirm but rather to give an example of why advice is hard to apply. She relayed in great detail an example Zhou Hong gave at a public lecture in Kunming—how he commended his daughter for getting one out of ten math problems right—and the lesson the audience was supposed to learn.

WEN HUI. Afterwards, I went home and felt like, "Should I go and be like this with my kid?" And then I felt like, *aiya*, why did I used to . . . I would scold. Sometimes I would even lose my temper, I even spanked him a couple times. This kind of thing has happened. So I wondered, "*Aiya*, why would I be like this?" *Mai*, and then you would start to think, just use Zhou Hong's method. He calls it "appreciate," so appreciate! But it didn't work. Two days of it and he just stopped listening.

TK. *(Chuckles) What do you mean? Didn't listen to appreciation? Or didn't listen to any reprimanding?*

WH. He would just say to you, if you said, "*Aiya*, Li Shengchun! Li Shengchun, you did *such* a good job! *Aiya!*" This and that. "*Ai*, mom, you're full of it."

When I asked Wen Hui if she thought that maybe her son didn't find her praise to be sincere, she thought, "Maybe it's because the kid is already older," even though Zhou Hong's daughter at the time of his story and Wen Hui's son at the time of the lecture were just about the same age. But then she started to imply that sincerity was in fact an issue: "He has his own opinion, and he really understands adult speech, what you mean when you say something. *Tsk*. So sometimes saying praising words out loud *aiya*, I would feel like, how did I . . . why would I say something like that? It's clearly a situation you should be angry about, yet you change to not-angry?!"

Although friends and acquaintances often complimented Li Shengchun for being an excellent child, Wen Hui felt that she could see only the things that made her angry.

WH.   He will make you angry every day. Every day. *Aiya*. He won't, you know, do things according to how you imagine it. Do the things he's supposed to, arrange the things he's supposed to arrange. He's always wanting to take it easy here, mess with that there. If you don't monitor him . . . If you want him to go to bed at exactly 10:00, he won't do it unless you monitor him! Otherwise there's no way he could do the things you want him to. He doesn't have a sense of time. He could stay up all night if he wanted to. *Mai*, he doesn't care.

Like Wang Yan, Wen Hui expresses frustrations over the issue of time management. Though Wen Hui does not represent her experience of contradiction in bodily terms, she describes second-guessing herself twice. First, after hearing Zhou Hong's talk, which she remembers in detail, she wondered how she could have scolded and even spanked her son. Then, after trying appreciation by saying words of praise, she wondered how she could have acted not-angry when anger was the correct response. Even her son could pick up on her ambivalence and would tell her "you're full of it."

CASE 3: SOMETIMES YOU'RE LEFT WITH
NO OTHER CHOICE

The first time I interviewed Zhou Huawei, she brought over an outline of topics she wanted to cover on a white index card, along with a pile of popular materials, including a stack of recent copies of the local newspaper *Spring City Evening News*. It had serialized excerpts from Intimate Sister's best-selling *Tell Your Child, You're the Best!* (Lu Qin 2004). Intimate Sister is the celebrity child-rearing expert who had the chance to interview Xu Li, the good student who killed his mother (chapter 2).

Zhou Huawei took pride in telling me a story about how she had once stuck up for her daughter in a meeting with her teacher. She wants to be her daughter's intimate friend so that "if she has something to talk about she can talk to me." At the same time, Zhou Huawei admitted, she could have a rather "anxious personality" (*xingge ji*). She began to describe for me the confusion she felt over what exactly constituted "family violence" (*jiating baoli*), a concept she had first encountered in the popular advice literature. She said, "If you don't give her this kind of lesson, it would be hard for her to become a useful person."

She presented two contrasting examples to illustrate her dilemma. The first, was the famous Chinese playwright Cao Yu, an incredibly tolerant parent who never hit or scolded his three children and always talked nicely to them. "But not one of them made something of themselves," Zhou Huawei pointed out. "Not one." Meanwhile, the internationally acclaimed Lang Lang was forced to play piano from childhood on. Zhou Huawei related an incident she had read about in the newspaper. One day, Lang Lang's father stepped out for some errands and came back to find his son playing with other children when he was supposed to be practicing. He immediately grabbed a bottle of poison and said, "If you don't want to practice, you drink half, I drink half. Your mom can die with us too." This bottle of poison continued to sit on top of the piano.

Zhou Huawei recognized how cruel this father was. As with the "good student kills mother" case, the public was shocked when the story came out, and it became a hot topic of debate. A training school even refused Lang Lang admission on the basis of what had been publicized. The mentor he wanted to study with did not want to be responsible for a potential family tragedy. But while recognizing that the father's measures were extreme, Zhou Huawei pointed out that his severity did produce a famous pianist. Now both of Lang Lang's parents live comfortably.

ZHOU HUAWEI. Lang Lang was probably spanked pretty hard! He . . . but he became something. This is one outcome. Some people, you spank them but they don't become anything. On top of that, they'll kill their parents. And they don't want to live either. This exists too. But is this called family violence? There are some that become something, and some that don't.

TK. *Is it family violence or a parenting method?*

ZHW. *Ai*, really.

TK. *Hard to say?*

ZHW. Really. So sometimes, I also feel like with this kid of mine, I've already told her once. I think she's heard. So she probably won't do it again today. Two days pass, and she commits the same problem. Then, if she doesn't listen again, there's nothing else you can do. You're left with having to give her a lesson. You're left with having to spank her, scold her. This way she'll remember. I'm not saying I will spank her right away. It's not that we hit her willy-nilly. We just want her to hurt a little bit. Not to spank her until she—

TK. *To the point of bleeding flowers.*

ZHW. *Anh,* bleed flowers, as you say. It's not like we're pulling her ears off, that kind of thing. It's just to let her hurt a little bit. Let her have a little pain of the flesh. Let her remember this lesson.

So this, I don't really know if this kind of style is suitable. But I just feel that if you don't punish her at all, it would *really* be hard for her to . . . And it's not like in America, right? One person can go to work, and one person can stay at home and specialize in having patience. If this was the case I could moderate. I would pour my entire heart into my kid. But that's not me. I have a pile of stuff to do.

Like Wang Yan, Zhou Huawei describes a limit to her patience. In an ideal world (as symbolized by America), she might be a more patient parent. In the practical world of having to both work and raise a child, Zhou Huawei faces a conflict that is illustrated in terms of an ambiguity surrounding two contrasting models: Cao Yu the playwright and the father of Lang Lang the pianist. Both models are simultaneously positive *and* negative. Cao Yu is closer to the kind of parent experts idealize, but his children did not achieve. Lang Lang's father used methods people find horrifying, but he cultivated an acclaimed musician. The ambiguity surrounding these two models prompts Zhou Huawei to puzzle over what constitutes "family violence."

THE RULE OF EMOTIONAL MANAGEMENT

When Wang Yan and Zhou Huawei attribute their lack of patience to their personality, they speak as if emotional experience were primarily an individual matter. When Wang Yan identifies as a weakness her inability to coordinate what her heart says and what her hand does, she personally takes the blame for not restraining her emotions more. Wang Yan, especially, describes her emotions as having a raw and spontaneous quality, thereby invoking a commonsense notion that the emotions are antithetical to reason. From an anthropological perspective, however, emotions are never an individual matter. They arise out of worldly engagement and are universally subjected to cultural rules for emotional control (or expression). In the ethnographic record, anger is commonly seen as a problematic emotion that calls for management and restraint.[7]

That mothers subject their anger and anxiety to thought and modification in contemporary China is quite specific to the historical context, in which we find a mass-mediated landscape populated by images of exemplary fathers such as Zhou Hong and good students who kill.[8] Zhou Huawei's reference to people who "kill their parents" indicates an enfolding of environmental influence by virtue of exposure to horrific and exemplary models. The influence in question is a local variation of what Nikolas Rose (1996) calls "psy"—a heterogeneous apparatus that assembles the psychological interiority of the modern person in relation to images of autonomy and self-realization and that simultaneously gives rise to the burden of self-doubt and self-reflection. This local variation is shaped by socialist techniques of government as well as by a time-honored preference for the use of exemplars in guiding human conduct.

Although much popular advice was moving through commercial channels by the turn of the twenty-first century, the distinction between commercial and state channels is by no means clear. Celebrity experts such as Intimate Sister, Zhou Hong, and Sun Yunxiao are associated with the state in different ways. Sun Yunxiao is vice director and researcher at the China Youth Research Center and has received honors from the State Council for his contributions. Zhou Hong is connected to the China Tao Xingzhi Research Association, an association composed of research societies led by high-ranking officials committed to education reform and bound by a shared interest in a Republican era education figure.[9] Intimate Sister has a column in *China Youth Daily* and is a member of a subcommittee of the China Working Committee for Caring about the Next Generation, a state initiative whose purpose and direction are formulated in relation to Jiang Zemin's "Three Represents."[10] Local experts in Kunming too are associated with the state to greater or lesser degrees.

This intimate relationship between the state and everyday life as mediated by popular experts and the various state organs listed above in no way indicates a duping of the masses. As anthropologists writing about transformations in knowledge/power in the post-Mao era have argued, the power of the state is best characterized in terms of governmentality—a Chinese sort that combines neoliberal logic with many other logics in a hybrid formation. *Governmentality* refers to a productive modality of power that depends not on constraint but on the capacity of individuals to act and to choose. It operates by acting on the actions of others and may be found in any relationship involving the guidance of conduct—for example, by experts, teachers, parents, life coaches, career counselors, or doctors—according to any number of techniques for subject formation, including advice, modeling, exercises, life goals, mantras, and so on (Rose 1999).

In China, techniques of enablement have become especially salient in the context of economic liberalization. The modernization strategy of the post-Mao Party-state is staked on unleashing the hidden potential of the market and of labor. Because the hidden potential of labor is seen to rest inside the human person, all adults involved in the education of children have a special responsibility for ensuring the liberation of that potential. In this context, the inner life of parents—or mothers more specifically—also becomes a critical terrain. Contemporary emphasis on the psychological interiority of the child, the putative origin of curiosity and creativity, obliges parents to conduct emotion work so that they will not obstruct the development of nation-transforming human qualities.

According to Sun Yunxiao, the time management issue that frustrates both Wang Yan and Wen Hui is one that must be approached with care and caution. In fact, it may be precisely because parents are so intent on instrumentalizing every moment of time that the child becomes slow. For this reason, Sun says, "Don't 'press' a child without understanding causes, nor should parents make rules about when a child ought to finish a task according to their own imagination. This will only place a psychological burden on the child" ([2005] 2006: 64). Sun goes on to say that a child's speed will naturally increase when parents "trust" and "understand" their child, both of which require "patience."

With the specter of undesirable or opposite results always looming, many mothers practice emotion work. This private, self-directed labor begins with the recognition of "feeling rules," which are found in "the pinch between 'what I do feel' and 'what I should feel'" (Hochschild 1983: 57). We see them at work when Wang Yan states, "I'm the kind of person who knows what I'm supposed to be doing at *that* moment," contrasting herself to parents who do not have any regrets over losing their patience. Wen Hui recalls the pinch she felt between the "do" and the "should" after hearing a Zhou Hong lecture. She wondered if it was right for her to lose her temper and sometimes spank her son. Zhou Huawei feels that she has an anxious personality that sometimes gets in the way of the friendship she tries to cultivate with her daughter. She expresses her sense of the "should" in terms of the patience she *could* achieve if only the circumstances were ideal.

As we see most clearly with Zhou Huawei, the parent who conducts emotion work is the mother. In an ideal world, as symbolized by America, labor is equally divided. A father can go to work, while a mother can "pour her entire heart into a child." In Wang Yan's case, I also observed a gendering of emotion work. Although she and her husband presented a united front when chatting with me—Mr. Wu had a personal interest in educational theories— it eventually became clear that Wang Yan carried the double burden of paid employment and primary responsibility for parenting. When it came down to it, Mr. Wu was the parent who enjoyed a "casual" relationship with Wu Linlin. He was the parent who got extra affection from her whenever Wang Yan lost her temper. He was also the one whom Wu Linlin would describe to her friends as the "better parent who doesn't criticize me."

Feeling rules and emotion work are not simply mechanisms for promoting a social order and perpetuating an unequal gender system, however, just as governmentality cannot be understood in terms of domination. Making the emotions an object of thought and modification belongs to a process of subject making that is simultaneously the outcome of both human technologies oriented toward a global economy and indigenous arts of ethical subjectivity. Expert advice reflects this hybrid logic in encouraging self-reflexivity and self-cultivation. For example, in discussing slowness and the need for emotional restraint, Sun Yunxiao links a child's psychological health to "the good self-cultivation of parents" ([2005] 2006: 69). When Jiang Xuelan, the author of *Decoding the Password* (2006), enjoins mothers to restrain themselves in the face of maddening behavior, she echoes prescriptions against yelling in anger found in Tang dynasty self-cultivation texts for women.[11] Meanwhile, for Zhou Hong, good parenting depends on cultivating an appreciative state of mind, one that *mutually* nourishes child and self. In this way, emotion work has broader implications for the shaping of an ethical subjectivity, informed by the Confucianist assumption that self-cultivation (*xiushen*) is a precondition for the harmonization of human relations.

Wang Yan seems to follow this logic when she wonders how she can fairly expect her daughter to be entirely self-motivated. She admits that it's contradictory—"Adults can't even do this, how can we expect children to do it?"— hinting that the solution to *maodun* does not lie in emotional control alone.

Wang Yan's friend Hu Qiuli, who is the envy of their social circle for her seemingly unlimited store of patience, said to her friends on one occasion, "Actually, reading these books and going to classes is not really about how to raise a child; there are personal benefits." In her case, regulation of the family extended inward in a project of self-transformation. This resonates with a Confucian virtue ethics that takes social relationships as "realms of selfhood" that symbolize potential for growth (Tu 1985: 58, 123).

In teasing out Confucian ethics, I do not mean to suggest that there is an unchanging cultural essence. Indeed, the past is a foreign country. But it would also be a mistake to ignore culturally specific resources that inform subject making in contemporary China.[12] If the past is a foreign country, then it is a deterritorialized country that travels along flows of information and cultural media, localized in the present according to contemporary logics and practical needs.[13] Popular experts rarely, if ever, mention Confucian ethics explicitly in the sense of self-cultivation, and arguments about bad parenting as a cultural problem often blame the Confucian ethics of hierarchy (i.e., *junjun chenchen fufu zizi*). Nonetheless, the ethic of *xiushen*, or self-cultivation, is often invoked in advice for, and in the practice of, emotion work—hinting at what Judith Farquhar and Qicheng Zhang have called "a space apart" (2005).

ANGER AND AMBIVALENCE: A RICH PERCEPTION AND INDEX OF THE SITUATION

Ambivalence stems from a desire to accord with contemporary ideas of both the good parent and the harsh reality of social competition. Rather than see the emotion of anger as spontaneous, harmful, and irrational, which is how anger is represented by both the experts and by mothers themselves, I ask, What is the story the emotion tells?

Anthropologists and other theorists of human emotion have worked hard to challenge the long-standing opposition between reason and the emotions in Western theories of the mind. This body of literature demonstrates that the emotions are social events indistinct from thought, that they indicate something about a person's involvement with the world and even negotiate with and act upon that world.[14] Against the "thoughtless natural energies" view, Martha Nussbaum ([2001] 2006) offers an especially helpful argument. She understands emotional response as a kind of evaluative judgment, though not in an abstract sense. Rather, the experience of emotions "contains rich and dense perceptions" of something that concerns what it means to live a good life (65). In her discussion of the role of literature in developing the moral imagination, Nussbaum argues that to be responsive is to be responsible. She writes, "We live amid bewildering complexities. Obtuseness and refusal of vision are our besetting vices" (1990: 148). In Nussbaum's view, moral achievement rests on the lucid perception of complex and irreducible particulars, a task that does not come easy.

In early Chinese thought, the human heart is the seat of affectivity, moved and agitated in one's "engagement and comportment with things and events" (H. Wang 2007: 210). In Daoist thought, the heart is a sense organ that perceives and processes information about flux, whether that flux pertains to situations, things, people, or the tendencies of grand phenomena (Bruya 2010: 213). In Confucian thought, the sympathetic nature of the heart is to be nurtured; to be fully sensitive is to be fully human and fully alive (Tu 1984: 386). Importantly, Confucian theories of human emotion also understand the emotions as central to living an ethical life, as they are thought to carry the capacity for moral action. A man who falls short of feeling affection for his parents, for example, will not be able to mourn properly (Y. Wang [2007] 2008: 356–57). Although sensitivity in this example does not concern irreducible particulars, as in Nussbaum's scheme, moral emotions are relationship or context specific. For this reason, emotions are related to the discernment of context, having a cognitive dimension.

Anger was justified and called for in Mencius's story of how King Wen, in a blaze of anger that was also a judgment of a particular situation, led out troops against an invading army and thereby brought peace to his empire (Y. Wang [2007] 2008: 361). But in certain contexts, emotional engagement is expected but can and should be avoided. What might be appropriate for one situation could be disastrous in another. Mencius believed that a nobleman should avoid educating his own son because his anger will be excessive, advising, "If [a father] becomes angry, his son will reply in kind with an injury to the father. . . . So, father and son end up injuring one another and it is bad for them to do so" (quoted in Im 1999: 6). The point here is that emotional control in the Mencian view rests, not on perfecting one's responses, but rather on manipulating the situation. This example illuminates the inseparability of emotion and situation, with the words in Chinese designated by the same character, *qing*.

If I am contradicting the preceding discussion of self-cultivation, it is because Chinese theories—and scholarly interpretations of them—are also contradictory. There is no consensus over whether the heart-mind (*xin*) is the problem or the solution (Plaks 2006: 115). Not surprisingly, ordinary people are contradictory too. While my informants felt badly about their lack of emotional restraint, wishing they could assert more control, they also, at the same time, believed their emotions were justified. There is a multiplicity of perspectives on one's own emotions, converging with indigenous and Aristotelian schemes that attribute importance to a certain passivity before external forces. In other words, for philosophers and ordinary people alike, ethical subjectivity is achieved in allowing oneself to be affected. One ought to be sensitive, vulnerable, and porous. Wen Hui, the mother from case 2, offers her own metatheory. After hearing Zhou Hong's lecture, Wen Hui feels bad for sometimes losing her temper and spanking her son. Then, she turns around and wonders how she could have effused words of praise. Her doubt does not simply concern the relationship between a felt emotion and outward expression. More importantly, it is a perception of an incongruity between emotion and situation. As Wen Hui put it, "It's clearly a situation you should be angry about, yet you change to not-angry?"

The situation in this instance involves particulars that cannot be generalized as expressions of the high hopes of parents or a refashioned cultural logic of hierarchy.[15] Anxious parenting behavior is related to immediate circumstances. Wen Hui's "angry every day," an emotion she is supposed to restrain, is synecdochical—shorthand for a situation that is perceived as vulnerable to reversal.[16] When Wen Hui feels as if she must constantly monitor her son, governing when he brushes his teeth and when he goes to bed at night, she is not simply nagging or exercising her authority over him. Her emotionally engaged reminders are "rich and dense perceptions" of the various contingencies that make up their situation: namely, Li Shengchun must go to bed at a certain hour so that he will sleep eight hours before he must get up again to go to school, which takes about thirty minutes on foot and by bus. If he is late, his teacher will scold him in front of a classroom of sixty other students, an event that may cause him to lose face, fall out of favor with his teacher, or even injure his self-esteem.

Of course these are all things that *could* happen *if* Li Shengchun does not go to bed on time. Because emotional experience is often linked to situations that agents do not control, the emotion serves as a "record" of that sense of vulnerability in addition to the agent's perception of unique particulars (Nussbaum [2001] 2006: 43). The possibilities I take the liberty of adding here are cobbled together from stories Wen Hui told me about the time she forgot to sign a homework assignment (thereby getting her son in trouble), about the son of a friend who fell out of a teacher's favor (he ended up having to transfer middle schools), and so on. The subjunctive elements are immediate possibilities that inform the situation.

Now, if "angry every day" speaks to the particulars of getting a child to school on time, what shall we make of the ambivalence my informants express? What is ambivalence a shorthand for? What kind of situation does ambivalence perceive? How should we interpret Zhou Huawei's puzzlement over whether she should be more like Cao Yu the playwright or Lang Lang's father? And are there other meanings to be interpreted from Wang Yan's confession that "parents are really contradictory"? Vanessa Fong (2007) found that parents in Dalian held mutually contradictory expectations of their teenage children: obedience, caring/sociableness, independence, and excellence. The first two clashed with the latter two—as when one teenager's internalization of the values of excellence and independence frustrated her parents' desire that she care more for family activities, or when one well-liked teenager's internalization of caring/sociableness conflicted with his parents' wish that he'd be more ambitious.[17] Fong notes, "Recognizing that their society was an uneasy mixture of Confucianism, socialism, and capitalism, parents I knew in Dalian tried to teach their children values that would enable them to fulfill all the roles that would be expected of them" (110).

Mothers also have different roles they are expected to fulfill. Their feeling of ambivalence is related to having to tack between competing claims and commitments. _Contradiction_ is a shorthand term for the expectation that mothers should raise a psychologically healthy child _and_ a competitive student who will succeed against difficult odds. Zhou Huawei's puzzle illustrates this best: one must discipline a child; how else will she or he become a useful person? At the same time, too much discipline and the child could explode.

This moral conflict must be understood in terms of the imaginative horizons parents simultaneously behold, both belonging to the broader historical situation. The first horizon is mediated by the metaphor of the child's heart-spirit (_xinling_), an entity that sits in the inner recesses of a child's heart-mind (_xin_). In some contexts, _xinling_ can refer to the "soul" in a secular sense.[18] For my purposes, I translate _xinling_ as "heart-spirit" to bring out a second meaning in the word _ling_, found in compounds denoting anomalous creatures such as sprites, fairies, and elves. I use the term _heart-spirit_ because the portrayal of _xinling_ in the advice literature evokes a living being.

The heart-spirit is often described as innocent and vulnerable; parents must take extra care to protect and ensure its healthful flourishing. Sun Yunxiao ([2005] 2006: 62) argues that time has become the intangible monster that pursues and swallows up the happy heart-spirit of children. Sometimes this living creature has physiological needs. Intimate Sister writes in *Tell Your Child, You're the Best!* "Forgiveness provides oxygen for the growth of the child's heart-spirit" (Lu Qin 2004: 85) Sometimes it is a creature that needs a home. In *Appreciate Your Child*, Zhou Hong titles a section "A Child Who Has No One to Have Heart-to-Hearts with Is Like a Heart-Spirit with No Home" (2003: 96) At times, the world of the heart-spirit is described as a physical location. The phrase used for understanding a child's heart-spirit is literally to "walk into." This location is often characterized as hidden, accessible only when one regulates one's emotions properly.

Sometimes the world of the heart-spirit is an agricultural one, requiring observation and care. A psychological health manual for primary school–age children likens self-awareness to tending the wheat field in which the heart-spirit lives: both need a watchful eye and cultivation (Zhou Ping and Xiong 2003: 35) Sometimes this world is described as having its own meteorological phenomena. According to Intimate Sister, having future dreams is like letting sunshine beam into the heart-spirit's world (Lu Qin 2004: 99). For Zhou Ping and Xiong Yan, addressing a child's emotional problems is like dispelling a dense fog (2003: 67), and failing to teach a child how to love causes the heart-spirit world to go arid (2003: 199). This first horizon, the world of the child's heart-spirit, helps to construct the importance of psychological health, the neglect of which can lead to terrible consequences.[19]

While the world of the heart-spirit is characterized by depth, interiority, and marked boundaries, the second horizon is vast, unbounded, and tremendously uncertain. Enumeration is a common rhetorical device for invoking this second horizon. Zhou Huawei said to me, "It's too brutal. Thirteen hundred million people. America only has two hundred million, we still have another eleven trying to compete with you! This kind of pressure is extremely heavy. If I let my kid go, I'm doing her harm." One year, ten million high school students took the college entrance exams. The mother who told me this exclaimed, "That's a whole country! Ten million people!" Fu Kejun, a reform advocate who authored a book titled *The Pain in the Hearts of Chinese Parents*, lamented that in the city of Beijing alone there were ninety-eight thousand graduating primary school students (2005: 233). And at least half of their parents could not bear to "resign themselves to the random selection of fate [*yaohao de mingyun*]" by sending their child to a bad school (233).[20] With only ten thousand places available for incoming students at Beijing's key-point schools, at least forty thousand students and their forty thousand families were sorely disappointed.

Finally, there is the immediate problem of school fees and tuition. Household registration or failure to get the right exam score can keep a student from attending a good school. Parents are more than willing to pay the exorbitant fees associated with good schooling because it is thought to secure the good life. The convergence of middle-class aspirations with the commercialization of education and the intensification of competition imposes a heavy psychological and financial burden on families. Certain middle schools in Kunming charge school-selecting families 20,000 to 30,000 RMB for three years. And sometimes a single point below an admission line on an entrance exam can make a difference between whether one pays extra fees or not. As one parent lamented, "One point really is worth tens of thousands."[21]

The point here is not to wonder about the accuracy of these numbers. Rather, enumeration shows how discernment and judgment take form. Enormous numbers in the tens of thousands and millions convey a sense of scale and stand in for the accumulated force of the present historical tendency, with which small-scale human actions must contend. The success of one's child *could* be determined by the random selection of fate, so parents must take every measure to maximize their chances. These measures include sending one's child to as many extracurricular classes as possible, vigilantly governing everyday habits and behavior, and ensuring that a child is well liked by peers and key teachers. While experts urge parents to exercise some restraint in order to promote and preserve a happy childhood, many parents are unwilling to take the risk. Fu Kejun writes in his incisive critique of the *suzhi jiaoyu* movement:

> Try "reform" and see what you get. Other people's kids are doing their homework; will you let your kid off the hook to play? Other people's kids are scrambling for their exams; will you let your kid watch TV, play games? The teacher has assigned this and that homework; you rack your brain and still can't figure out the weird trick questions. So you tell your kid, precious, don't tire yourself out, there's no point in doing these, let's do something else. Are you willing to try? If you're willing to experiment like this, that will be the end of your kid! Your kid will be treated as a "bad student," kicked out of the classroom, kicked out of school. Your kid will be eliminated. (31)

Given that academic success is still measured by examination scores, schoolchildren in Kunming learn in a competitive environment. Teachers too are under enormous pressure to produce high-scoring students and have little patience for deviance. Reforms efforts to create a student-centered curriculum that facilitates active learning are usually difficult to implement because of classroom size (averaging fifty to seventy students in primary and middle school) and limited resources. At the same time, many Chinese maintain that an examination system makes the most sense given population size and is still the fairest option in a culture where advancement is too easily bought with gifts and favors. Thus, between ensuring a childhood and attending to psychological health, *and* cultivating virtuous learning habits and endowing a competitive edge in a child, urban mothers are faced with a moral conflict between incommensurable goods. Ambivalence constitutes a recognition of this conflict.

THERE IS ALWAYS MORE TO THE STORY

When Richard Shweder asserts that the emotion is the "whole story," he has this in mind: the emotion is inseparable from social appraisals of whether it is a virtue or a vice, inseparable from the perception of an event and of that event's implications for the self, and inseparable from a plan for action. All of these components are experienced simultaneously (2003: 154–55).

But there is also more to the story.

The emotion is merely what gets recognized within a durable context— durable in the sense that asymmetrical relations of power have been firmly institutionalized. In the historical situation considered in this book, *durable context* refers to a population improvement project that targets parental thought and behavior as objects for modification. The notion of "too emotional" is a product of the kind of reduction that often happens in durable contexts—a reduction of a much broader interplay of things into reified categories. To think of emotion in this way is to also recognize that the emotion is, simultaneously, an extension of affect, broadly conceived. Emotion plugs a subject into a broader interplay of things both as an affected subject and as an effective actor. It is connected to a virtual realm of potential—a "pressing crowd of incipiencies and tendencies" that hovers above and around individualized experience (Massumi 2002: 30). To explain, allow me to draw from Brian Massumi's discussion of the color experiments of David Katz.

Katz asked a research subject to match a color patch provided in the laboratory with the blue eyes of a certain friend in the absence of that friend. The subject made a "mismatch," choosing a patch that was "too blue." The case initially suggested that the research subject's fond memories may have led him to choose an exaggerated color, but Massumi draws a more complicated picture. The "too blue" result arises from a process in which the singularity of the color blue "struck" the context of the laboratory study (2002:211). The mismatch belonged less to the personal subjectivity of the research subject than to the *impersonal subjectivity* of the color (211). Yet in the context of the laboratory study, characterized by an asymmetrical relationship between researcher and subject, the event of "too blue" is chalked up as a mistake and "owned up to" by the subject. "Too blue" is attributed to "emotion" when in fact the event arises out of dynamic interaction between everything in play: the researcher, the subject, fond feelings, the institution of fact production (i.e., the staging of a mismatch), and the color blue, not to mention the three dimensions of brightness, saturation, and hue (221).

"Too emotional" is a mismatch between the discursive expectation that mothers exercise emotional restraint and their failure to do so in everyday life. But it is in reality the expression of a dynamic interaction that involves a number of factors in play—factors related to gender, discourse, and the singularities of the historical situation (competition) and immediate circumstances (mean teachers). The singularities of situation and circumstance strike the context, giving rise to "too emotional," which is then owned up to by the mothers in question. They, in turn, revirtualize "too emotional" in asserting ambivalence, for if *contradiction* is a shorthand term, then it points to a mode of "virtual knowing" that reconnects everyday practical actions back into the ongoing and unfolding of China's contradictory social reality.[22] If self-doubt is partially molded by a mass-mediated landscape populated by certain images that act upon actions (the capacity to be affected), then virtual knowing in the mode of ambivalence is just the beginning of the discernment necessary for artful disposition (the power to affect).

The indigenous logic of propensity embodied in the Chinese term *shi* points to a cultural understanding of the coexistence of the virtual and the actual. A tendency in its incipient stage may be manipulated by human action. But a tendency that has accumulated force, one that has passed the critical point between the virtual and the actual, will be more difficult to manage. Therefore, to wisely time the taking of initiative is crucial: it begins with the judgment of a given situation. The heart, as a sense organ that perceives and conveys information about worldly fluctuations and situational tendencies, is like a hinge. It is paradoxically the most active when it is passive. It participates through responsiveness and sensitivity. Its confusion gives rise to meaningful action.

FOUR

Creating Tiaojian, *or,*
The Art of Disposition

ONE POINT THREE BILLION PEOPLE living in China, ten million high school students taking the college entrance exam, ninety-eight thousand graduating primary school students in one city, three to four hundred million primary school students, 30,000 *yuan* in school fees—these totals convey how odds are perceived and how they pose, for urban Chinese parents and their children, the problem of *how to stand out against the crowd.* How to be outstanding in a classroom of sixty or seventy other classmates who also want to be outstanding? How to stay on the path that might lead to a decent life, with competition and risk all around? These questions highlight the uncertainties that surround raising a child in urban China, questions that concern the issue of "existential control" (Jackson 1998). What can I control as a parent? What is within my sphere of influence? What am I responsible for? Many of the mothers I knew answered these questions in a mode of action they referred to as "creating" or "providing" *tiaojian.*

Tiaojian is invoked in a wide variety of contexts and can be translated as "conditions" or "circumstances." It can refer to the conditions of a physical space, as when a rental agent flatly said to me after showing an apartment I could not hide disappointment toward: "Around here, *tiaojian* is simply like this." It can refer to the conditions of a physical environment, as when a teacher I observed asked her students to describe the natural *tiaojian*—weather, view, and color—in an outdoor exercise. *Tiaojian* can also refer to social conditions or circumstances, such as a person's economic status or financial situation, as when a parent told me that he regretted not having the "economic conditions" to live on the first rather than the seventh floor, so that his toddler could play outside more. *Tiaojian* can refer to a person's family background in the newly stratified society. Whereas *jieceng* is a more formal and differentiated way of talking about socioeconomic differences, *tiaojian* is unspecific.[1] Either one's family background is good (*jiating tiao- jian hao*), or it is not so good (*jiating tiaojian bu tai hao*).

When invoked in conversations about children and education, *tiaojian* serves to link economic means to one's ability to access information, educa- tion, and opportunity. For example, families who can afford to pay support- ing fees to attend schools outside their assigned district are families with good conditions. *Tiaojian* also links economic means to the physical spaces of human development, as when a parent is quoted in a newspaper as saying that a small living space means that "conditions for studying are not so good."[2] Opportunities embedded in social relationships are a form of *tiao- jian*, as seen when one mother scolded her son for not practicing his English with me, saying, "Such a good condition! [And you're not taking advantage of it!]" I had joined their two-day vacation during a Labor Day holiday, but her painfully shy son did not interact with me much.

Coming from a family with good conditions is not always advantageous, however. This is the case as far as the child's well-being is concerned because families with good economic *tiaojian* tend to overpack their child's learning schedule. One friend explained, "Like my niece, she doesn't even have time to eat a piece of watermelon." Children from families with good conditions also lack certain skills and virtues. It is a common sentiment that children from families with very good conditions typically lack independence, whereas children who do not come from a family with good conditions are admirably more independent, though they are more likely to have an inferiority com- plex (*zibei gan*). The twenty-one-year-old clerk at my neighborhood conven- ience store, who described her own *tiaojian* as not too good, felt that city kids didn't seem to know how to do anything. She reiterated this point many times when she told me that she regularly sent money home to her parents back in the countryside. The many exemplary stories concerning children who grow up under very poor conditions (*tiaojian hen cha de jiating*) but manage to test into Peking and Tsinghua University suggest a belief that good economic conditions can sometimes be a limitation. One such story— encapsulated in the proverb "Pierce a hole for some light" (*chuanbi yin- guang*)—goes as far back as the Han dynasty. It concerns a peasant boy named Kuang Heng whose family was so poor he had to create a hole in the wall they shared with a neighbor so as to have some light for studying. Through sheer effort and determination, Kuang Heng eventually entered the officialdom.[3]

Teachers use *tiaojian* when speaking about pedagogical infrastructure, as when a junior middle school geography teacher lamented that his *tiaojian* had limitations. Sometimes he would like to print material off the Internet but is not able to do so. *Tiaojian* in this sense is often what makes a good school a good school in popular understanding. It is well equipped and has good facilities, such as computer and science laboratories, television monitors for every classroom, and a running track.

Policy documents are littered with calls for creating or providing *tiaojian* so as to facilitate the implementation of particular directives. We find in the first section of the 1999 Resolution for *suzhi jiaoyu* this statement: "In order to fully move *suzhi jiaoyu* forward, we must persist in addressing the needs and realities of the entire student body and creating corresponding conditions [*tiaojian*] for the well-rounded development of students" (Ministry of Education 1999: I.1) This document later devotes an entire section to creating conditions. It lists a number of areas for reform, some of which include admission and examination reform, curriculum reform, and reintegration of higher education with various industries. In discussing the importance of extracurricular activities in cultivating well-roundedness in students, the document also asks that various domains of society "provide the necessary conditions" so that students may participate in practical activities.

Tiaojian can encompass human geography. People often expressed surprise that I chose Yunnan Province over other, more developed areas for my study. It is a relatively poor, remote area far from China's cultural and economic centers, so *tiaojian* in Yunnan are generally limited, people will say. Parents in Kunming supposedly do not have the same access to information that parents in other cities have, and a student could be a provincial top scorer on the national college entrance exam but find him- or herself at the bottom of a class at an elite university.

Sometimes, *tiaojian* can refer to the sum total of everything that has conditioned a particular (socially constructed) aspect of human development, as when *tiaojian* is modified by the terms *social* and *historical*. A study of population quality published by the Chinese Communist Party states, "A population's psychological *suzhi* is inevitably constrained by social and historical *tiaojian*" (Wu 1991: 146). The market economy is also a condition, as seen in the advice given by one parenting expert on child rearing "under the conditions of the market economy" (Wang Lingling 2004). While some of the earlier examples refer to relatively smaller scales of socio-structural conditioning—economic circumstances, family background, geographical location—these examples refer to the broad scale of historical experience.

Tiaojian can also refer to a person's physical constitution, as when athletic potential is discussed in terms of biological *tiaojian* (Huang 2001: 30). Ensuring that a child eats enough and eats the right food can be referred to in terms of *tiaojian*, as in "ensure nutritional conditions." *Tiaojian* may even be invoked to refer to a more ephemeral kind of physical conditioning, as when one popular expert advises that taking an after-lunch nap "ensures the basic *tiaojian* for high-efficiency learning in the afternoon" (Jiang Xuelan 2006: 40).

These various ways of invoking *tiaojian* express an enduring emphasis on the role of natural, social, and economic environments in shaping human development in Chinese philosophy and educational theories.[4] They also resonate with Hannah Arendt's assertion that "whatever touches or enters into a sustained relationship with human life immediately assumes the character of a condition of human existence. . . . Human existence is conditioned existence" ([1958] 1998: 9). In my conversations with parents and teachers, in popular parenting advice, and in national policies for education reform, human development is recognized as *conditioned* development. Conditions, or *tiaojian*, include anything that touches or enters into a relationship with a human life, from weather to architecture to socioeconomic differentiation— even taking a nap. While some *tiaojian* are natural and others are social, all forms of *tiaojian* possess a conditioning power.

When parents invoke *tiaojian*, they recognize that the life and future of a child are conditioned by external circumstances—which include, from the perspective of parents, the agency of the child, his or her willingness and ability to work hard. In invoking *tiaojian*, parents also recognize that some conditions must be actively provided or created. The mothers I knew would often say that their only responsibility was to create *tiaojian* and that what happened thereafter was out of their control. It is the purpose of this chapter to "treasure this odd way of speaking," by presenting *tiaojian* creation as a metatheory that makes a certain assertion about the nature of reality and the place of humans in it (Latour 2005). The maternal effort made in creating and providing *tiaojian* constitutes artful disposition, a practice that privileges "relations of force" over human subjectivity. The logic behind creating and providing *tiaojian* resonates with antihumanism, as it too operates with the premise that humans are essentially assembled.

The discourse and practice of creating and providing *tiaojian* share with certain strands of philosophical thought a recognition of the intermediate space between the conditioning power of external circumstance and the possibility of meaningful human action. *Tiaojian* creation has something in common with Hannah Arendt's philosophy, which recognizes the condition of plurality—men living with other men—as a constraint on individual sovereignty and mastership, while proposing at the same time that taking initiative, making promises, and forgiving make up a meaningful repertoire of human action. It also and more importantly corresponds with the Chinese logic of propensity, crystallized in the word *shi,* variously translated as "potential born of disposition," "deployment," "setup," "propensity," or "tendency." Although *shi,* unlike *dao* or *li,* has not been recognized as a major philosophical concept—it is nevertheless fundamental to Chinese thinking (Jullien [1992] 1995). It can go a long way in explaining how contemporary Chinese try to make their way through the world.

The logic of propensity privileges relations of force over human subjectivity, while proposing that "every kind of reality" may be "worked to one's advantage." Artful disposition starts with accurately discerning a given situation and acting in a timely manner (Jullien [1992] 1995: 15).

For the seventeenth-century writer Wang Fuzhi, the historical process was generated by tendencies that gave way to change as a matter of course and could not therefore be attributed to the personality of great figures. But Wang Fuzhi also believed that human initiative and management were important, for if one wanted to influence a course of events, or to avoid a particular state of affairs, one had to divert a tendency in its incipient stage. Otherwise, any effort would be insignificant in the face of accumulated force (Jullien [1992] 1995: 191).

In middle-class parenting, competition is perceived as an ineluctable force that has the absolute power to arbitrarily eliminate, thereby posing a serious challenge to personal striving. Yet, despite the givenness of this force, human initiative is possible, even required. Like the strategist imagined in early Chinese texts on the art of disposition, parents work to exercise discernment and to identify opportunities for managing tendency. Competition as historical tendency is conceived in relation to enormous numbers that pose the practical problem of how to stand out against the crowd. Its management takes the form of consuming educational goods that promise to endow the child with a competitive edge. Competition as historical tendency may also have more immediate manifestations, namely in emergent situations that involve a teacher who has decided that a child is no longer worth the effort. Managing such a situation involves the artful arrangement of things, aimed at diverting negative tendencies that may lead to "elimination" (*taotai*).

In crowded classrooms where misrecognition can easily take place, mothers—especially—will deploy whatever resources they have at hand to set up and establish a situation that could eventually run a positive course. As banal as middle-class parenting may appear, creating and providing *tiaojian* is a significant mode of human action that points to a modality of power that corresponds with the art of government: the "right disposition of things, arranged so as to lead to a convenient end" (quoted in Foucault 1991: 93). Antihumanist thought in Western social theory insists on the assembled nature of human beings—the passive side of affectivity or the capacity to be affected. Contrarily, what *tiaojian* creation insists on is the active side of affectivity, the capacity humans have to assemble things, to create conditioning external circumstances. Even if the power to affect is itself assembled—as some anthropologists might argue—its exercise belongs to something more fundamental: the human capacity to manipulate reality, engender effects, and extend oneself. It is no coincidence that mothers speak of their responsibility in terms of creating and providing *tiaojian*. In doing so, they invoke a grand term that cuts across vastly different scales of human conditioning, situating themselves as makers rather than as made.

Human development is conditioned by environmental, biological, economic, material, nutritional, social, and historical *tiaojian*. But mothers, as primary caretakers, experience themselves as agents in creating *tiaojian* and in managing the uncertainty of their children's future. This mode of agency is by no means something to romanticize. It is a moral burden fraught with the fear of potential or actual regret.

DELIMITING MORAL RESPONSIBILITY

Creating *tiaojian* is a moral practice that involves drawing lines between what one can and cannot control in an unpredictable world, what one is and is not responsible for. Consider this conversation I had with a mother of an eight-year-old girl. Let's call her Mrs. Huang.

MRS. HUANG. Parents now, we're all born in the 1960s, 1970s. Think about it . . . I haven't really learned anything, I didn't have the *tiaojian* for learning. So right now, I want to create *tiaojian* for my daughter to learn.

Let her not regret and say, "Ah, my parents didn't create these *tiaojian* for me," right? So now, I've created them for you. If you pick it up or don't pick it up, that's another matter. But the point is, you won't regret.

TK. *You have fulfilled your responsibility.*

MRS. HUANG. Ah, right, right. Your parents have tried their best to fulfill their responsibility.

Mrs. Huang went on to explain that Chinese parents care for their children well into adulthood, and we eventually got around to talking about Xu Li, the good student who had killed. She knew the story quite well and cited a television show where Intimate Sister talked about his case. Mrs. Huang was much more sympathetic to Xu Li's mother than Intimate Sister was and felt that she had been only looking out for her son's best interest.

MRS. HUANG. See, there's another thing about Chinese parents when it comes to their child. To enable the child to be a useful person, that parent will keep . . . One thing is intellectual cultivation. Another is to enable the child to be self-sufficient later when he is grown up. He has to find a job, after all. Think about it, right now work is very hard to find. Right? If you don't have ability, how are you going to look? You have to create the *tiaojian* and let him have a definite level of ability. Mother Xu's starting point [*chufa dian*] was good. But can the child take it?

The kind of responsibility Mrs. Huang feels toward her daughter is shaped by her perception of her own past, as shaped by present values, and also by what she imagines the future to hold. "Right now work is very hard to find," she states. A child's future employment is a matter over which an individual parent has little control save her ability to create *tiaojian* in the present. The first time Mrs. Huang invokes creating *tiaojian* here, she is referring to paying money for extracurricular classes in hobbies such as piano, violin, and English, or for some kind of sport. She says she has not learned anything in her own lifetime, though this is not technically true. In fact, she is an educator by profession and teaches accounting to college undergraduates. What she has not learned are the cultural skills that have come to be so highly valued in the reform era. These skills confer cultural capital in the form of *suzhi*, and it is in this area that she is supposedly lacking.

The second time Mrs. Huang invokes *tiaojian*, she more explicitly links a parent's responsibility for creating *tiaojian* to surviving the competition, while acknowledging at the same time the vulnerability of a parent's good intentions to external contingencies. Just because one sends a child off to learn this or that special talent does not mean the child will pick it up, let alone like the new hobby. And just because a parent works to create *tiaojian* in the form of constant supervision, as Mother Xu tried to do, does not mean the child will respond in a positive way. When mothers say that what happens after *tiaojian* are created is not up to them, they are making an assertion about the ethical importance of initiative. Here the parallel between creating *tiaojian* and Hannah Arendt's philosophy comes into sharper focus. Action is always cast out into a web of already existing relationships composed of an innumerable number of distinct and unique individuals with their distinct and unique intentions ([1958] 1998: 184). This web of relationships will inevitably subvert an actor's original purpose, so that outcome rarely corresponds to intention. Thus one need not judge a person for the consequences of his or her actions because any actor can take responsibility only for what he or she initiates.

This explains Mrs. Huang's admiration for Mother Xu: although her constant supervision drove her son to matricide, her intention, her starting point (*chufa dian*), was good. Mrs. Huang also finds comfort in being able to draw a boundary between initiative and consequence, as one may forestall regret by taking responsibility for the little that one could in fact control. The moral reasoning behind creating *tiaojian* can be summarized in this way: "I've tried my best, given the means I have at my disposal. Don't blame me later for not having tried." One can try to do everything a middle-class parent is supposed to do and possibly free oneself from future blame. Or one can simply make no effort and risk the discomfort of moral judgment.

On Regret

There are many parallels between the creation of *tiaojian* and Hannah Arendt's understanding of the human condition. But in real life, people often blame one another for consequences that individual actors are not entirely responsible for, and actors themselves often take responsibility for things they clearly could not have controlled. The famous case of Azande witchcraft demonstrates how a society has normalized mechanisms of blame in such a way that the morally unfortunate will voluntarily accept responsibility for causing another person to suffer—for one *might* be a witch without even knowing it (Evans-Pritchard 1976). In a more familiar example: funerals are commonly events that unleash torrents of guilt and regret. This is because the death of a loved one involves much more than the end of a life; it is also the end of possible action within a given relationship. "I could have been a better daughter/son/husband/wife." "I shouldn't have held those grudges." "I should have been more helpful." "I could have eased his suffering." "I should have told her how much I really love her." Even if people rationally know that life is lived within all sorts of constraints (e.g., "My job prevented me from being a better caretaker") and that most of life is muddled through (e.g., "I didn't realize he was suffering"), they still blame themselves. In moral philosophy, this called "moral luck" (Nagel 1979; Williams 1981).

In the context of middle-class child rearing in China, self-blame is commonly bundled with potential or actual regret—the idea that a given situation might be different had one acted otherwise. The kind of regret indicated by Mrs. Huang is more general in character, as the regret she feels has more to do with the course of history. She does not take responsibility for her lack of cultural sophistication because she belongs to a generation that did not have the conditions for learning how to play the piano, et cetera. In the ethnographic cases to which I will soon turn, we observe the kind of regret that stems from self-blame. This second variant of regret—what Bernard Williams calls agent-regret—is commonly a motive force behind intensive child rearing.[5] Agent-regret in the cases to follow intersects with the logic of propensity. To illustrate what I mean, allow me to quote Jullien at length: "Historical tendency possesses a great potential force; a seemingly insignificant precedent may alter the course of history for several centuries. Once a certain groove is followed it later becomes nearly impossible 'to change the line or get out of the rut.' Hence the extreme caution *constantly* required of all who play a role in the course of history: the first, false step is so simple to take, and, as time passes, it becomes difficult to correct that waywardness" (Jullien [1992] 1995: 191, emphasis added). Similarly, a seemingly insignificant precedent in the course of a child's academic career can have profound implications, yet "the first, false step is so simple to take." Thus the demand for constant vigilance in China's competition regime.

The mothers in the cases to follow learn this lesson the hard way, and their experience of agent-regret involves regret over obtuse perception and slow timing. This regret is both moral and metaphysical; it is a burden that derives from the recognition that human agency is simultaneously very limited and very important. The question for these actors is not whether human agency and control are possible in the face of determinism, but rather where and when action is possible, necessary, or futile.

Because the logic of propensity does not conceive of uncertainty as an issue—so long as one discerns accurately, and disposes wisely, the desired course of action is ineluctable—the lived problem of moral luck may be all the more tragic for middle-class Chinese mothers. "If things do not go your way, you really only have yourself to blame because you missed an important opportunity for action."

Yet at the same time, paradoxically, ineluctability may also be a source of tremendous empowerment. For those who manage to dispose of things in a wise and timely manner engender worldly efficacy and extend themselves by riding on the powers immanent in a given process. We will return to this idea at the end of the chapter.

CASE 1: I'M TRYING MY BEST

I met Zhang Xin the same night I met Wang Yan (from chapter 3). Wang Yan, Wen Hui, and Zhang Xin were all good friends, as were their children. Zhang Xin's son Deng Siwen was a year younger than Wang Yan and Wen Hui's children, seven years old when he and I first met. Like her friends, Zhang Xin put a lot of effort into her son. This group of women, avid consumers of the parenting literature, believed in the importance of creating a learning environment and in the idea that a parent's responsibility did not end with dropping the child off at school or bringing him or her to special talent classes. One should take a participatory role, and grow up together with the child. One thing Zhang Xin worked particularly hard at was creating an English-speaking environment beyond the classroom. While friends and colleagues sometimes took the night off to go out or go to the gym, Zhang Xin stayed home with her son to study from his *New Concept English* book. Even though Zhang Xin confessed that it was hard for her to put sentences together, she often tried to converse with her son, as well as myself, entirely in English.

But I eventually learned that Zhang Xin hadn't always had this kind of time, something she felt agent-regret over. For the first six years of Deng Siwen's life, Zhang Xin was occupied. In her midtwenties, right around 1996 when Siwen was born, she decided to go back to school because expectations for higher degrees in the workplace were increasing. (She was a health care practitioner.) She went back and studied the high school curriculum and participated in the national college entrance exam, since she had only a diploma from a technical high school. She went on to college from there, and then to Beijing for advanced studies, before she finally had time to actively engage in parenting. In the meantime, her husband was constantly going out of town for work, so the couple hired a nanny and sent their son to preschool at a very young age.

Zhang Xin attributed Siwen's ill temper to those many years of not having had a relationship with him. "Sometimes, his temper is a little, you know . . . really weird. It makes me feel like, maybe it's all because I didn't do a good job guiding him, you know?" Although Zhang Xin felt that regret is pointless, sometimes she still blamed herself.

She told me a story about a fight that had occurred between Siwen and his three-year-old cousin, Zhang Xin's younger sister's son. Siwen was sitting on the sofa while his little cousin climbed about. The cousin, who was six or seven years Siwen's junior, started playing rough and accidentally caused the back of Siwen's head to hit the wall. The impact made an audible *thunk,* sending Siwen into a rage. According to Zhang Xin, Siwen began to kick his cousin relentlessly, accusing him of intentionally wanting to hurt him. Zhang Xin immediately tried to resolve the conflict and reason with her son. But Siwen was unstoppable. Zhang Xin lost her temper and resorted to giving her son a taste of his own medicine.

Feeling regret for her reaction, Zhang Xin said to Siwen, who was sitting with us at this point of the interview, "Mommy shouldn't have been like that either, right? But Mommy had already tried to reason with you. If I didn't adopt some action, there wasn't any way for you to calm down! I felt like I had no other choice."

She then turned to me, asked me what she should have done in the situation, and went on to say this:

ZHANG XIN. That's why I feel like it actually isn't easy for a parent to really, *tsk,* well, raise a child to adulthood, *oh?* Because he, he's also exposed to a lot of outside things. You have to pay attention to his development. Avoid waywardness. Kids these days . . . some kids are very smart. If the kid does something bad out there, he might not come home and tell you truthfully. *Tsk.* This kind of thing is very dangerous. Like my classmate, she also works at the hospital, now her situation, let's see, she's . . .

TK. *The kind of kids you're talking about are older, right?*

ZX. Pretty much around Deng Siwen's age. That kid's temper is . . . I feel is . . . It isn't good. *Tsk.* His mother is also very dutiful. Because she is also . . . the father is also . . .

TK. *Oh, divorced.*

ZX. Divorced. She is raising the kid by herself. Also a very exhausting thing.

TK. *Right right right. Right.*

ZX. Mmm. That kid used to be at the same school as Deng Siwen. And then he had to transfer.

TK. *Because of what?*

ZX. Because in class he would . . . he was actually quite naughty. And so he didn't give the teacher a good impression. The teacher was especially, especially you know . . .

TK. *Not fair to him.*

ZX. Right right right. Simply felt like, "You're *just* that kind of kid. That kind of, you're the *bad* type." This is the worst scenario. I feel like teachers, teachers in China,

TK. *Once a teacher makes this kind of determination . . .*

ZX. Right! A set determination is not good. Right. So my friend felt like this wasn't good. Her son shouldn't be in this classroom anymore, this is harmful to a child's development. Even though he . . . some of his classmates especially liked to, even as young children . . . (*lowers voice to a whisper*) I'm really not clear, and that was the fourth grade at the time. They would gamble. It's really strange.

TK. *Really?*

ZX. Because there are some kids that come from really rich families. They give their kids a lot of spending money. So sometimes the kids will gamble between themselves. So her son hung out with those kids. *Tsk.* And so he received some negative influences. So maybe this kid learned some of those bad habits. Dime-plucking gangs.[6] Those things from the adult world.

TK. *(Laughs) I've heard of dime-plucking gangs.*

ZX. And then, *unh!* Thank goodness, his mother felt that it was not good. This child cannot stay in this class like this anymore. If he stays any longer the outcome won't be good. It'll destroy the child's life. Because I think with such a good kid, he could still change. He's only going along because it's fun, he doesn't know anything. Right? But if he continues and gets deeper, then it'll be very dangerous. So she transferred him to a different district.

Afterwards I asked her about her situation again once they got over there, and she said things were much better. I think leaving this kind of environment is very important.

Zhang Xin went on to explain that the really rich families she was thinking of were those that came from the countryside and had suddenly gotten very rich. Otherwise known as the nouveau riche, these entrepreneurs successfully exploited certain market niches as the Chinese economy underwent liberalization and tended to have lower levels of formal education.

Zhang Xin felt that classrooms were increasingly being polluted by children of wealthy peasants who lacked *suzhi*. In the opinion of teachers and urban middle-class parents like Zhang Xin, these children were simply handed over to the schools by parents who provided very little guidance at home. For this reason, Zhang Xin felt that a good school was important and that parents played an important role in how a child turned out. She continued, directing her statement to Siwen, who was still sitting with us:

ZX. So, the point is, what we can do at home we try our best to do. What we can do for him, should do for him, I've done it all! I don't have any regrets. (*To her son in a sweet voice*) One day, when he is all grown up, I will feel very happy.

If things turn out otherwise, and I look back on things, I won't have any regrets. I will feel like I've tried my best. I don't wish that he becomes anything necessarily, just grow up and that's good enough, (*to her son*), right?

With this invitation to join our conversation, Deng Siwen took the opportunity to lodge a complaint: "Your education method really is a failure. You don't even have patience." Zhang Xin laughed, nervously. I laughed too, to dispel the tension. The two had already exchanged gestures of reconciliation after the incident, but clearly not all was forgiven. Rather than admit to her wrong again, Zhang Xin tried to make very clear that she was doing the best she could. While she had expressed feelings of regret over missed years only moments ago, here she insisted on having no regrets, now that Siwen was sitting next to us:

ZX. The point is, everything Mommy should do, Mommy's done, don't you think? I've done everything I was supposed to. And I haven't wronged you. And I don't have any regrets. Down the line, what you need to put effort into, what you know is important, you ought to put in the effort yourself. Because that's how it is in China, *ah?* Such a big population. Yet so few opportunities. Able persons are as common as air.

(*Turning to me*) That's why I tell you, it'll be even scarier for their generation. Our employment environment . . . their environment later is very grim.

Thinking with Stories about Waywardness

As Zhang Xin moves from the particular to the general, from a story about losing her temper, to a story about a friend's gambling son, to the situation of the nouveau riche in Kunming, and finally to the broader problem of what Siwen will have to face in the future, we can observe a train of thought that illustrates a parent's sense that raising a child from birth to adulthood is fraught with uncertainty. This is especially the case for parents of boys, who are more likely to be seduced by gambling, Internet addiction, fighting, and joining dime-plucking gangs. In the story about her classmate's son, Zhang Xin suggests that the child himself was maybe involved with a dime-plucking gang. In telling this story, Zhang Xin expresses anxiety over the pollution of children by "outside things"—in this case, gangs and gambling, "things from the adult world." Because she associates gambling children with the nouveau riche, namely wealthy peasants with "low *suzhi*," her concern expresses a classist anxiety over class boundaries, and also an existential worry over the many things that can impede a parent's good intention to set her child on a straight path. It is not easy to raise a child to adulthood, Zhang Xin muses.

But exposure to "outside things" is not the only danger that makes the pursuit of the good life for one's child vulnerable. One must also ensure that a child's teachers, especially the homeroom teacher, do not develop a negative impression, as this can have immediate and far-reaching consequences for a child's academic career. Being labeled as the "bad type" is the worst-case scenario, as core curriculum teachers follow their students up to graduation. Because there is so much at stake in these relationships, a teacher is an ally at best and an adversary at worst. In the case of Zhang Xin's friend, it was important that she get her son away not only from negative peer influences but also from a teacher who had already determined that he was the bad type. "A set determination is not good," Zhang Xin explains. After a transfer to a different school district and a new beginning, things turned for the better for this classmate and her son.

All of the mothers I knew felt an acute, future-oriented anxiety over the possibility of being crowded out by the competition. This anxiety was largely shaped by stories about the children of friends who had been negatively labeled. I heard such horror stories on many occasions. In one story I heard, told by one parent to another in a conversation about the importance of the *suzhi* and the mental health of teachers, a conflict that had arisen between a high school student and his math teacher led to a situation where the student was getting criticized every day. The parents in this story eventually transferred their son to a different school, but the boy had already become so discouraged he couldn't even look at math anymore, let alone take the college entrance exam. In another story I heard, a perfectly lovable and emotionally intelligent child was pressured to transfer to another school for being a bad student. The parent telling me this story related that the teacher felt the child was not pleasing to the eye, and was unforgiving of the child's absentmindedness. My interlocutor told this tale while expressing gratitude that her daughter's teacher had yet to summon her for an admonishing conversation. Whatever her troubles in parenting were, they could be worse.

Stories about getting a bad label constituted a subgenre of horror story; they paraded the possibility that elimination was an ever-present threat, even for the well-intended parent and the good-natured child. Getting a bad label was worrisome because it meant that the teacher had decided your child was no longer worth the effort. When Zhang Xin started to say, "I feel like teachers, teachers in China . . . " she was indicating that the phenomenon was rather widespread, common enough to be a serious concern. This is a phenomenon that has, in fact, come to the attention of the *suzhi jiaoyu* advocates. Because schools and teachers are evaluated according to rates of promotion and student test scores, they inadvertently focus on nurturing the promising students while rejecting the bad students. One reform advocate gives the unfair treatment of bad students a name: "educational discrimination," found in both primary and secondary schools. Treating students unfairly is just one of many modes of gradual elimination, along with holding them back, suspending them, or expelling them (Man 1997: 22). Educational *discrimination* can also include subtle pressure to leave "voluntarily."

A teenager I knew experienced *discrimination* at one of Kunming's three elite key-point high schools. By the time I met Linda, she had already withdrawn from school, given up on the prospect of taking the college entrance exam, and sought psychiatric help as an inpatient for sleep problems. High school was a very bad experience for her. All she ever wanted to do was sleep.

She would often sleep past the beginning of the first period, and she still wanted to sleep at the end of the day, when she was supposed to be completing her homework assignments. It was in the context of trying to locate possible sources for the intangible pressure she felt during high school that she mentioned how her school and her teacher had threatened her with expulsion. In her understanding, they could not arbitrarily ask you to leave because you were underperforming academically. "They would find some behavioral problem," she told me, "and then, you know, kick you out." It could be poor attendance, missing homework, or a lack of diligence during the cleaning period. "Ah, you don't love to labor! Don't like the class collective!" So those who were left, she reasoned, had "*extremely* good academic records," thereby preserving the school's excellent reputation. Linda, meanwhile, assumed that her life was completely ruined because she failed to finish high school.[7]

To return to Zhang Xin's case, educational discrimination had not happened to Siwen, but it was imagined as one of many possible ways in which a child's life could go off the rails. Parents often think with stories—not only with the public stories circulated in the media and in popular advice (chapter 2) but also with cases concerning friends, former classmates, and coworkers. Stories can underscore how the unknown lurks just around the corner and how the "anomalous event" can thwart moral projects (Mattingly 1998a: 128). Because so much uncertainty surrounds the pursuit of the good life, the lives of others offer materials for contemplating one's own.[8]

For Zhang Xin, the story about her friend's son taking up gambling and transferring schools hit close to home for many reasons. Having gone to school together, now working for the same employer, and having sons of the same age who, previously, had attended the same school, Zhang Xin and her friend already lived parallel lives. Unlike her friend, Zhang Xin was still married to her husband. But she undoubtedly felt like a single parent because he was constantly going out of town for work, sometimes for as long as nine months. For this reason, what happened to her friend put her on the alert. She immediately thought of her friend in reflecting on the justness of physically punishing her son for kicking his cousin.

Further noticing that older children of other friends had turned out every which way, Zhang Xin sensed that there were many things outside her control. This was the moral of the gambling boy story, which featured something "really strange." Knowing that action is always cast out into a web of already existing relationship, she made a judgment about what to take responsibility for and where to concede. Her parenting philosophy was that her duty was to provide *tiaojian,* according to the best *tiaojian* she had at hand. "I think the starting point of every parent is like this," she said. She could not undo her absence in her son's first six years of life, so she channeled her agent-regret into making effort in the present. Zhang Xin now did everything she possibly could to be an actively engaged parent, whether it involved punishing her son when he behaved badly, even if it broke her heart, or sending him to extracurricular classes, or studying *New Concept English* with him every night. "If things turn out otherwise," she said, she could at least look back without regret. And she expected that Siwen would not have regrets either: "If you don't pick something up, there's nothing I can do about it. Just don't blame me later for not having tried."

CASE 2: YOU CAN'T LET YOUR TEACHER HAVE ANYTHING TO SAY ABOUT YOU

Yang Ruihong and her husband Yang Zhonghai were unlike many of the other parents I followed. I never saw them raise their voice or nag their son Xiaoming, who was twelve years old when I first met them. They never said things like "Study hard and you can do x, y, z," which was so common with the other families I knew. ("Study hard and you can visit Teacher Kuan in America!") Many of the families I followed were affectionate, but this was particularly the case for the Yang family. Xiaoming, already in his preteen years and getting quite tall, was always draping himself all over his parents. They were one affectionate bunch, and they spoke some kind of secret discourse that I was never quite able to penetrate.

But it would be a mistake to assume from all the mutual affection that Xiaoming's parents were the laissez-faire type. Yang Ruihong did not buy all the business about not spanking one's child. "Why do you think Xiaoming is so obedient?" she once asked rhetorically.

Xiaoming was enrolled in a variety of extracurricular activities and classes: basketball, composition writing, the study of Chinese classics, and of course English. His involvement was an expression of Yang Ruihong's sense of parental responsibility, the creation and provision of *tiaojian* for success. She once told me, "We feel like creating *tiaojian* is our responsibility. And then learning is the kid's responsibility." But her notion of this responsibility once expanded to include exercising vigilance over homework assignments. "When he was in the third or fourth grade, we didn't have much time to take care of him. And then maybe when his teachers or we weren't paying attention, his passion for learning was hurt," she began. Xiaoming was taking all night to finish homework that should have been finished within an hour. Yet he would still turn in unfinished assignments to Chinese class and incorrect answers to math class. At the time, Yang Ruihong wasn't sure if he had an "intellect problem" (*zhili wenti*) or if he figured he could get away with turning in unfinished homework.

YANG RUIHONG. So then the math teacher criticized him. I think the teacher said . . . I don't know what was said exactly, he's never told me. And then he, *tsk,* I just thought that when he was doing his homework he was having a really hard time. So I sought out the teacher and we discussed this. She said, (*sucks in air*) this problem of his, one is he doesn't ask questions, another is he doesn't enthusiastically speak up in class.

I talked to the teacher, and the teacher said, he doesn't have a sense of responsibility. He is lazy. He doesn't want to do it, et cetera et cetera. I think if you say this kind of thing a lot, it could be a little harmful to a kid's psychology. "Oh well, I'm inadequate. I'm lazy anyway." And then the kid won't be willing to . . . As soon as the teacher said this to me, I felt speechless.

TK. *You didn't agree with her.*

YRH. *Unh.* But with the teacher, you know, I didn't agree with this kind of method. I think kids, of course they're going to be naughty, of course they will do things they aren't supposed to do. But how to not hurt their self-respect, I think it's really important.

Here a parent describes her own child's brush with educational discrimination, an event that Yang Ruihong causally relates—speaking in terms of a *we*—to having been busy at work. She does not know how it happened exactly, but only that her son was having a really hard time doing his schoolwork at home. He was "just especially slow."

Yang Ruihong guessed two causes for the problem: Xiaoming either he had an intellectual problem or was just being naughty. The teacher, on the other hand had already made up her mind: Xiaoming didn't ask questions, didn't enthusiastically speak up, didn't have a sense of responsibility, and was just being lazy. Xiaoming, in the eyes of this teacher, had definitively become a whole suite of negative traits. Not only was he a bad student, in terms of marks, but he also had characteristics that were much worse than naughtiness and intellectual deficiency. Naughtiness is accepted as a childhood trait, and intellectual deficiency is not a moral deficiency. On a different occasion, Yang Ruihong explained to me that a teacher's impression is very important because teachers treat good students a certain way and bad students another. This echoes the kind of concern Zhang Xin expressed in our first case in observing that "a set determination is not good."

YRH. I didn't know how it could be. He didn't talk to me about it either. But when he was doing his homework, I saw for myself, he was just especially slow. And then I talked to the teacher, twice. But we weren't communicating so well. The teacher thought the problem was the kid's laziness. But I thought, it should be a problem of how to muster up his enthusiasm and passion. If you let him feel like he is simply a certain kind of person in class or in front of his classmates, he won't have any motivation.

TK. *Right. He will feel like, "Okay. This is how I am."*

YRH. There's also "I *don't* want to be like this." He also earnestly feels, "I don't want to be like this." But he will have that psychological barrier once he's in that environment. That's why I later said: the first step, forget what the problem might be, he must finish every homework assignment the teacher gives. Don't give the teacher a reason to bring up this homework problem ever again. I would keep him company while he did his homework until 11:00, 12:00 at night. Sometimes 1:00 in the morning! My heavens.

TK. *Aiyo.*

YRH. It wasn't because the teacher gave a lot of homework. He just had difficulty doing it. And it's not that he didn't know how to do it. At that time you know, he would sit himself in front of the desk, and for one character he would have to look so many times! Actually he *knows* how to write that character. But that brain didn't know how to direct his hand (*laughs*). *Aiyo,* once it got a little late, he was just very tired and would want to sleep. "You want to sleep? No way, let's go running. Let's go downstairs for a lap and finish after that. Still not okay? Let's go run again, wake up a little. Or wash your face." And then that wouldn't work . . .

Yang Ruihong monitored her son like this every night for a month or two. But it was not because she wanted to improve his marks or to teach him the kind of discipline homework required. She wanted to reconfigure the situation by artfully disposing the resources at hand: her own time and energy. Resonating with early Chinese antihumanism and the logic of propensity, Yang Ruihong's reasoning privileged external circumstance over human interiority. As she said, "Forget what the problem might be, he must finish every homework assignment."

For Yang Ruihong, her effort was aimed at diverting what had already become a wayward tendency, one she spoke of in the psychological terms of the *suzhi jiaoyu* movement. At stake was his self-respect. "If you let him feel like he is simply a certain kind of person in class or in front of his classmates," Yang Ruihong thought, "he won't have any motivation." With the aim of engendering a new course, one that began with the first step of changing the environment by giving the teacher no reason to bring up the homework problem, Yang Ruihong quite literally coached her son in the manner a coach might train a boxer—stimulating the senses with cold water and physical motion in the wee hours.

Not completely understanding the point of her story, I asked if she thought at the time that she was tutoring him. She clarified,

YRH. Well, not tutor exactly. Actually he knows how to do it *all*. He was just *slow*. Just, looking at this stuff, and then he would go to write, and he would keep getting it wrong. Like the word for *good*, he would keep writing another character. I actually think it was a kind of psychological barrier. It was hard for him to do these things. Not that he had . . . anything. Just a psychological—

TK. *Not that he didn't know how to write the character for good.*

YRH. Regardless of what the problem actually is, you have to finish your teacher's assignments, so the teacher doesn't have anything to say about your homework problem, let your teacher feel that you're still . . . And then, slowly, homework time was shortened. I had already tried many methods. *Aiya*, I was worried. At that time, my scalp was numb (*laughs*).

In the end, Yang Ruihong felt that it wasn't an intellectual problem but rather a situation where things had taken the wrong course, starting with Xiaoming slacking off a little. Xiaoming's math teacher may have then said something harmful to him that hurt his self-respect, engendering a fear of school. Yang Ruihong even felt that he had reached the point of becoming "sick of learning" (*yanxue*), a psychological barrier that made completing homework assignments extremely difficult. She asked Xiaoming if he wanted to see a "psychological doctor" (*xinli yisheng*) about his difficulties.

Like Zhang Xin's story, this second case involves a working mother and agent-regret. Whereas Zhang Xin blamed her son's ill temper on her having pursued higher education during his early years, Yang Ruihong summed up this episode as follows: "This situation, you know, it was when I had neglected, when I hadn't noticed, that he got to this very terrible place." I believe this was a significant episode for mother and son. Yang Ruihong had told me a briefer version of this story the first time we met, many months before I sat her down for this interview. When we first met, she explained to me that one reason why it was not easy to apply popular advice was that parents had to work so much. By the time she got home, she was too tired to figure out what a certain problem is all about.

Her parenting philosophy had been pretty typical. "We feel like creating *tiaojian* is our responsibility. And then studying is the kid's responsibility." Working itself, bringing in a second income, provided the basic foundation for creating *tiaojian*. But this episode demonstrated to Yang Ruihong that responsibility did not necessarily end there. Xiaoming's school had an excellent reputation and attracted a large number of school-selecting students, students who paid extra money to attend a school outside their assigned district. This factor contributed to large class sizes—as many as sixty-nine students in the case of Xiaoming's classroom. Between the factor of size and the school's imperative to preserve its reputation, "misrecognition" (*kancuo*), a term used by the parent in the next case, was also more likely to happen.

This is a concern, because there is an even greater multitude in her vision of her child's future. If misrecognition can so easily occur in a classroom, what will the adult world be like? This episode expanded Yang Ruihong's notion of creating *tiaojian* to include ensuring a child's likability in the eyes of a teacher and self-respect in relation to his classmates. If well established, a new, positive situation engendered by the initiative she took to change the environment could potentially run its own course. Deploying the resources at hand—her own time and energy—Yang Ruihong engaged in the art of disposition.

CASE 3: SHE'S GETTING BETTER NOW, MORE "SMOOTH"

Unlike many of the other children in her daughter's first-grade classroom, Zhao Jiajia had not yet learned basic arithmetic and character recognition. Zhou Huawei and her husband simply did not have time. Everyone was just "one busy mess." With a long and arduous road ahead, why bother? "It's just preschool," they thought. But once Jiajia entered primary school they began to worry:

zhw: We realized, she was starting the race behind everybody else. She really was not the same. I don't know what it's like in America, I doubt that parents squawk about pouring in all kinds of things during preschool. There is a lot of that here! I suddenly realized that my kid was downstream. On top of that she was small in physique, and not very pretty.

While Zhou Huawei took no issue with the fact that her daughter was behind her preschool peers—"So what if she's stupid?"—she was unwilling to be laissez-faire about primary school. She felt bad that Jiajia had fallen behind because she hadn't started squawking about pouring in all kinds of things right away. On top of that, Jiajia's homeroom teacher had already developed a negative impression.

Zhou Huawei once ran into this homeroom teacher on the street, so she figured she would make some conversation and ask about Jiajia's behavior. The teacher responded haughtily, according to Zhou Huawei's account: "Ye-oh! That Zhao Jiajia of yours. *Aiya,* doesn't speak much. It's like she's deeply afraid she's going to do something wrong. Personality is a bit introverted." Although Zhou Huawei was in disbelief that this teacher had already made such a conclusion, she acted deferentially and promised that she would go home and try her best to work on her daughter. In her mind, however, the teacher's assessment was unfair. Maybe Jiajia was the type of person who preferred to suss out a situation before she revealed herself. Zhou Huawei thought, "More than anything this indicates a person's maturity of mind," not a deficiency in personality.

Meanwhile, Jiajia was often picked on and scolded by the teacher, and she felt very stifled.

zhw. She often felt sad over not getting 100 on a test. Would cry. Because everyone else got 100. Because everyone else has learned before! How can you be like someone who has learned before? Right? Of course she's going to be different. So she was very sad. So then I noticed this and I was sad too. Because if she has pressure, I have pressure. This pressure is two-sided. It's not that I give the pressure to the kid and I don't have any pressure. I have pressure too. So I *immediately* spring into action, you know? I'm gathering things as fast as I can. I want to improve her grades.

Here, "sad too" forms the agent-regret expressed in a spring to action. Seeing that she could no longer let things run their course naturally, Zhou Huawei started tutoring Jiajia in math, even though she personally hated looking at numbers and had poor methods that rely on memorization rather than technique. It did not matter, for the time being, that such a method would be harmful in the long run because it worked. Jiajia was one of two students to score 100 points on a first-grade final exam. Zhou Huawei recalled, "I felt like I wanted to show them, to what degree my child was bad. 'You want to insist that I'm so bad, well, I'll show you.'"

Scoring 100 on the math exam gave Jiajia the self-confidence she had previously lacked. By the second grade, she had completely transformed her standing in class by publishing compositions in local newspapers—compositions Zhou Huawei sweetened up.

ZHW. She published! She got 50 *kuai* in royalties. We got it already. And so, she was very proud! Extremely proud!

TK. *Really?*

ZHW. *Unh*, extremely proud. And then, their homeroom teacher suddenly saw her—

TK. *Differently.*

ZHW. Differently. Because when you publish in the newspaper like this, their homeroom teacher teaches Chinese, it brings benefit to their teacher. There's a sense of success because it's her own student. And then you know, it adds points to their class.

TK. *Because it will say so and so from the second grade from such and such primary school.*

ZHW. *Eh! Eh!* Zhao Jiajia, and then this and that, this is for point keeping. This establishes a foundation for the outstanding homeroom teacher. So this got published. And then she suddenly changed. She felt this was very—

TK. *Her self-confidence really . . .*

ZHW. Became much stronger.

TK. *Established.*

ZHW. Right, right. And then her teacher saw her differently too. So when her teacher's leading a class, you know, the kind of attitude she has, it leads the other students, how they should treat her too. A teacher's attitude *definitely* shapes the attitudes of students.

Jiajia said that in the past, when she went to school, she played by herself. The people around her rarely played with her. So if she brought a lot of fun toys to play with, because one time they had a special interest class, she brought some toys. So if she has a magazine, she's the only one looking at it. No one's paying attention to her (*laughs*). It's different now. As soon as she brings something, everyone's fighting to see what it is. They just want to hang out with her. It's like they think she is, how to say, someone worth befriending. That's how they see her.

See, our environment is like this.

When Zhou Huawei says, "See, our environment is like this," she points to the political nature of classroom relationships, between a student and his or her teacher, and between students themselves. People would tell me that children worshipped their mothers in early childhood and then their teachers in primary school. This certainly seemed to explain the power of a teacher's influence on peer-to-peer relationships in the classroom. Given such an environment, reconfiguring a child's social standing in class would begin with the first step of changing a teacher's negative impression. As in the previous case, Zhou Huawei's efforts in tutoring her daughter and in helping her publish were primarily aimed at diverting a negative tendency.

When Jiajia entered the first grade, she had difficulty making friends. No one paid attention to her and her teacher did not treat her well. But with an improvement in test scores and with two publications in a local newspaper—which listed her grade, her classroom number, and the name of her school, thereby bringing honor to her homeroom teacher—Jiajia's social status changed. Her teacher began to see and treat her differently, and her classmates consequently followed. Jiajia, a small, skinny, and timid girl, became someone worth befriending.

Zhou Huawei explained to me that there were a number of ways a parent might try to curry favor with a teacher and ensure extra care. They might treat a teacher to a facial or go shopping with her. Those who sent their child to what was called "little lunch table" could especially count on extra care. The teacher would feed and take care of your child during the lunch break, for a fee. Zhou Huawei, an unusually blunt person, contended that this was to be expected, "They have a kind of economic relationship. They have a kind of benefit-seeking relationship." Zhou Huawei was not at all interested in playing such games. When I asked if it was true that parents gave teachers "red-packets"—ritual envelopes filled with cash—Zhou Huawei said, "Absolutely. But I won't even give a blade of grass to her." She described her relationship to Jiajia's teacher as circumspect and did not want to mix with her any more than she needed to. But she was also perfectly aware of the importance of a teacher's impression, which she illustrated for me with a horror story.

One of Jiajia's classmates, who sat right behind Jiajia, had very low social status. The child had once said to Jiajia, "I am nice to everyone. But no one is nice to me." Zhou Huawei was not totally clear on the details of the situation but only knew that this child might be a low-achieving student. The situation was so bad this student even wished to transfer schools. To make matters worse, something extremely embarrassing had happened. Apparently this student came from a family with very good *tiaojian*: both parents drove private cars, and a nanny brought the child to school and back home every day. Around the Mid-Autumn Festival, this classmate's parents sent an expensive box of mooncakes with the child to give to the teacher as a gift. Zhou Huawei relates, "Maybe the kid didn't know how to give a gift" and did not understand the cultural taboo against public gift giving. But the child presented the gift in front of everyone, and the teacher rejected it, just as publicly. "With this," Zhou Huawei points out to me, "this person's status in the class is even lower, just not anything. Think about it, this is really sad. This kind of thing can really injure a person."

It is significant that Zhou Huawei told me this story. In contrast with the first case in this chapter, where storyteller and protagonist lived parallel lives, Zhou Huawei did not have much in common with the parents in this story. (She and her husband were teachers, while the parents in the story were businesspeople.) But her daughter had been in a similar situation of being seen and treated a certain way. Knowing the classroom environment, she wanted Jiajia to have good social relationships and felt more than willing to help "build a foundation" (*dianding jichu*). Zhou Huawei had professional experience in publication and had the social connections to make it happen. Having these things at her disposal, she felt compelled to take some initiative to manage the situation.

Popular experts would likely disparage her "sweetening" of Jiajia's compositions as "meddling in the affairs of others." One of Jiajia's two compositions was, in fact, unrealistically clever for a second grader. Titled "Memoirs of an Official," it recounted Jiajia's experience of being the world's smallest official. The appointment came after some improvement in her academic performance and was a responsibility she often complained about to her mom. As the world's smallest official, she didn't understand why she had to work so hard while officials above her did nothing. Jiajia complained to her mother about it. So Zhou Huawei encouraged her daughter to express her feelings and taught her the art of social satire: if you have grievances, you can express them indirectly with humor. In the essay, "the P.E. committee-members go and climb the jungle gym, for the sake of strengthening one's muscles; the art committee-members in the corridor wiggle their necks, wiggle their butts, for the sake of beautifying their physique; the learning committee-members take huge gulps of fresh air, for the sake of taking inspiration from nature." Meanwhile, the author drenches herself in sweat fulfilling her duties as a lowly assistant to the chief.

According to Zhou Huawei, the teacher liked this composition so much she read it out loud to the class, and the entire room roared with laughter because so much of it was true. From an adult perspective, the composition cleverly offered a critique of an endemic social problem in China—the pursuit of gain on the part of high officials while those below struggle along. Social critique was couched in the innocence of playground politics. Thus it was obvious Jiajia did not write this on her own.

ZHW. Of course everybody is going to say, your kid published something in the second grade, it's actually fake. She can't possibly write something so good! That's true, I can admit that. You think her teacher doesn't know? Of course she knows! Who doesn't know who was responsible? They all know! But this is something very easy for me.

From Zhou Huawei's point of view, whether she had "meddled" in Jiajia's affairs was beside the point. The purpose of this project was strategic—artful disposition. Like the bad tutoring method that might be harmful in the long run, the intrinsic meaning of the action mattered less than the action's potential efficacy in reconfiguring an immediate circumstance.

When Jiajia's teacher underwent a complete change of heart once she produced a perfect math score, exclaiming, "*Ye-oh!* How outstanding she is!" Zhou Huawei thought, "Their teacher misrecognized again. Misrecognized *again!*" But since the tendency had changed in her and Jiajia's favor, there was no need for correction. Jiajia was now getting more "smooth" (*you*, literally "slick"). "More experienced. More daring, unafraid to talk back to the teacher." Having built a foundation, Zhou Huawei could now look forward to letting things run their course, at least for the time being.

TO BE WITH TIME

Børge Bakken observes that environmentalism occupies an important place in Chinese theories of learning. Chinese environmentalism assumes human persons to be highly porous and susceptible to influence—rich in their capacity to be affected: "Socialization is everywhere around us, spontaneously and constantly exerting an influence" (2000: 156). Earlier in the reform era, educators and party leaders argued for making use of this susceptibility in the engineering of educational environments. For example, researchers in the early 1990s wrote about creating "campus culture" with the design of material space and education plans that would consciously exploit unconscious processes (159–60). Bakken rightly notes that environmentalism is an ancient idea, one famously expressed in the story about Mencius's mother moving three times.

The affective power of environment is explicitly invoked in all three cases presented here. With regard to the story about the gambling boy, Zhang Xin states that things turned for the better for her friend and her son once they transferred school districts. "I think leaving this kind of environment is very important," she said. In the second case, Yang Ruihong says, "He will have that psychological barrier once he's in that environment" when making sense of her son's difficulty with homework. While Xiaoming's teacher located the homework problem inside him, Yang Ruihong locates the source of his problem externally. Finally, in the third case, Zhou Huawei invokes the environment in describing the dynamics involved in who gets befriended and who gets mistreated. "See, our environment is like this," she says, as if to suggest some resignation on her part.

Middle-class parents are keen on creating and providing *tiaojian*, or opportunities for learning, with the purpose of ensuring a child's competitiveness. *Tiaojian* fever, if you will, is a response to a broad historical circumstance where a person's worth is primarily measured in relation to educational attainment—schools attended, degrees earned, and cultural skills learned. As such, *tiaojian* creation and *suzhi* discourse are related phenomena. But there is also an environmentalist logic behind the practice of *tiaojian* creation, one that assumes that anything that touches or enters into a relationship with human life possesses a conditioning power. Thus the great concern over the environment of everyday classroom life and emergent situations involving a misrecognizing teacher. The environment in this context refers to an external circumstance that must be adapted to, manipulated, or simply left behind. In the second and third cases, mothers adapt to the political nature of classroom relationships by staging the appearance of a certain kind of child—one who is not lazy or timid, a good student worthy of fair treatment and the respect of peers. In the first case, a mother—as depicted in a told story—simply took her son out of an unfavorable environment where a teacher had already determined that he was the bad type and where young boys gambled among themselves.

Thus, while comparisons could be made between middle-class child rearing in China and practices found in middle-class America—the most relevant being, as far as this chapter is concerned, the tendency of mothers to intervene in unfavorable situations (Lareau 2011)—there are important differences. China is still a developing country, one challenged by imbalances of all kinds—for example, between population size and available resources, between the overproduction of college graduates and an economy unable to absorb the surplus of white-collar labor.[9] This generates a kind of intensity and insecurity that is uniquely Chinese, which in turn mobilizes scripts for action that are also uniquely Chinese. Here the hero is less interested in struggling against the odds than in adapting to existing circumstances. Hence the proverbs "She who discerns timing and situations wisely is a hero" and "Accord with propensity and all will go well" remain popular to this day. I have had many a conversation with parents about the American ideal of following your dream and doing something meaningful with your life, as opposed to pursuing the kind of job that merely provides financial security. My interlocutors would recognize the appeal of such an idea, but they also felt that it was an impractical luxury given China's situation.

So there is this dimension of constraint, to be sure, but adaptation is not a passive mode of action. Its meaning is rooted in a certain ethical and cosmological formulation, found in texts as old as the third century: it is virtuous to partner with the fluctuations of the world (Jullien [1991] 2004: 59–63). In twenty-first-century China, this cultural logic is expressed in the notion of creating *tiaojian*.

While the conventional anthropological reading would look for how power operates through the unconscious conduct of everyday life, I would like to propose that *tiaojian* creation constitutes a modality of power that corresponds to the exercise of power at the level of the state. Like the art of government, *tiaojian* creation involves artful disposition. Like the art of government, *tiaojian* creation concerns the "imbrication of men and things." While Foucault uses the metaphor of the ship to explain what this means— to govern a ship means not just taking care of the sailors, the boat itself, and the cargo but dealing with "all those eventualities like winds, rocks, storms and so on" (1991: 94)—I would argue that *tiaojian* creation can mean not only providing educational opportunities but also dealing with immediate eventualities such as mean teachers, exposure to negative influences, and psychological injury, as well as imagined future eventualities. When Zhang Xin says, in making a statement about the importance of effort both on her part and on the part of her son, "Such a big population. Yet so few opportunities. Able persons are as common as air," she suggests that the future is fraught with uncertainty and best managed by putting one's best foot forward.

Foucault offers a second illustration of the art of government with the example of the household, the governing of which is not limited to safeguarding family property: "It means to reckon with all the possible events that may intervene . . . and with *all the things that can be done*" (94, my emphasis). This bears a resemblance to the logic expressed in creating *tiaojian*, which concerns what can be done to manage the long journey of raising a child in the face of intervening events and eventualities. *Tiaojian* creation recognizes human actors as sufferers and doers, made and makers, affected and affecting, assembled and assembling.[10] Expressing the logic of propensity, *tiaojian* creation presumes that humans are capacitated within particular assemblages, while also recognizing at the same time a human capacity to arrange things in ways that generate spontaneous effects. The *Sunzi* (*Art of War*), for example, asserts that the virtues of an individual soldier, whether he is intrinsically cowardly or brave, are not as consequential as the means by which he is deployed. Not dissimilarly, Yang Ruihong was less interested in what the homework problem actually was than in reconfiguring the immediate circumstance. Her actions make the assertion that circumstance is prior to subjectivity.

The word for propensity (*shi*) is closely related to the concept "to be with time" (*déshí*), which may be further understood as referring to the attainment of power and efficacy by making one's efforts coextensive with the process *of* time. In fact, "to be with time" is often translated as riding with Lady Luck. This idea is central to the logic of propensity, which proposes the possibility of maximizing worldly power by adapting to a propensity at work in a timely manner. "One who can 'pull back' when the tendency is running against him and resume the initiative when the tendency becomes favorable again is never 'under pressure' and eventually 'obtains everything.' In a bad situation, what is essential is to ensure one's own safety in order to manipulate chance better later" (Jullien [1992] 1995: 202).

Ironically, this idea sets actors up for moral tragedy—one that differs from the tragedies Greek heroes face—as they have only their poor discernment and timing to blame if situations do not turn out favorably. Although mothers find comfort in making distinctions between what they are and are not responsible for—pulling back when appropriate—all three cases involve obtuse vision and poor timing. It is especially regrettable to miss opportunities for taking initiative in a world where so much seems to be subject to impersonal forces of tremendous scale. Yang Ruihong said it best: "This situation, you know, it was when I had neglected, when I hadn't noticed, that he got to this very terrible place." Because she had failed to discern and to act when the situation was more incipient, she had to work hard to change the teacher's mind.

In this chapter, I have argued that the effort involved in creating and providing *tiaojian* is something one *can* control in an uncertain world. It is within one's domain of possible action. Even if the mothers in the three cases were slow to act at critical moments, there were remaining cards to play.[11] This is indeed what Yang Ruihong and Zhou Huawei did in reconfiguring their child's status in the classroom in the wake of misrecognition. A favorable tendency, once established, is a tremendous achievement.

In the spirit of total antihumanism, one could argue that control is a necessary illusion that blinds these mothers to structurally rooted impossibilities. One might further argue that *tiaojian* creation is an effect of a neoliberal social order that depends on the ability of ordinary people to take responsibility for their own lives. Parents *must* create security-providing *tiaojian* in a society where the state no longer provides the security that it used to. Moreover, *tiaojian* creation could be understood as a manifestation of the logic of competition, which has become central to contemporary Chinese governance and the organization, or disorganization, of social life. These parents are simply acting in accordance with the demands of competition.

While the larger historical circumstance certainly conditions human possibilities, I hope this chapter has shown how acting or not acting, or acting sooner rather than later, makes a significant empirical difference from the point of view of the moral agent. It is like the difference between 0 and 1, to borrow an illustration from Gregory Bateson.[12] It is the difference between remembering to report one's taxes or not, doing the dishes or not, remembering to sign your child's homework assignment or not. The responsibility to do these things is shaped by the regimes of taxation, hygiene, and school discipline—respectively. But doing or not doing these things has consequences that go beyond achieving conformity with rules and conventions. The difference between 0 and 1 has consequences for whether one can live comfortably with oneself.

FIVE

The Defeat of Maternal Logic in Televisual Space

SET IN BEIJING, the 2009 television serial *Who Shall Decide My Youth?* (*Wo de qingchun shei zuo zhu?*) tells the story of an extended family of women headed by a widowed matriarch. It is a coming-of-age story that follows the lives of three cousins, related through their mothers, as they look for love and deal with the challenges that come with entering adult society. In carving out a space in the world, each cousin must battle her mother in a fierce contest of will and strategy. Qingchu (literally "Clarity"), the eldest of the three cousins, is fresh out of law school and refuses to return home despite her mother's insistence. Xiaoyang (literally "Little Sample"), having "only" a vocational degree, runs away from her home in Yinchuan with a boy she has just met to realize her dream of living in Beijing, where her maternal grandmother lives. Pili (literally "Thunderclap"), the youngest and most affluent of the three cousins, has lived in London for three years as a high school student. Under extreme pressure to get into Cambridge, and failing to do so, she pays for a counterfeit admission letter and uses money meant for tuition to start a restaurant in Beijing, hoodwinking her autocratic mother with photoshopped pictures of her life in England.

I was introduced to the television drama *Who Shall Decide My Youth?* by Yang Ruihong (who figured in the previous chapter). This show was one of many shows she recommended to me during an after-dinner chat where we cracked our way through many ashtrays' worth of sunflower seeds. Some were productions from the 1980s, some were set during the Cultural Revolution, and a good number of them were about modern life. Directed by Zhao Baogang, *Who Shall Decide My Youth?* originally aired on China Central Television in 2009, receiving very high viewer ratings. In a joking manner, Yang Ruihong told me that as an "elderly person" she felt that watching *Who Shall Decide My Youth?* helped her understand her son and his age group. (Xiaoming was in his late teens at this point.) In what felt like an overwhelming amount of detail, she recounted a couple of story lines from this TV drama, one of which concerned Pili, the child who wanted to be a chef. I tried my best to listen.

That Yang Ruihong chose this one to recount out of the many plotlines that make up the show was indicative of her viewing position. The producers of *Who Shall Decide My Youth?* intended for the show to be enjoyed across generational divides, with the moral of the story being family harmony and the importance of communication in resolving conflicts. Depending on one's viewing position, there are different lessons to be learned. For the youth generation, the show provides a lesson on the importance of perseverance and of struggling against the odds. It is generally described as a "motivational drama" (*lizhi ju*), and although the show features good-looking actors and trendy settings—the characters drink Starbucks, drive Audis, and hang out around Marc Jacobs stores—Gao Xuan and Ren Baoru, the writers of the show, insist that it is not "idol drama, fantasy, or romance."[1] Instead, it intends to present ideas and to explore social issues—namely, how the post-1980s generation might adapt to reality, learn from their mistakes, take on adult responsibilities, work through confusion, and aspire toward great things.

For the parental generation, the show argues for giving children an autonomous space in which to grow and make decisions. Yang Ruihong was most struck with the story line that most definitively argued for a child's right to decide his or her own life. In the summer of 2010, she too found herself in a position where she would have to balance her own ideas about her son's future against his individual interests, as Xiaoming had recently received his college entrance examination score and would soon have to make a decision about which school to attend. It was important to Yang Ruihong that Xiaoming choose with some foresight rather than base a decision on interest alone. Xiaoming was interested in animation, but she felt that he ought to study something else while learning animation on his own time. She told me that a story I had told her about a good friend of mine inspired her thinking—a friend who worked in graphic animation but had majored in literature. Her final words to me the day I left for the airport that summer were "Wherever he chooses to go, whatever he chooses to do, I will support him."

Yang Ruihong's attempt to encourage a certain direction while still expressing unconditional support is the very conflict represented in *Who*

Shall Decide My Youth? This show explores the tension between a child's right to autonomy and a mother's good intentions. Although the mothering practices depicted in the drama are extreme and exaggerated, they reflect practices of *tiaojian* creation in everyday life, thereby making the characters in the parental generation very relatable. The intensity of maternal control concerns personal efficacy in the face of uncertainty, symbolized in the show by "society" and "reality." When the mothers in the show act autocratically and overprotect—an abomination as far as the popular experts are concerned—they are engaging in a practice I call "potential born of effort," to be explained shortly.

The show represents "potential born of effort" with felicity. But it ultimately dismisses maternal reasoning in favor of youth autonomy thanks to convenient happy endings that suggest the young were right all along. This dismissal is one of many inversions in the show: youth power triumphs over parental power, women determine the value of men,[2] and an elitist fantasy displaces brute social realities. Moving between an analysis of the show and viewer responses collected from popular online discussion forums such as *Sina, Sohu,* and *NetEase,* this chapter will argue that the assertion of modern values such as "autonomy" and "freedom" depends on papering over social and economic realities and trivializing the concerns of well-meaning mothers.[3]

INSPIRING ASPIRATION

Television in general and television dramas in particular occupy a significant place in contemporary Chinese social life. Just as China has the greatest number of Internet users and English speakers in the world, it also has the greatest number of television viewers. As of 2005, there were 1.188 billion viewers, penetrating 95.6 percent of the population (T. Zhang 2009: 172). The television drama is one of many genres popular with viewing audiences, from domestic and international news to variety shows (172).

Who Shall Decide My Youth? shares features found in popular TV dramas previously discussed by anthropologists and media studies scholars. Like *Yearnings,* popular in the early 1990s in China, *Who Shall Decide My Youth?* reflects the concerns of a particular historical moment. If *Yearnings* taught the art of longing just after the crisis of Tiananmen, then *Who Shall Decide My Youth?* teaches the art of aspiration and determination, as the country's first generation of only children come of age and join the workforce (Rofel 2007). Like *Tokyo Love Story*, a Japanese equivalent to *Dallas* once popular in East Asia, *Who Shall Decide My Youth?* expresses a particular vision of modernity. In this case, Beijing rather than Tokyo provides the backdrop for staging what it means to be cosmopolitan and modern. It too follows the romantic and working lives of the young, through a variety of urban scenes such as the office, lobbies, trendy restaurants, outdoor patios, shopping promenades, freeway overpasses, and *hutong* neighborhoods. Like the "post-trendy" or idol dramas of Japan and Taiwan, *Who Shall Decide My Youth?* cultivates consumer desires and provides a space for indulging in fantasy.[4] A comment one viewer makes about the character Qingchu is especially illustrative: "The clothes that she wears are very pretty, and well-styled, appropriate for a white-collar woman, I really like it. (She never wears the same thing twice.) It's all worth my learning from."[5] A rather different kind of viewer, however, resents the writers and director for making young people salivate over what they cannot have.[6]

The most noteworthy feature, however, is one that has been found in Japanese TV dramas: the use of drama to inspire the young. In the late 1970s, a genre known as the "urban youth drama" emerged in Japan, offering stories about the struggle of rural youths with urban life. According to one study, these dramas "saw the prominence of the message 'to strive hard and to struggle hard,' or *'ganbaru'* in Japanese" (Leung 2004: 90). Dramas from the 1990s continued the *ganbaru* theme, featuring characters committed to overcoming life challenges in pursuit of the good life. Similarly, *Who Shall Decide My Youth?* depicts the working and romantic lives of urban youths who overcome obstacles and learn from them. For this very reason, the show, the second of a trilogy of youth-themed TV dramas by the director Zhao Baogang, has been labeled as belonging to the genre of the "motivational drama." The first in this trilogy, *Struggle (Fendou)*, is also a coming-of-age story that focuses solely on a group of friends. Although *Who Shall Decide My Youth?* largely concerns intergenerational relationships, it continues themes explored in *Struggle*, with each character striving for his or her ideals. As one viewer commented, the show was "something that calls on young people to aspire."[7] Another said, "I like this—I've watched *Struggle* five times, *Youth* three times so far. You can make it if you try; the show can function as a horsewhip for our lives."[8] In the same vein, a viewer arguing against the show's critics wrote, "One cannot only look at the surface. One must watch at a deeper level, and you will be inspired, regardless of your class level."[9]

The comment that the show will inspire regardless of class refers to a debate between netizens online, which primarily centered on the question of whether the show depicted reality accurately. Viewer responses indicate that a large majority of young viewers felt that the show was too distant from their lives, alienating those who could not relate to the material conditions it represented or to the success of most of its characters—particularly the all-too-perfect Qingchu, who starts taking cases shortly after graduating from law school, having breezily landed her first job, and who manages to buy a brand-new red Audi by episode 18, all before the age of thirty. For such viewers, the characters in the show are able to achieve self-realization only because their economic *tiaojian* has allowed them to do so; they see what the show argues for as an inaccessible luxury for the elite. At the other extreme are viewers who reproach the critics for being jealous. One comment I found even went as far as saying, "This show was not meant for you poor people in the first place. (By poor I mean poor of heart; by poor of heart I mean people who don't dare to create, don't dare to aspire, and only know how to complain and only wish that everyone else could be as petty as they."[10] Between the show's critics and supporters are viewers who argue that some people take the show too seriously, that to expect accuracy of a TV drama is itself unrealistic, and that looking past its flaws, one can take away a meaningful lesson on how to better oneself.

The dialogue in the show is indeed replete with moral pedagogy, with each character serving as a mouthpiece for a particular set of values. As such, the show turns out to be a hybrid between commercial entertainment and social-ist realism, an approach to representation that casts society not in terms of how it is but in terms of how it ought to be. At a news conference related to the premiere of the show, the president of the Shanghai Film Company expressed hope that the show would help to facilitate social transition in China and that it would have a good social influence.[11] It is very hard to imag-ine an American studio executive saying the same thing about a soap opera.

TELEVISUAL ADVICE: REFORMING PARENTS

While the show provides lessons on aspiration and determination for youth viewers, it is also an attempt at reforming parenting behavior. Expertise is directly invoked in a scene where the grandmother advises Xiaoyang on how to deal with her mother's nagging.

GM. Your mother wouldn't be able to live with herself if she didn't say those things. Just let her nag. If you don't want to listen, just pretend it's wind.

XIAOYANG. Her gust of wind has a terrible influence on me. She hurts a person's confidence as soon as she opens her mouth. Education experts say: children ought to be protected. My body-mind development is this unhealthy, yet I don't know who to lodge my complaint with.

GM. (*with mirth*) Why do you appear so healthy to me? Very sunny.

XIAOYANG: That's only because my ability to resist is strong.[12]

The idea that words can injure often appears in popular advice, as does the idea of a child's vulnerability to threats that come directly from the behavior of a parent. Xiaoyang argues that the only reason she is able to maintain her health is strength of resistance, a certain kind of immunity that has little to do with anything that her mother has done. Here, the notion of resistance pits the ethical subjectivity of a parent (to do the right thing and to speak one's mind as soon as concern arises), against the psychological subjectivity of a child (vulnerable to psychological injury). In the next episode, Xiaoyang once again invokes the language of the experts after a discouraging day at a job fair. As soon as she opens the front door to her grandmother's apartment, she makes a firm gesture and announces, "To protect my heart-spirit [*xin-ling*], please do not ask about the details."

Meanwhile, the story line concerning Pili makes an argument for the importance of communication between parents and children.[13] By the time we meet Pili, she has lived in England as a high school student studying abroad—a part of her mother's grand design for her life. Back in Beijing, her parents have divorced one another after many years of marital unhappiness. They have decided to keep their divorce a secret so as to not disturb Pili as she prepares for her A-level exams. When Pili learns the truth, she cannot accept it and schemes to break up her father's relationship with his working-class girlfriend, hoping to bring her parents back together again. In classic soap opera fashion, she manipulates the situation to her liking whenever an opportunity arises, even going so far as to acquire a counterfeit bank statement indicating that her father's girlfriend has been keeping a secret stash of money. She drops the statement off in her father's mailbox, causing the couple to break up shortly thereafter.

Indeed, one could read such behavior as wicked, as Pili sabotages a struggling woman who is trying to support her own child with wages from a waitressing job. According to the show's reasoning, however, Pili's actions were merely responses to her parents' dismissal of her psychological needs, namely a need for the sense of safety that comes with having a whole family. When her father learns of her schemes, he writes it off as immaturity rather than wickedness and takes responsibility for what he sees as the natural outcome of poor parenting. As happens throughout the show, it is the wise and, according to Internet commenters, not true-to-life grandmother who steps in to parent the parents. In one scene, she lectures Pili's mother for not giving Pili what she really wants—close attention. When Pili's mother learns about the counterfeit bank statement in the last episode of the show, she is surprised to know that the divorce has affected Pili to such a degree. Grandmother responds, "From this you can know the extent to which she felt fear over the dissolution of your marriage, the extent to which she yearned for a complete family. Many parents never know what imprints they have left in their child's heart. Since you now know, don't go on muddle-headed anymore."

For many viewers, the insightful grandmother who always comes to the defense of the young, arguing for their freedom while scolding her overprotective daughters, is unrealistic. But it is interesting that the director and writers created such a character, as the grandmother serves to combine the expectation that women rule the domestic sphere with well-reasoned expertise. "Laolao" (Maternal Grandmother) is a well-respected law professor with practical experience—a member of the intelligentsia. In many scenes she has the last word, imparting perspective on ongoing conflicts between her daughters and their daughters.

The makers of *Who Shall Decide My Youth?* intend for the show to be taken seriously. On the official blog page, one entry describes the show as a "family manual for parents." The same entry raises the question "When exactly should parents intervene? Keep their silence or jabber on and on?"[14] An article reposted on *NetEase* from a news website gives advice to parents for how to interpret the show, reporting interviews with education experts advising parents on how to deal with a child who is like Qingchu, Xiaoyang, or Pili. Interestingly, a comment following this post poses a parenting question to other viewers: How can I get my teenage daughter to study harder? This viewer gives her daughter's life story in the comment, explains that she has not been able to get any help from her daughter's teacher, and continues, "This TV drama, I have seen it, but I could not find an answer to my problem. Can some netizens please give me some suggestions?"[15] This viewer received two responses: one that there must be something wrong with the child's environment and the other that this mother listen to her daughter's heart's desire before making any suggestions.[16] In the same discussion thread, one viewer scolds other viewers on both sides of the "is it realistic" debate for missing the point of the show, writing, "If post-1980s people were to have their parents watch the show, their parents would surely be stirred. That's the main point of this show, yet so many people don't get it!"[17]

SOCIAL RECOGNITION VERSUS SELF-REALIZATION: PARTICIPATION OR SEPARATION?

The pedagogical dimension of *Who Shall Decide My Youth?* is fairly overt: young viewers are to receive inspiration on how to aspire, while parents are to reform their behavior. That modeling and commercial entertainment can coexist in the form of a soap opera sponsored by Audi is a fascinating mini-aturization of China's hybridization of capitalism and socialism. But most interesting of all is the way the show pits deeply incommensurable cultural logics concerning human agency and moral responsibility against one another, throwing the debate over what it means to be a good parent into stark relief. Battle metaphors pervade the dialogue. In the following, I will discuss the Pili story line, as this one most explicitly argues for a child's autonomy while representing maternal logic in its clearest form.

When we meet Pili at the beginning of the show, she has already lived in London for three years as a high school student, something she holds a grudge against her parents for. Pili's mother, Yang Er, the CEO of a built-from-nothing lingerie company that exports goods to Western countries, claims to have sent her teenage daughter abroad to give her a competitive edge and insists throughout the show that her purpose in life is to provide for her daughter. Yang Er is an autocratic mother who completely overshadows her ex-husband—a low-earning academic with a meek personality. In a scene where Pili's father gently reminds her that her mother has only wanted the best for her, Pili argues, "I am the bullet in her barrel, I shoot to wherever she points. I have absolutely no autonomy."

Because of her mother's personality and her single-minded insistence on high A-level scores and a Cambridge admission, Pili feels she has no choice but to keep her interest in cooking a secret. When Pili doesn't get admitted to Cambridge, she purchases a counterfeit admission letter and returns to Beijing with her tuition money in hand, eventually starting a Western-food restaurant as the head chef with the co-investment of a friend. She continues to bamboozle her mother by sending photoshopped pictures of her life in England, deferring the inevitable so as to have some time to "self-realize" without her mother's interference.

When Yang Er eventually learns the truth, she is beside herself with rage: "The truth is that you want to be a cook? I spent a million to raise someone who makes meals?" For the next few days, Yang Er loses her sense of life purpose and stops going to work. She also forbids Pili to leave the house. It is Pili who initiates their first attempt at communication. They debate the meaning of life, social recognition versus self-realization, two ideals that represent very different orientations toward the world. Pili rejects the life plan her mother has designed for her. Yang Er is perplexed that her efforts are not being appreciated.

> YANG ER. *Ei?* Your outstanding life *tiaojian*, you get to go abroad at such a young age, come back and join the business world, I'm forcing all this on you? You don't appreciate any of this. So what is your ideal then? Be a cook? That's willful, child's play. That kind of ideal has no value. An ideal worth some gold is to transform self-value into social recognition and wealth to the greatest possible degree.
>
> PILI. As long as you have ideals. Ideals differ only in kind, not in value. You might think that this person doesn't have any value, but that's because you're using your own individual value system to measure someone else. Who has the right to evaluate someone else's lifestyle and life quality?
>
> YE. My values are the values of the masses.
>
> PILI. So you admit it? You are a follower, it's a simplistic value system. A slave to the common ways of the world, you will always live for being in somebody else's view.
>
> YE. Well, where else am I going to live then, huh? Where should I live?
>
> PILI. You? It is what it is, you can't be reformed. I don't want to be driven by fame and fortune. I'll just seek my own happiness.

Pili's position is "Western" in orientation. She espouses the liberal ideals of tolerance for all, of going against the grain, and of pursuing individual happiness and the actualization of a "true" self. To pursue "self-realization" (*ziwo shixian*) is more authentic than seeking "social recognition" (*shehui renke*); to seek the latter is to be a slave, while to pursue the former is to find liberation. Interestingly, her argument resonates strongly with the "soft individualism" of upper-middle-class families living in Manhattan, as depicted in Adrie Kusserow's (2004) ethnography of American individualisms. And the fact that Pili invokes the milestone age of eighteen later in the scene to further her argument for independence suggests that the show takes America as a point of reference.

> PILI. You and I ought to have our separate lives after I reach eighteen years of age, not live the other's life goal. And a pure mother-daughter relationship should not be one of investment and the actualization of investment value.
>
> YE. Why are you talking as if you're doing business?
>
> PILI. Such meaning is already in there. Chinese-style education has created a payout-and-return kind of style. This goes against the nature of kin relations. Mom, I want you to be happy, I also hope that I can be your pride, but not under the premise of sacrificing the self. Mom, how about if you go and realize your dreams. Go to Cambridge, just pretend I'm a fart and let me go.

For Pili, self-realization corresponds with separation, an assertion made quite literally when she says, "You and I ought to have our separate lives after I reach eighteen years of age, not live the other's life goal." She (or the show) makes a case for separation at another level too. Stating, "A pure mother-daughter relationship should not be one of investment and the actualization of investment value," Pili suggests that a self cannot be realized when it is entangled in obligation. By removing expectations of payout and return, by removing the pollutions of economic behavior, a mother and daughter could achieve something more authentic. Such an assertion is a fantasy, of course— a fantasy of disembedment specifically, which invokes classical economic theory and its presumptions of the free market and the free individual.[18] It flies in the face of well-established and well-understood practices of intergenerational reciprocity, where children repay their parents' efforts by studying hard and achieving academically.[19]

Pili's insistence that kin relations should be pure, and that to follow the masses is to be enslaved, expresses a cultural logic that idealizes true agency in terms of separation. It is an "ethos of elective distance from the necessities of the natural and social world," characteristic of the bourgeoisie (Bourdieu 1984: 5). Yang Er on the other hand, makes no separation and wonders why her daughter is talking as if she were doing business. Yang Er's position seems to smack of rational utility, but beneath rational utility lies a deeper moral concern over what a parent is responsible for and what it means to be an effective human being. François Jullien's discussion of the notion of potentiality is illuminating here. It will gives us a different vantage point from which to view what Pili (or the show) sees as blind conformism. If not in this world, Yang Er wonders, where else am I going to live?

In *The Propensity of Things*, Jullien draws a contrast between Western versus Chinese modes of thought and action. For starters, Jullien argues, the heroic is absent in the Chinese tradition. In early Chinese military thinking, victory is not won on the battlefield; but secured through a strategic disposal of things, which engenders an ineluctable course of actions tending toward victory. In the Greek tradition, victory is decided on the battlefield in broad daylight ([1992] 1995: 35). Jullien illustrates his contrast with two images: the spear and the crossbow. If the spear, "both instrument and symbol of this heroic confrontation" (36), is decisive and direct, then the crossbow—weapon of choice in early Chinese militarism—is the perfect symbol of strategic engagement, and more importantly, of what Jullien calls "potential born of disposition" (35). The use of the crossbow and the ability to dispose of things strategically achieves "the maximum effect from a distance" with minimal effort.

Jullien further notes that the hero in Greek myths is a tragic one; he will fight against the odds to utter exhaustion or even death, which from the Chinese view is a rather futile expenditure of human effort. In the Chinese tradition, contrastingly, the good general, politician, poet, or painter acts in accordance with the propensity of a given situation, with the understanding that every situation is characterized by a particular tendency: for example, water moving along the side of a mountain will tend downward. A good strategist discerns the objective features of a given situation as lucidly as possible, so as to exploit its potentiality to the maximum degree possible (260).

This idea of maximization within a given context is expressed when Yang Er says, "An ideal worth some gold is to transform self-worth into social recognition and wealth to the greatest degree possible." Whatever the self may be capable of, the worth of a person is contingent upon what can be recognized in a given context. Operating at the level of the concrete, Yang Er's theory of self-worth is rooted in the present historical circumstance of a society that, for better or for worse, has come to value status and wealth above all else. Yang Er does not think to go against (or transcend) this situation because this is the situation that exists. It is the concrete social reality before her, so she acts according its tendency, exploiting its potentiality so as to benefit from it with as little exhaustion as possible on her part. This is why she has no qualms in stating, "My values are the values of the masses." When her daughter tells her she "will always live for being in somebody else's view," Yang Er asks perplexedly, "Well, where else am I going to live then, huh?" When Pili rejects fame and fortune to insist on seeking happiness, Yang Er wonders, "*Ei?* How did I raise you to be someone who sees money as dirt? You were supposed to be very carefully guided toward success by me, but it turns out you've rebelled to the point of nihilism."

One would not expect to find parallels between early Chinese thought and a commercial, turn-of-the-twenty-first-century TV drama. But they are indeed there, and I highlight them to show how China's transformation may involve much more than economic restructuring and subject making. The very idea that the moral agent is one who pursues self-realization and is not afraid to go against the masses—however self-evident that may sound— proposes a mode of thought and action that is radically incommensurable with a deeply embedded folk theory concerning how to make one's way through the world. The sage, Jullien explains, does not "aim to assert his liberty"; rather, he participates *with* the course of reality. The human agent in this scheme of things partners in solidarity, which can result in "a power of influence that can be at once invisible, infinite, and perfectly spontaneous" ([1992] 1995: 264; [1991] 2004: 61). While Pili sees her mother as a conformist, Yang Er would be better understood as a strategist. In fact, in a production note published online explaining how the writers came up with the characters' names, all three mothers in this show are described as "women-generals."

There are of course limits to the analogy that I am drawing here. Yang Er invokes the notion of *tiaojian* in this dialogue, which concerns human effort and what one ought to take responsibility for given circumstances that are not within one's sphere of control. When Yang Er lists her daughter's outstanding life *tiaojian* as one of the many things Pili fails to appreciate, she is pointing out that privilege does not come from nowhere; it is engendered through the painstaking efforts of a parent. The notion of *tiaojian* is invoked one other time in this story line when Pili's father first discovers the truth behind the monstrous lie; he reminds his daughter of how hard parents work to create *tiaojian*.

Contemporary parenting practices articulate a variation on Jullien's "potential born of disposition," thereby making an assertion that I call "potential born of effort." Like the generals addressed in the *Sunzi,* modern parents aim to affect from a distance, a temporal one in their case. But potentiality is related more to effort than to disposition. While the *Sunzi* does not conceive of uncertainty as an issue so long as one exercises accurate discernment, in the case of modern parenting strategic disposition does not offer an absolute guarantee. One does, however, have control over the individual exertion of effort. Trying is both the least and the most anyone can do.

PROTECTING AGAINST A CRUSHING REALITY

Bubbly and defiant, Xiaoyang is the least disciplined and the least ambitious of the three cousins. She lands herself in absurd situations, and her obsession with money and fast results gets her in trouble time and again. For this reason, Xiaoyang bounces from job to job and from one interest to another with little idea of what she wants or can do in life. When she gets fired from her job as a salesgirl at a real estate company for violating the terms of her employment—no direct sales for the first three months—Xiaoyang doesn't understand why the consequence of the highly advocated "self-realization and putting yourself out there" is actually ruin. (She signed a contract with an elderly couple impressed by her willingness to spend three hours with them.) Xiaoyang's mother Yang Shan long believed that she would not be able to survive in Beijing, thinking she had little innate ability and would fool around without purpose. Yang Shan's prophecy seems to fulfill itself in her daughter's romantic ambitions.

While Pili defies her mother's designs to realize her dream of becoming a chef, Xiaoyang is determined to date the boy she ran away from Yinchuan with, a blue-collar car mechanic named Fang Yu. Her mother disapproves of the relationship from the start, not only because the young man is to blame for her daughter's running away but also because he belongs to a lower socioeconomic class. Like Pili's mother, Xiaoyang's mother Yang Shan appears to be excessively concerned with socioeconomic status; she sees Fang Yu as nothing but a little tramp and plots to break up the young couple at multiple points in the show. I will briefly summarize her attempts so that the later discussion of how "potential born of effort" plays out in this case will make sense.

The first attempt follows an incident where Xiaoyang has gotten injured trying to defend Fang Yu in a fight he got himself into. Yang Shan travels to Beijing to personally make sure that her daughter will return to Yinchuan where she can keep an eye on her. For Yang Shan, Xiaoyang's injury is proof that she is not capable of taking the right course. Meanwhile, Xiaoyang and her boyfriend plan an escape and agree on a rendezvous point at the train station where she will be with her parents the next day. The conflicting wishes of a parent and child lead to a dramatic turning point in the story: on the day of the rendezvous, Xiaoyang's father is hit by the young couple's getaway vehicle. He suffers an injury to the spinal cord that leaves him paralyzed from the waist down.

The second time Yang Shan tries to break up the young couple is more strategic and less direct, thanks to the advice of her two sisters—who are engaged in their own battles with their daughters. At this point in the story, Xiaoyang and her parents are back in Beijing as a family, so as to have "better" access to rehabilitative care.[20] Xiaoyang continues to see Fang Yu in secret, practicing "underground love" (*dixia qing*). Meanwhile, Yang Shan sets her sights on a young doctor named Gao Qi, a kindly single man who happens to be present every time someone in the family lands in the hospital, providing whatever support they need. (A soap opera is not a soap opera without multiple hospital scenes, of course.) Although Gao Qi has a crush on Xiaoyang, he insists that helping people is his joy—invoking the spirit of the socialist culture hero Lei Feng. When Xiaoyang and her parents return to Beijing to seek rehabilitative care, it is Gao Qi who finds them an apartment to stay in, one that is conveniently close to the hospital. Impressed by his character and reassured by his profession, Yang Shan plots to make him a son-in-law. She organizes a weekend trip to the suburbs for the family and invites him along.

The third interference takes place toward the end of the show. Fang Yu has been imprisoned for inadvertently getting involved with a gang that resells stolen cars, thanks to overtime work he took on to earn money for Xiaoyang's family's medical expenses. Yang Shan pays him a visit in jail and gives him a carefully reasoned speech that encourages him to leave her daughter in the name of love. Sentimental piano music provides the soundtrack to this scene as Yang Shan, who has been very tough on the young man, expresses appreciation for everything he has done. She describes reality as crushing and suggests that the couple's breakup will make both of them happier. He will be able to free himself of his responsibility to their family, while Xiaoyang will be free to date a more economically and morally stable man—the young doctor. She ends with saying, "Sometimes, love may not bring the person you love happiness, but letting them go could." Fang Yu agrees and subsequently refuses to see Xiaoyang during visiting hours.

A viewer could easily find this mother's persistence problematic. While the show seems to argue that the paralyzing accident could be entirely blamed on Xiaoyang and her insistence on autonomy, one cannot help but think that Xiaoyang's parents should have never interfered in the first place. After all, this character is a twenty-one-year-old woman.

Juxtaposed against the notion of "potential born of disposition" however, the moral logic that informs this mother's stance becomes easier to understand. Although the entire story line is exaggerated for entertainment, there is a logic to the strategic reasoning represented, one that feels familiar to many young and middle-aged viewers. In fact, this was the other story line my friend Yang Ruihong had recounted to me in great detail when she recommended the show (although she remembered Fang Yu as being a rural youth rather than an urban, blue-collar worker). Viewers posting in online forums readily recognized that the behavior of the mothers in this show represents a common parental wish: to do things for the good of a child. What this actually means in practice, however, is precisely the question posed by the show.

If the theme expressed by the story line concerning Pili's dream of becoming a chef is a daughter's quest for self-realization against her mother's insistence on social recognition, then the theme expressed by the story line concerning Xiaoyang and her mother's determination to direct her love life is best captured by a popular Chinese saying: "The whole world pities a parent's heart." Underneath Yang Shan's cold and unyielding disapproval of her daughter's relationship with the car mechanic—as problematic as it is from the Western liberal view—beats a tender concern for doing everything possible to minimize a child's suffering in life. She wants to ensure "prosperity, security, and peace" as much as she possibly can.[21]

In a scene where Yang Shan and her husband have a serious talk about bringing their daughter back home to Yinchuan, related to the first attempt described above, Yang Shan admits she can see why the two make a happy pair. But, she continues, "Society isn't as simple as it used to be," referring to a time in recent history when dramatic socioeconomic differences did not exist. "This society we have now keeps getting more and more complicated. Competition is intense, the pressure of daily life is heavy, even marriage has become a comprehensive subject of study." She argues that factors such as salary and occupation are crucial elements in holding a marriage together; "Otherwise as soon as you encounter a real problem, fragile feelings will not be able to sustain a single blow." Since the children have nothing but feelings, this mother asserts, "We have to see farther than they can, we have to have a deeper discernment of reality."[22]

Like the mothers I knew in Kunming, this fictional mother feels deep uncertainty about her child's future. While my informants were still overseeing the completion of homework tasks and classroom visibility as a way to manage uncertainty, this fictional mother sees a good marriage as a way to fortify against possible future troubles and whatever might come a young couple's way. Romance and affection do not stand a chance against the strength of "this society," while stable material conditions do. The character is not so much materialistic per se as in search of security. The mothers in this show exercise a kind of magical thinking that correlates economic well-being with worldly power, meaningful agency, and the ability to solve life problems. Thus they aim to engender a potentiality that might lead to life security. The economic and the moral are intertwined here, as exemplified by a later scene in which Yang Shan says to her daughter, "Don't think your mom is thinking like a profiteer. One day when you and Fang Yu are fighting about daily necessities, how much purchase will feelings have?"

The Fang Yu character concurs, feeling dejected because it was the kindly doctor who was able to provide the family a rent-free apartment close to the rehabilitation hospital, while all of his efforts to build up his supportive capacities by earning money in a variety of ways have brought him nothing but trouble and misfortune. Over the course of the show, he gets beat up, chased by gangs, and imprisoned. In one humorous incident, he is hassled by a policeman for having no advertising permit for his sidecar motorbike, which he has rented out as a billboard to make extra cash.

For the parent in this story line, reality calls for a mother's efforts to dispose of things in a way so as to generate potentiality. Yang Shan believes the kindly doctor can provide for her daughter better, and her two sisters completely support her. But one sister, Pili's mother, doesn't support her approach to the situation, pointing out that mere disapproval will achieve nothing. Yang Er says,

YE. This attitude of yours is too passive, it's like doing nothing. A mother must have farsightedness and have the ability to direct. Sever with one

stroke if you disapprove of the two, don't leave any margin. If you think
Gao Qi isn't bad, then guide Xiaoyang. Actively bring the two together.
Doesn't Xiaoyang have good feelings toward Gao Qi? Influence!
Deal with Xiaoyang as you would administer water. Block the places
she shouldn't go to. Dig out the places you want her to go toward.
Imperceptible influence and transformation, don't you know?

This advice perfectly expresses the logic of propensity: Xiaoyang already has
good feelings toward the kindly doctor, so as far as her aunt is concerned it is
simply a matter of tapping into the existing tendency of her feelings for the
man and promoting its development. Rather than creating a relationship out
of nothing, Yang Shan should exploit the opportunity at hand. This exemplifies a kind of reasoning that conceives of human agency in terms of influence
rather than action, or rather, action conducted not in broad daylight but
imperceptibly. It privileges the scene of embryonic development over the
scene of battle. Xiaoyang may not love Gao Qi now, but she could. Manage
as one would water.

Managing reality is of course easier said than done, and some forms of
material or personalities are more likely to tend in a particular direction than
others. Thus, Yang Shan's joking response to her sister's advice is "I'm worried
that Xiaoyang is not like water, she's a stone." Xiaoyang is stubborn and does
not take advantage of the opportunity before her.

An Ethics of Trying

If the premodern texts idealize minimal effort and maximum efficacy, contemporary middle-class mothers privilege effort over efficacy in recognizing
the possibility of futility. They think like the strategic general addressed in
the *Sunzi* as well as the vulnerable actor the neo-Aristotelians have in mind
(see chapter 4) . While Chinese mothers are often shown in popular representations as controlling, I contend that mothers are most compelled by an
ethics of trying. This too is reflected in *Who Shall Decide My Youth?*, especially in a scene where Yang Shan gives her daughter the same speech she gave
her husband about the complexity of society and the necessity of a man who
can provide life security. Xiaoyang maintains her stance and informs her
mother that her words are futile. Her mother's response is: "Futile, but at
least I have tried. One day when the rain comes, and my daughter will marry,
there is nothing I can do. But as long as I am in the position of mother for
another day, then I'm compelled to conspire for the good of another day's

affairs."[23] The advice is unsolicited and falls on deaf ears, but Yang Shan makes an effort to exert an influence all the same. A slight kick of the foot sets a rock in motion; a pull on the bow shoots an arrow into the air. Where the rock ends up, what the arrow may pierce, is not entirely up to the human agent. Efficacy starts with trying, an assertion ordinary mothers also make when they tell me that their only responsibility is to create *tiaojian* and that what happens thereafter is out of their control.

In the end, the show favors the pursuits of the three daughters. And as one might expect of a soap opera, conflicts resolve themselves all too conveniently. Pili, the cousin who dreams of becoming a chef, is operating a successful restaurant by the end of the show. Her mother, Yang Er, comes out of the mother-daughter battle feeling more enlightened and more receptive to the wishes and viewpoints of other people. Xiaoyang's mother finally yields and gives her blessings in the last episode. Meanwhile, Fang Yu, the blue-collar boyfriend, is surprised with a shiny new auto repair shop of which he has been made a co-owner. That all signs point to happiness and prosperity for these youngsters suggest that the concerns of the mothers, especially Yang Er and Yang Shan, were unnecessary, thereby arguing that sheer determination will get you what you want and that parents do not necessarily know better.

The autonomy of the characters to pursue a particular career or love interest is achieved at the expense of not only dismissing a particular cultural logic but also ignoring social reality. Here I would like to return to the voices of the critics for perspective—those viewers who felt that the show was too distant from their lives. A long essay posted by a viewer named "cityofangell" in a *Sina* forum articulates at length what many expressed in short comments. Cityofangell takes issue with the idea that someone could do something like take a parent's money to gamble on something as risky as opening a restaurant. It raises the question "What is the actual relationship between making your uniqueness known and your life *tiaojian?*" The character Pili is able to start a business with money meant for tuition because "Pili's mother could afford to let her lose. Isn't it just buying a lesson and an experience for a few hundreds of thousands? Yet Director Baogang failed to realize how much those of us who have worked for almost ten years have had to struggle to pay a mortgage so we could grit our teeth and purchase a flat for living in." Cityofangell would also like to make his uniqueness known, but "family background and traditional upbringing do not allow me to be too over-selfed." Cityofangell begrudgingly studied science, a more practical path he nonetheless accepted. He dreams of opening a small audiovisual store that specializes in the music he likes, but unlike the fictional Pili, he feels that expressing himself is merely "something to play with in one's mind."[24]

Ironically, the representation of the youth generation by *Who Shall Decide My Youth?*, a drama that argues for youth autonomy and freedom, generated tremendous controversy among young viewers. Yet I saw virtually no disapproval of the show's depiction of the parental generation; in fact, many viewers—both young and middle-aged, saw correspondence between the fictional mothers and real life. As disagreeable as their behavior was, autocratic and interfering, viewers were even sympathetic, seeing the good intentions behind their problematic parenting behavior. I would argue too that part and parcel of good intention is a willingness to discern and confront contemporary reality openly and directly—something the show fails to do as a whole. The hyperpragmatism, hyperconcern for wealth and status, and utilitarian thinking of middle-class mothers grows out of the intensity of competition in China today. There is much to compete for: good grades, a good job, a good home, and, ultimately, life security.

My friend Zhou Huawei started to tell her daughter Jiajia the truth about society early on, in the second grade, admitting that she might not necessarily be correct to do so. She noted that there were two ways of describing the lesson she tried to impart about status differentiation—one easier on the ears, the other more "vulgar." However you put it, though, the reality is the same: difference exists.

> ZHW. You can say, "*Ai*, all people are equal." In reality, people are not entirely equal. Once we've gone the path of market reforms, it becomes more and more clear. This kind of inequality is multifaceted. Politically, economically, culturally, mentally, the factors are multiple. Whether you see it as equal or not, inequality exists. It's really obvious. But our ideological education, they say we have to be equal. That's ideological education. But if you want your child to think more realistically, you know, not let her live in a fictitious world, then I want to tell her now, "People are differentiated according to status."

Vulgar on the surface, the lesson ultimately concerns ethics, or self-conduct, and is given to remind her daughter of the importance of hard work: "With differentiation, it's up to you to work hard. Whether you can reach a certain status, you have to rely on yourself. We adults can help you. But we can't do everything. We can only help." Zhou Huawei has the kind of social and cultural capital that will give her daughter a competitive edge over children from other backgrounds. But this mother works hard to teach her daughter that she is by no means entitled to anything. Zhou Huawei's bluntness provides a contrast to Kusserow's observation of upper-middle-class parents in Manhattan: "In a world where people are *not* equal, where everyone is *not* your friend, and where sometimes people *are* bad, great efforts were made to get the child to feel and believe the opposite" (2004: 166).

As vulgar as it is to instill status consciousness in a child, there is something moral at stake here. I never had a chance to speak to Zhou Huawei about the show, but when I mentioned *Who Shall Decide My Youth?* to Jiajia on my last trip, she rolled her eyes because she preferred *Harry Potter*. But her mother loved the show. She would sit in front of the television for hours, Jiajia told me, delightfully immersed. Having in mind their story about the "fake" publication (chapter 4), I could imagine how much Zhou Huawei must have related to the moms in the show, especially their good intentions. As one viewer put it, "The whole world pities a parent's heart; in order to let a child avoid adversity, parents inevitably have a utilitarian mind."[25]

TELEVISUAL DENIAL

This chapter has offered a close analysis of a single television drama, one that embeds popular parenting advice in mass-mediated entertainment. But my primary reason for examining *Who Shall Decide My Youth?* in such detail has to do less with its pedagogical content than with its representation of scheming, overprotective mothers—its crystallization of the moral logic of "potential born of effort." I am interested less in how this show has affected behavior (it was "the behavior" that came first) than in what this show could reveal about my friend Yang Ruihong's concerns. What compelled her to recommend this show to me, that evening when we cracked our way through many ashtrays' worth of sunflower seeds? Why did she insist on recounting, in great detail, the story lines of Xiaoyang and the car mechanic's forbidden love, and of Pili's aspirations to be a professional chef? Her joke that the show helped an elderly person (*laoren*) such as herself understand her own son and his age group is telling. I believe the show helped her make some sense of her own life situation as a parent, as she tried to balance warm support with firm guidance in helping Xiaoming make an important life decision.

That she could *think with* this television show has something to do with the felicity with which the writers have represented maternal reasoning and the emphasis put on *tiaojian* creation. And it is significant that it was this aspect of the show that was the least controversial among the netizens. Surely the popularity of *Who Shall Decide My Youth?* could be attributed to the fantasy of cosmopolitan life offered to young viewers. But I would argue that the show did something more, at least for the parental generation, and that its significance was not unlike the significance of a Balinese cockfight.

Who Shall Decide My Youth? is a cultural text that "renders ordinary, everyday experience comprehensible" by crystallizing and displaying major themes pertaining to modern family life (Geertz 1973: 443). It helps coordinate impressions about life that otherwise remain "loose and disorganized."[26] Why was *Desperate Housewives* a flop in China, even though it also features scheming middle-class mothers?[27] Why was the reality show *Where Are We Going, Dad? (Baba qu na'er?)* a smashing success in 2013? Answering these questions would require not only an understanding of the Chinese ethnographic context but also an understanding of the texts themselves. Popular texts, in turn, can enrich our understanding of an ethnographic context by providing a glimpse of the virtual world of cultural and personal imagination.

To the show's discredit, maternal logic is ultimately defeated in favor of youth autonomy, thanks to convenient happy endings that suggest the youth were right all along. *Who Shall Decide My Youth?* ultimately trivializes the concerns of well-meaning mothers, echoing the voices of China's popular parenting experts with their presumption that what parents are doing is misguided and anachronistic. Moreover, it makes assertions about the importance of values such as autonomy and freedom by dismissing harsh social realities—realities that remain when the show is over, leaving those who do not have the luxury to realize an "authentic" self feeling excluded. As problematic as hyperutilitarianism might be, the denial of necessity may be worse.

In comparing the child-rearing styles of three different New York neighborhoods, Adrie Kusserow found a collision of class cultures in a working-class preschool, where teachers and printed school materials encouraged the "soft individualism" of the upper middle class—a "psychological pedagogy of self-expression that conflicted with and made no sense" to working-class parents (2004: 179). A certain form of violence occurs when teachers encourage parents to practice affirmation, as in one case: "When a mother says, 'I'm sick of her,' and Mrs. Costado replies, 'No, you're not,' the mother's reality is in some ways being denied" (179). For Kusserow, the problem with the discourse of "soft individualism" is that its image of naturalness obscures class-based biases. In other words, the naturalism of psychologized child rearing is blind to the liberation of a child's "true self" as a class-based practice, creating dissonance not only for the working class but also for immigrant families in many classroom contexts. Meanwhile, what we have in the case of urban China is a conflict of theories on a global scale. Even though my informants were middle class, they saw their children as facing a grim reality and consequently felt ambivalent about granting them freedom and autonomy.

SIX

Investing in Human Capital, Conserving Life Energies

> Of course Dinka hope that their rites will suspend the natural course of events. Of course they hope that rain rituals will cause rain, healing rituals avert death, harvest rituals produce crops. But instrumental efficacy is not the only kind of efficacy to be derived from their symbolic action. The other kind is achieved in the action itself, in the assertions it makes and the experience which bears its imprinting.
>
> MARY DOUGLAS, *PURITY AND DANGER*

THE CLASSIC MARXIST DEFINITION OF IDEOLOGY is encapsulated in the sentence "They do not know it, but they are doing it." This conception presumes that people act in ways that reproduce relations of capitalist production without knowing that they are doing so and that ideology masks or distorts reality in the minds of social actors. Related to the Marxist conception of ideology is the idea of the fetish, which helps to conceal objective social relations of production. Money is a classic example. People mistake wealth as intrinsic to money when in fact it is nothing more than "a condensation, a materialization of a network of social relations" (Žižek 1989: 31).

The Marxist argument is often invoked to interpret parenthood or motherhood under capitalism, as when motherhood itself is said to constitute an ideology that serves to mask the oppressive conditions in which mothers produce children. In such a framework, mothers are seen as laborers who have freely internalized an ideology that supports the reproduction of the capitalist workforce, without knowing that they have done so.[1] In the context of post-Mao China, one could, following this line of argument, say that women have been interpellated into taking up the role of the "good mother" who is entrusted to rear a "high-quality child," subject positions created by the population improvement project. Moreover, one could point out how childhood has become increasingly commercialized with economic liberalization. Many commodities on the market—infant formula, nutritional supplements, educational toys, test-prep materials, and special-talent classes—have offered and continue to offer the promise of enhancing the physical and mental potential of a child.[2] Meanwhile, the phenomenon of "school selection" has led to a commercialization of education whereby parents willingly pay to send a child to a school outside their assigned district for schooling that would otherwise be publicly funded.

Thus, when parents deploy their economic *tiaojian* to create *tiaojian*, they are effectively engaging in economic behavior that converts monetary capital into embodied capital, in the form of *suzhi*, thereby contributing to the nation's biopolitical project while effecting social differentiation and inequality. Under this regime, according to one interpretation, the body of the child becomes a "repository" of stored value, thought to be responsive to "capital inputs" promising to improve and enhance (Anagnost 1997a, 2008). Using commodities to improve and enhance, the argument goes, constitutes "a form of fetishism which endows material things with magical powers to effect miraculous changes" (1997a: 218). This kind of analysis suggests that parents are doing something without knowing what they are actually doing: furthering economic development and producing high-quality persons for the good of the nation.[3]

I would like to suggest a revision to the classic Marxist formulation: "They know it, and they have no choice but to do it." Middle-class parents are well aware of the social relations of production, and of the kind of privilege their child has over children from other backgrounds. Their efforts in ensuring or sharpening a child's competitive edge have less to do with a mistaken belief in the intrinsic value of *suzhi*-building commodities than with a fine-tuned discernment of the historical situation in which they find themselves. Of course they hope that *suzhi*-building commodities will enhance the potential of their child. Of course they hope their investments will secure the good life. But the consumption practices of middle-class mothers are directed less to the achievement of particular ends than to the ethical work of figuring out the boundary between what one can and cannot control. Fetishes are not always sources of mystification, a point well demonstrated by classic studies of religion in Africa. They may also be used as devices for channeling attention and energy in situations involving uncertainty—whether one is hunting for an animal or hunting for a job. The efficacy sought is both instrumental and moral. Fetishes externalize intention and can, in fact, generate empirical differences in the physical world (Lienhardt 2008), differences that matter a great deal to the moral actor.

In this chapter, I discuss two conceptions of good parenting, juxtaposing the advice of a parenting expert based in Kunming, Teacher Wang, with the position of an ordinary parent, Mr. Deng. Keeping in mind that the management of uncertainty is practiced in relation to culturally specific idioms—in Africa, for example, they include fetishes, rituals, clan spirits, cursing, and sorcery—I will argue that it is in and through economic thinking and behavior that these two individuals offer or exert some measure of control over the contingencies posed by social competition. Both use economically oriented language to speak about the work of parenting. One invokes the terms *invest* (*touzi*), *profit* (*shouyi*), *asset* (*zichan*), *produce* (*chanchu*), *production unit* (*shengchan danwei*), and *human capital* (*renli ziben*), and the other invokes *overdraw* (*touzhi*) and *expend/expenditure* (*xiaohao*). These terms may be taken as metaphors that serve as purposive guides, both sharing a single key metaphor: human capital.

"Human capital" is especially potent for guiding action because it reiterates connections between vastly different scales of phenomena, namely the macro-level scale of the market economy writ large and the micro-level scale of human activity. It is a metaphor that operates less by means of transference, borrowing from one thing to make sense of another, than by articulating unitary principles of energy and resource organization—principles that imply an ontological correspondence between things large and small. The conception of human capital to be dealt with here shall not be confused with human capital as a mode of neoliberal governmentality (Anagnost 2013). It is more closely related to the moral agent's problem of artful disposition.

Taken together, the cases will challenge the idea that the work of parenting operates under a kind of false consciousness. They will suggest that in is in and through economic thinking and behavior that people try to have some say over their lives. Indeed, middle-class parents willingly subject themselves and their children to a regime of competition that encourages the voracious consumption of educational goods and the empty pursuit of status. But this economic orientation disguises and renders invisible a deeper, more significant dimension: that of ethics. Competing and consuming are less expressions of rational calculations made in the pursuit of gain and class status as ends in themselves than expressions of an ethics of trying to survive what Allison Pugh has called the "economy of dignity" (2009)—a concept that articulates with Chinese concerns with "face" (*mianzi*). In her study of consumption among American families of various socioeconomic backgrounds, Pugh found that the emotions connected with consumption "hint at a deeper mystery, of the meaning of things, of care, and of belonging" (13). In an economy of dignity, families consume in the pursuit of social visibility and recognition. In the context of urban China, families consume so as to *survive* a rather cruel economy of dignity, with clear-eyed knowledge that the system is in fact arbitrary, but ignored at one's own peril.

THE FAMILY REPLACES THE COMMUNE AS A PRODUCTION UNIT

Wang Lingling is a native of Kunming who publishes nationally and lectures locally at a wide variety of venues, from Parent Schools organized by the Women's Federation to privately organized events. By all accounts, she is well liked and respected. One mother told me that Teacher Wang had "a lot of love" because she didn't charge any money for phone consultations. Another expressed admiration, noting that she had once been a "rusticated youth."[4] One teacher told me that unlike other experts who speak too abstractly at lectures for parents at the middle school where she works, Teacher Wang is able to keep her audience's attention. A university teacher who had never met her before shared with me an anecdote she had read in the *Kunming Daily*: Teacher Wang used to bathe her infant in the outdoor courtyard where she lived, with the intention of strengthening her daughter's constitution. Every time she started downstairs, her neighbors would sneer, "The crazy one's coming down." Of course the joke is now on them, my interlocutor seemed to be suggesting, as Wang's daughter eventually went to the reputable People's University in Beijing.

I met Teacher Wang at a dinner one of my friends arranged. It was attended by seven other women, all mothers, three of them participants in my study. Teacher Wang was the last to arrive, and when she did, everybody stood up and a full table of dishes suddenly appeared. My friend Wen Hui, who had been sitting to my left, immediately vacated her seat so I could sit next to the night's guest of honor.

After everyone had introduced themselves, dinner and conversation commenced. The conversation alternated between discussion and Teacher Wang's taking specific questions from individual mothers. "What do Ma Jiajue and Liu Haiyang have in common?"[5] "Why travel and go to McDonald's and KFC?" "Howard Gardner found that humans have eight kinds of intelligence." "How do I get my daughter to be more efficient?" "Do I have my daughter signed up for too much?" "When should a parent stop monitoring a child?" "Is it bad for a boy to spend too much time with his mother?" "Did encouraging your daughter to be social conflict with study time?" "Did you ever hit and scold your daughter?" "What should I do about my daughter's rebellion?" "My daughter roughhouses with boys. Should I explain the sexes to her?" "My son worries he isn't good at anything—what should I do?" "I forgot to sign my son's homework and his teacher punished him for it."

Wang had an answer or suggestion for every question and concern. Her advice to parents does not differ much from advice given by the celebrity child-rearing experts who populate the national scene, especially with regard to the importance of psychological health, of respecting children and their developmental stages, their rights and dignity. Where she differs from other popular experts is her unromantic emphasis on spending procedures, the economic practices by which one creates *tiaojian*. Having studied history and politics, and being a faculty member at Yunnan Finance and Trade College, Teacher Wang is sharply aware of the socioeconomic conditions that shape parenthood in China today. In a pamphlet she distributes at her talks, Teacher Wang writes, "Family is no longer just a life unit within the planned economy, a cell of society; it is the production unit [*shengchan danwei*] within the market economy, it has the function of investing and producing [*touzi chanchu*]" (2004: 1–2). Because the family has replaced the commune as a production unit, the responsibility of parents is much greater. Parents are responsible not only for the many aspects of a child's psychological development but also for managing resources and making choices about educational investments. Teacher Wang has no qualms about mixing motherhood with consumption. Good parents spend money, particularly on cultivating special talents—"music, dance, performance, and various kind of *suzhi jiaoyu* training classes" (63). She adds: "Parents know, relying on book knowledge in the future will be far from enough. When the child of another family surpasses one's own child in a special talent, yours could forever be behind. No matter how frugally you have to live, you must ensure investment in a child's learning. ... There will be payoff [*huibao*] from investing in a child's future. However small, it is all worth it" (63).

With this advice, Teacher Wang establishes a rational basis for educational consumption, arguing that spending constitutes an investment that will yield a return in the future. One might think it odd that Wang would speak in such direct terms, but her bluntness about economics derives from her background of having lived through the socialist planned economy, where economic production and output constituted the central focus of collective life—an expression of the glory of socialism. Rather than industrial production quotas, it is now human capital that is at stake. In her pamphlet, she explicitly draws on economic theory to promote the importance of investing in education, even though she is addressing a nonacademic audience. She explains: "Nobel Prize winner Theodore Schultz has endowed a significant economic character to education with his 'human capital theory.' Degree and direction of educational investment correspond with the increase and appreciation of human capital [*renli ziben*]. The goal of educational investment is profit [*shouyi*]. Speaking in abstract terms, this profit is expressed in terms of the increase in human capital, a kind of intangible asset [*zichan*]" (66). In its original context, Theodore Schultz's human capital theory sought to reframe public spending on education as a kind of investment, challenging a view that saw such spending as a form of consumption that took away from public funds (1981: 20–21, 34). Similarly, Wang seeks to convince parents that there is a solid rationale behind spending on education. The "profit" (*shouyi*) that comes from investment is not direct; rather, it comes later in a child's life—when he or she tests into a key-point middle school, moves on to higher education, and finds employment in the professional labor market (Wang Lingling 2004: 65–67). Just as managers of monetary capital ought to calculate wisely, so should parents, as managers of the family "production unit" (*shengchan danwei*).

In the pamphlet she distributes, Teacher Wang makes two important divisions between what parents are responsible for: preparing "hardware" and "software." While the latter section discusses interpersonal relations and behavioral and subjective qualities (the nature of children, rights, dignity, habits, abilities, sociality, and moral virtues), the section on hardware, for the most part, frames a discussion of spending and educational investments. In the pamphlet she writes, "Educational investment must be scientific, maximum gain with relatively little investment" (66). One example of a piece of practical advice concerns when not to spend: Wang lists and describes a number of websites offering free services as an alternative to costly private tutors and after-school classes. In another section, Wang even offers a mathematical equation that reads:

$$\text{talent} = (\text{grades} + \text{diploma}) \times suzhi$$

Pragmatic through and through, Wang's advice for rational calculation should not be seen as a means to an end in itself, namely profit and the increase of human capital. The trying enacted in the calculation is an end in and of itself, with rational calculation having little to do with the freedom of rational choice. One must calculate out of necessity because the intensity of competition *leaves* you no other choice. Concurring with a sentiment widely held by parents themselves, what is really at stake is survival—maybe not in terms of a child's "bare life," but certainly in terms of having a dignified life.

Unlike Schultz, Wang also encourages spending on noneducational goods, which she puts in the categories of social spending and entertainment spending. When it comes to birthdays and holidays, children will need to give cards and gifts to friends and teachers. "These things have all become the inevitable expenditures of children," Wang explains (63). Some will have to throw a birthday party, to reciprocate for another birthday party. Each must be better than the one before. Wang explains that if you do not participate, "then it means that you have no relationships, no position, no friends" (64), thereby highlighting the ethical dimension behind what can appear on the surface to be a competition for status and a form of vanity. Providing for social expenditures constitutes a modality of care, thereby expressing appropriate concern for a child's dignity, esteem, and face in the presence of peers (Pugh 2009). Parents who resist the social reality of having to consume risk making their child an outcast.

Wang even goes so far as to educate parents about pop culture, explaining that children have already turned from Hong Kong and Taiwan pop stars toward those from Korea. From H.O.T. to NRG to Baby V.O.X., children swoon over Korean boy bands and girl groups. This entails a significant amount of spending, from posters to concert tickets. Buying music, playing video games, and watching the latest movies all determine whether children will have "something to talk about" among their peers (Wang Lingling 2004: 64). Even if parents do not support this kind of spending, Wang explains that children will save their breakfast and lunch money.

This advice is significant because many parents would not think that there was a solid rationale behind spending on noneducational goods. Surely, some parents have no problem with supporting a child's spending habits. (A teenager once told me that some of her classmates get a new mobile phone every time a new model comes out and that some even get as much as a 600 RMB monthly allowance). But they do not necessarily have what Teacher Wang calls the task of "preparing hardware" in mind. The advice is also significant because most parents do not understand or support a child's adoration of pop stars, which, in local language, is satirized: children take commercial popular culture so seriously that their adoration has assumed the form of an "-ism," as in "chasing star-ism" (*zhuixing zhuyi*). Other parents do not support social spending at all, let alone socializing with peers. One unusually strict parent I knew forbade her twelve-year-old son to attend *any* birthday parties, as she felt that socializing was the business of adults.

For Teacher Wang, reservations about consumption are unreasonable. She advocates this kind of spending, but not because there is value intrinsic to commodities themselves. At the dinner I attended, Wang explains that the attraction children have for Western fast food has nothing to do with the food itself; rather, their self-confidence is at stake—a practical argument that happens to resonate with the academic arguments found in the East Asian anthropology classic *Golden Arches East* (Watson 2006). Rather than deny a meal at McDonald's, she suggests, communicate with them and discover the root of their desire. This advice is in the pamphlet as well: "Eat some Western fast food, wear some name brands, use some luxury goods, go to tourist destinations, there are more choices in the lives of children. There is no need to inhibit their desires. You have no choice but to satisfy their desires. Otherwise, your child will have no face [*mianzi*] in a group, and their self-respect will be harmed. The loss caused by an attack on self-respect is beyond calculation" (Wang Lingling 2004: 64). Self-confidence is a topic of frequent occurrence, as is its opposite: the inferiority complex. In the section headed by the afore- [*Constant*] mentioned equation, talent = (grades + diploma) × *suzhi,* Wang states: [*Comparison*] "What a child will do in the future when they're grown up is not important. What is important is that the child have some kind of hobby. When other children are flaunting their own hobbies, your child will not feel inferior" (70–71). In 2004, the problem of having an inferiority complex was especially at the forefront of Kunming people's minds as a consequence of the Ma Jiajue incident, involving the Yunnan University student who, provoked by a card game dispute, murdered four of his own classmates. A poor child from the countryside, Ma Jiajue wrote a poem while incarcerated that went viral on the Internet describing how he had been made to feel inferior—the mockery he had suffered for dressing and acting differently. While classmates rented apartments to cohabit with girlfriends, Ma Jiajue could barely even afford a cell phone, let alone a pair of slippers. Wang has Ma Jiajue in mind when she emphasizes the dangers of losing self-respect and feeling inferior, even though her advisees are urbanites.

Surely much of Wang's advice serves to effect socioeconomic differentiation, reinforcing the growing distance between the have and have-nots and securing the class position of her middle-class audiences. Wang promotes the creation of cultural capital, to be sure, which will serve to distinguish its possessors while securing better access to economic opportunities.[6] From Wang's perspective, however, the issue is less about distinguishing oneself than about fostering a sense of security. She once asked me rhetorically, "Parents who spent most of their childhood in a planned economy find it hard to find certainty in the present; how can they feel any sense of certainty about the future?"

Posing a question that simultaneously holds structural determination and meaningful human action in the same view, she starts her pamphlet by asking, "In this social transition period, we and our children have been tied to the crazy chariot that is the market economy. What course to follow?" (1). This question is at the heart of a parent's dilemma, as far as Wang is concerned, the necessity of having to make choices. Contrarily, in the socialist planned economy, one only needed to follow the Party line and everything would be okay. I have heard Teacher Wang say many times, "You can count on the milk being there, you can count on the bread being there." A family's livelihood was secured in the work-unit. Contrastingly, the market economy "will not be moved by tears." For Chinese children who "face the cruelty of the market economy's survival of the fittest as soon as they are born," life is a long-distance race where differences only get starker and starker over time (2–3). To put her argument in the framework of the art of disposition: making appropriate consumption choices would constitute adapting oneself to the propensity of the historical circumstance; failure to do so in a timely manner could engender a negative tendency that would be difficult to improve.

It is in this context that ensuring a child's self-confidence—by spending money—becomes paramount. Rational calculation is not simply a means to an end in itself. It is a strategy for managing uncertainty. I believe this is the reason why Wang is so popular with parents in Kunming: she seems to understand the moral-existential dilemma faced by parents. Oddly enough, Teacher Wang includes ensuring a child's likability in her discussion of the task of "preparing hardware," which suggests that the distinction between hardware and software does not strictly correspond to the material versus the psychological/cultural domain. To "prepare hardware" is to set up a kind of protective infrastructure, one that protects the child not only against the eliminating force of competition but also against the force of social differentiation within a single classroom.

Not all children experience the same environment in the same way, for teachers often make determinations based on "personality" (77). Even students at the best schools can find themselves in an environment adverse to learning, Teacher Wang points out, invoking the problem of "educational discrimination." She writes, "A group of children who all go to the same really good school eat the same rice. But that doesn't mean that every child will develop really well in this kind of environment. Every social environment has differentiations. Just as in an organization, some are cadres, some are commoners" (76). How a teacher sees a child has enormous consequences for development and achievement.

One of the practices Wang advises against is giving gifts to a child's teacher to ensure special care (77). Gift giving, Wang stresses, in place of a cultivating a good personality, can only create a vicious cycle where a teacher commends falsely, thereby attracting the dislike of classmates, which "places the child in an even worse situation" (77).

That Wang places spending money and cultivating a likable personality under the section of "preparing hardware" indicates that investing money and energy is more an ethical matter of artful disposition and arrangement of *tiaojian* than one of pure economic instrumentality. Like the parents she advises, she is attuned to the issue of social visibility and esteem and to fears of losing the race. Developmental problems could very well begin with a seemingly insignificant precedent, such as a teacher's attitude, which might then influence something as seemingly fixed as level of intelligence (77). For this reason, ensuring a child's likability by developing the child's social virtues is just as important as spending and investing.[7] Both protect against uncertainty by establishing a favorable tendency that will gather a force of its own.

TWO PEOPLE ARE IN A FOREST, AND HERE COMES A TIGER

Much to his wife's dismay, Mr. Deng repudiated participating in the competition. While Zhang Xin felt that one ought to try one's hardest (see chapter 4), her husband wanted to let go. Many fathers in my case families felt more casual about a child's education. But Mr. Deng was not simply casual: he adamantly rejected China's competition regime. Like Teacher Wang, Mr. Deng also conceived of a child's life as a long-distance race. Unlike Teacher Wang, who felt that small differences would only become larger later in the race, Mr. Deng insisted that winning the race depended on conserving one's energy. While Wang encouraged spending, Deng insisted on saving. In one conversation we had, he emphatically reiterated that he did not want to "overdraw" (*touzhi*) on his son's motivation, his emotions, and his intelligence. "If you take the latter fifty years of a person's whole life and compress it all into the first twelve years, and take care of this kid at this time, this isn't realistic and it isn't scientific." At stake were his son's psychological resources. If Wang saw talent and skills as human capital to be created through monetary investment, Deng saw the "life energies" (*huoli*) as a limited resource to be conserved.

Reasoning with stories, Mr. Deng gave many examples to argue that real success comes later in life, something schooling does not have any direct correlation with. He pointed out that China's many millionaires and billionaires had not gone to school and that best-selling authors did not study literature. He had also observed in his own field that education did not necessarily translate into career success. Top leaders were those that had ability, not good grades. He invoked an academician at the Chinese Academy of the Sciences:

DENG. His experience is extremely rich. He's organized the biggest construction projects. Someone with a doctorate, who dares to give him millions of *yuan* to direct? But people are willing to give it to this guy, he's led tens of thousands of workers. He's already led thousands of people by twenty-seven years old, to do work. He has experience, he knows how to manage people. He also knows how to use money. He also knows how to use power. So he has what they call emotional intelligence. While these, those students who have made it to Tsinghua University—learning various kinds of engineering skills, those who have passed through the entire curriculum, all you have is knowledge. Is someone going to tell you to organize millions of *yuan*?

The issue Mr. Deng raised here has long been a subject of debate in China, one concerning the relationship between meritocracy and the value of academic degrees, the use of social connections in career advancement, and the importance of applicable skills and abilities.[8] The academician Deng spoke of did not do well academically. But because he had rich life experience and high emotional intelligence, he had risen to the top. Deng contrasted this to the adolescents who start training early on, the Olympic math champions who completely lose interest in math by the time they reach adulthood. "Why?" Deng asked. "It's like I was saying, he's already overdrawn [*touzhi*] on his knowledge. He's also overdrawn on his emotions. He doesn't even want to think about math."

For Deng, the risk of overdrawing could entail something even more severe than loss of interest. He gave a number of examples of people who have died from overwork: ITs in Shenzhen in their twenties, a company CEO who had died of a heart attack at thirty-eight, and a thirty-six-year-old general manager at Shanghai Volkswagen who had leaped out from the seventeenth floor of a building. While in children the demands of competition could lead to loss of interest, for adults the demands of economic productivity could sometimes lead to death.

DENG. They're all dead. Died from overwork. This cohort . . . because they couldn't run any longer in the second half of the race. They couldn't eke it out anymore. But there are those who kept eking. China's elite are *too* diligent. Even more so than the Japanese. Have given up their rest. And then as soon as you look, like her [referring to his wife], her brother-in-law, a worker! A mechanic. Hasn't had a day of rest since last year. Your boss gives you a task, your manager gives you a task, if you don't go overtime, if you don't work on Saturday, Sunday, there's no way you can finish.

For Deng, a deep cultural logic had informed everything—from education, to work, to economic policies. The same logic that informed the exploitation of natural resources also informed the exploitation of human resources: the life energies. He invoked the rush to industrialize during the Great Leap Forward and more recent developmental projects to make his point.

DENG. We've taken all of China's big rivers, whatever we could dam we've dammed. It's pretty much all done. . . . So we can only go and seize [resources] in the Third World. That's why our businesses have all rushed out. Road building, China's pretty much built all the highways she can build. So we can only build roads outside.

TK. *Go to Southeast Asia.*
DENG. We don't go to Southeast Asia anymore! Now we're going to South America and Africa. We're building electric stations in South America and Africa. Drilling oil, from South America right over to Africa. Excavating steel ores, from South America over to Africa. So these ways of doing things, and you get to our children, and none of the things they're learning are useful. What he will face in the future is something no one can predict. What's the best for him right now? Take care of his body, ensure his life

energy [*huoli*]. Ensure his curiosity. Or his enthusiasm. That's enough. When new things appear in the future, when everybody else has already expended [*xiaohao*] their talents and intelligence, to the point of being sick of learning, that'll be the time for him to go.

Mr. Deng traversed the world and the span of history to explain and justify his attitude. His perspective was of course unique to his professional background and his own complicity in the exploitation of natural resources, effortlessly drawing a parallel between relations of production around the globe and relations of production at home. Mr. Deng identified an economic logic that structured not only the extraction of natural resources but also the human "expenditure" of life energy, identifying a correspondence between macro- and micro-level processes. This had come to China late, Mr. Deng noted—having Britain's industrial revolution in mind. But China already had a cultural practice that involved the needless expenditure of life energy: the imperial civil service examination system. In Deng's opinion, success in this system depended on knowing things, better than any one else, that had no practical value in the officialdom. The current exam-oriented education system was a continuation of an old tradition:

DENG.   You have no choice but to cope with Chinese education. It wants to select, out of the population of Chinese people, a small portion of people who can live well. And then another portion who have no *way* to live well. In order for the other portion to live well. In this situation, China has adopted the fairest method possible, because test taking is only test taking.

As emphatic as Mr. Deng was about his point of view, that he was right to "let his son go," he admitted that he was not as free to act as he wished. He found some consolation in the fact that his colleagues felt the same way about child rearing, as informed by their years of study and professional experience.[9] "We all feel it's terrible. But it's useless to know, you still have to let your kid go and study. You know clearly that this is completely irrational, but you still have to execute." Like the mothers in chapter 3, he too felt ambivalent. Mr. Deng put the reality of competition like this, again, in life-and-death terms:

DENG.   So people have this story: two people are in a forest, let's say two Chinese people. We don't even have to mention foreigners. Two Chinese people are in a forest. The tiger has come. In the beginning both of them are running. Later one of them gives up. He says, "*Aiya*, I can't. How can we outrun a tiger? A tiger is fast. We're not even long-distance running champions, we can't win this race." The other person now, very smart. "[We can't] outrun the tiger, that's for sure! Neither of us can outrun the tiger. But as long as I run faster than you, that's good enough. Once the tiger eats you, I can live."

So I don't need to be a long-distance running champion. I don't have to have the ability. And my *speed* doesn't have to be high either. As long as I can outrun you, that's good enough.

In this allegory, the tiger is social competition, one that aims to separate the wheat from the chaff. Those who are not selected are then eliminated, or eaten. Mr. Deng does not want his son to be eliminated, but he doesn't want to overdraw on his life energies either. So he shouldn't run his fastest, but only fast enough to survive.

This is a delicate balance Mr. Deng is trying to strike. If the balance tips too far in one direction or another, the repercussions are not easy to predict. I wondered what it was like for Mr. Deng's son to be part of a peer group— often thrown together because their mothers were friendly—where he was the least, to speak in Chinese terms, "excellent." Two of these children were elected class monitors, and the other was extremely enthusiastic about learning and was seen by all as a remarkably obedient. That Mr. Deng's son Deng Siwen had scored 40 out of 100 points on one particular test was everybody's business. "Of course his mother is worried about him!" one of the others exclaimed to me; her own daughter had scored 80 on the same test.

I had my own concerns as his supposed English teacher. Every other Sunday I had Deng Siwen and his three learning-mates over at my apartment. I had an arrangement with the four mothers that I would teach their children English with games, and I used games from my own childhood, such as "Simon Says," "Go Fish," "Memory" and "Chutes and Ladders," recreating the latter two with white paper and colored markers. While these games worked well with other groups, it was particularly difficult with this one. American children's games are all competitive: they sort players into winners and losers. Deng Siwen was always the loser, last to get to the top in "Chutes and Ladders," for example. It wasn't that he wasn't able to answer the questions I created, which allowed players to move one, three, or five steps ahead. Deng Siwen just wasn't interested in getting ahead. When he was in a square where he could take the ladder to skip a number of steps, he chose not to. On a different day, after losing interest in a game, he simply packed up his backpack and left right in the middle. "I don't want to play anymore," he stated simply as he walked toward my front door. His refusal and resistance frustrated me tremendously.

Deng Siwen's attitude affected his status in the group. My suspicion that my competitive games were not good for him was confirmed when I learned from one of the other mothers that the day we had played "Chutes and Ladders," two of his learning-mates had run downstairs from my apartment bragging about who had won and who had come in last. Deng Siwen refused to come to my apartment again after that, which the other mothers did not look upon too well. How could he have so little ability to bear failure? they wondered. Life is full of it. Consequently, on a different learning-date, led by a different English teacher, Deng Siwen was not invited. In fact, his mother Zhang Xin was sometimes not invited to events she probably would have liked to attend. For example, three of the four mothers were present at the dinner with Teacher Wang, and the one who had arranged the dinner, normally good friends with Zhang Xin, explained to me that she had not invited Zhang Xin because there were simply already too many people.

I wondered if the intensity of social competition could in fact weaken otherwise easy friendships. I sensed that Zhang Xin's friends saw her son Deng Siwen as a bad influence and did not always include them for this reason. Could his refusal to compete be attributed to his father's outlook?

It was important to Zhang Xin that she have her husband's support. Because he was so often out of town, she felt like a single parent, which might have been just as well given their disagreement about how to raise their son. She confided, "Sometimes I feel when I'm with him at home, if his dad isn't around, he's a good kid. So I say maybe one person is better than two, especially if you have different ideas." Zhang Xin felt that her husband spoiled their son too much, making it difficult for her to teach him important values and practical abilities.

Be that as it may, this couple might have agreed more than they were able to admit to. On the way to dinner one night, Mr. Deng played a game with his son as they held hands in the backseat. He play-interviewed his son, something he also liked to do with Deng Siwen's schoolmates when he was waiting at the gate after school. The conversation went something like this:

"Which do you think is better, going to school or playing?"

"Definitely not going to school!" Deng Siwen said.

I joined in and asked, "Well what would do you with all the free time?"

"Do the things I like to do!"

"But you live in China, so you have no choice," his father said. "You must learn a few things and make yourself stand out."

This conversation moved from the playful to the pedagogical. Mr. Deng already knew what the answer would be, as he had posed this question to schoolchildren many times before. But he acted as if he didn't know, and created a suspended space where his son could temporarily resist school discipline, only to tell him he had no choice but to work hard. Mr. Deng and his wife actually concurred in the view that hard work was not a matter of choice: it was a brute and inescapable necessity that belonged to the larger historical circumstance. Recall from chapter 4 that Zhang Xin said to her son: "What you know is important, you ought to put in the effort yourself. Because that's how it is in China." Mr. Deng had to execute, even though he would have liked to do otherwise, "because the choices my son faces are really, really cruel."

As much as Mr. Deng would have liked to simply let his son go, he did indeed execute in his own ways. When I first visited their home, Deng Siwen gave me a tour of his bedroom. In addition to the typical artifacts of a middle-class childhood—toys upon toys, books upon books, and large glossy studio photographs of him in various costumes—there were yellow Post-it notes everywhere. Every Post-it note had a different English term scribbled on it, not by—to my surprise—his mother, but by his father, who wanted him to run only fast enough to survive.

TWO GENRES FOR MANAGING UNCERTAINTY

In the two cases presented, good parenting is formulated in explicitly economic terms. One invokes the terms *invest* (*touzi*), *profit* (*shouyi*), *asset* (*zichan*), *produce* (*chanchu*), *production unit* (*shengchan danwei*), and *human capital* (*renli ziben*); the other invokes *overdraw* (*touzhi*) and *expend/ expenditure* (*xiaohao*). While Teacher Wang's use of economically oriented language is deliberate, informed by her acquaintance with Theodore Schultz's theory of human capital and her faculty work teaching economics at the college level, Mr. Deng's is less deliberate, though it is certainly shaped by his professional background.

The economically oriented terms found in these two versions of good parenting are metaphors. And they all point to one *key* metaphor: human capital. Mr. Deng does not actually use the term *human capital* as Teacher

Wang does, but his concern with conserving his son's life energy—enthusiasm, emotions, and intelligence—constructs a theory of human capital that sees the above as nonrenewable resources that can run out. I juxtapose the two views so as to better illuminate what is at stake in the rational calculation that Teacher Wang encourages, and the fervor with which mothers pursue extracurricular education for their children. We should not mistakenly view Wang's advice or maternal fervor as pure obsession with status and competitive success: what they are really concerned about is ensuring survival—though not in terms of a child's bare life—and exercising some measure of control over uncertainty. Mr. Deng shares the same concern but has a different strategy. For Teacher Wang and the many mothers who practice what she advises, survival depends on creating human capital through monetary investment, while for Mr. Deng survival depends on conserving the life energies, one's psychological resources.

The idea of human capital is metaphorical in the sense that *capital*, in its conventional sense, refers to money, or to seeds and farming implements in the agrarian context—neither of which can be embodied by the human being. Similarly, to speak of the family as a "production unit" (Wang), or of "overdrawing" on life energies (Deng), is to conceive of matters in metaphorical terms.[10] Production units in Maoist China produced material goods and industrial products, not human beings. *Overdrawing*, in its literal sense, refers to taking out more money from a bank account than one has saved, or getting paid salary one has yet to earn—one cannot literally withdraw one's stock of life energies. These metaphors support a basic premise found in theories of metaphor: they forge congruities between unlike categories and experiences.[11]

In their seminal *Metaphors We Live By*, Lakoff and Johnson consider "labour is a resource" and "time is a resource" as metaphors "culturally grounded in our experience with material resources" (1980: 65). Both labor and time are immaterial. But like a material resource such as coal, labor and time are used in producing a product, can be quantified and given a value, and get "*used up* progressively as the purpose is served" (65). They constitute what Lakoff and Johnson call "ontological metaphors," rendering something intangible into an entity amenable to human purpose (25–29, 66). By speaking of labor and time as if they were discrete entities, we can reason about them (25).

In the same way, speaking about human capital and life energies as if they were discrete entities allows Teacher Wang and Mr. Deng to reason about them. Like "labor" and "time," these immaterial aspects of experience are grounded in their cultural experiences with material production. Wang's conception of human capital is grounded in her personal experience of life under Maoist socialism, when production quotas determined the output of material and industrial goods, and where the achievement of targets served to express the glory of the planned economy. Now that communes have been dismantled, she argues that it is the family that has become a "production unit," responsible for the output of individuals high in human capital. Mr. Deng's conception of human capital is grounded in his professional involvement in developing infrastructure for harnessing energy in Southeast Asia. Just as developmental logic can extract natural resources to depletion, the demands of economic productivity in China can result in the total "expenditure" of a person's life energy.

The Pragmatic Value of Metaphor

When Lakoff and Johnson identify ontological metaphors as rendering something intangible into entities amenable to human purpose, they point to a rather underemphasized aspect of the metaphorical process. Metaphors have not only cognitive value but pragmatic value. This is certainly the case with the metaphor of human capital—as conceived in its original theoretical context, as used explicitly by Teacher Wang, and as constructed by Mr. Deng in his concern with a person's stock of life energy. Specifically, the metaphor of human capital serves as a purposive guide for managing and controlling uncertainty. The end to which purpose is directed—the control of experience—is ultimately ethical in nature (cf. Lienhardt 2008).

In its original theoretical context, human capital is understood as allowing farmers to control for risk, that is, to subdue the impersonal forces of nature, "host to thousands of species that are hostile to the endeavors of farmers" (Schultz 1981: 17). Embodied human capital allows farmers "to perceive, interpret, and respond to new events in a context of risk" (25). For Teacher Wang and Mr. Deng, the risk lies in the impersonal force of market capitalism. Though the risk is not as severe as famine, it can be as severe as loss of self-confidence or unemployment (Wang), and loss of interest or death from overwork (Deng). By conceiving of human capital as a tangible entity that one can create with monetary investment, an entity that Wang also refers to as an "asset," she offers parents who have the economic resources a sense of control over the risks posed by competition. By conceiving of life energy as a tangible entity that one can conserve rather than "overdraw" on or "expend," Mr. Deng feels a measure of control over the impersonal force of developmental logic by going easy on his son.

But the reason why the metaphor of human capital can serve as a purposive guide is not sufficiently explained with Western metaphor theory. Chinese metaphor theory, on the other hand, can reveal how potency is related to the fact that the metaphor is less novel, as Western metaphor theory would have it, than reiterative. In an essay titled "Metaphor and *Bi*," Michelle Yeh asks whether metaphor is a universal feature of poetic discourse. She finds that metaphor in Western poetics, with its "emphasis on tension, disparity, and incompatibility," is rather at odds with the use of *bi* in classical Chinese poetics (1987: 252). *Bi* "suggests a matching of two members of the same kind" (245–46), a more prominent feature in Chinese poetics. This feature differs from Western uses of metaphor in a number of ways, the most important of which is its ability to cast the world in terms of affinity and correspondence. "To *bi*, to create an analogy or metaphor," Yeh argues, is to "present a pair of images that are paradigmatic of the ontological correspondence or 'resonance' between things in the organic universe. Instead of the tension and disjunction that we have observed in the Western concept of metaphor, *bi* presumes affinity and complementarity" (250). While metaphor demonstrates the creative genius of its creator or user in Western poetics, the Chinese *bi* reiterates immanent connections between things (250).

The economic terms used in our two cases, which I have identified as having the quality of a metaphor, reiterate the socioeconomic logic that shapes social life in contemporary China. Surely the "human capital" metaphor derives its meaning from material capital (Schultz and Wang) and natural resources (Deng), which seems to imply a structure of transference. But it also casts the world in terms of affinity and correspondence, reiterating a unitary principle that informs both economic development and human development. For Deng, it is the principle of energy exploitation. For Wang, it is the principle of cost and benefit. As in farm or factory production, so in family reproduction: one must spend and invest to be economically viable. Both principles are associated with the broader logic of market capitalism. For both individuals, this logic is impersonal and inhuman. For Wang, the market economy is a crazy chariot that cannot be moved by tears. For Deng the market economy will exploit to utter depletion, just as all the rivers in China have been dammed, all the oil in South America has been drilled, and all the steel ores in South America have been excavated.[12]

While the logic perceived is inhuman, Wang's and Deng's theories of human capital suggest that the life of capital ultimately depends on human activity, thereby offering a guide to action. One can actively create it, or actively conserve it. The human capital metaphor provides some reconciliation between the scale of the market economy writ large and the scale of the everyday. The theories constitute two genres for recognizing the coexistence of inescapable constraints and the possibility of meaningful human action. Teacher Wang's version of good parenting is hopeful for those who follow her recommendations, tragic for those who do not. Mr. Deng's version of good parenting starts with a tragic view—what you are supposed to do as a child in urban China is worthless—yet is hopeful in suggesting that things will sort themselves out eventually. Both offer metatheories for how to dispose of things at hand, using economic language as a device for negotiating the boundary between what can and cannot be controlled.

CHILDREN AND ECONOMIC VALUE

What happened to the economic value of children in relation to old-age security and the moral tradition of intergenerational reciprocity? The mothers I knew were less overtly interested in the value of children in this sense than in building value into a child. Few expected their efforts to be returned with old-age care. Though they commonly saw selfishness as a widespread problem among urban only children, they also blamed themselves. Many felt that they had raised their child in a way that did not foster caring for others. They identified this as an outcome of rising standards of living and of the one-child policy. Most urban children have grown up with many adults orbiting around them. During family meals, an important site for practicing care for others, parents have become accustomed to giving their child the best food on the table. They feel satisfaction simply in seeing the child eat something. Urban parents of primary school–age children also lower their expectations for old-age care when they see how older children of older friends have turned out. They see in grown only children a defiant sense of independence, and they see how career paths can geographically separate families rather permanently. Some parents feel that it is not fair to expect a child to return care in old age. As one mother said to me, "You could not possibly do it, as an only child, especially if both married children are only children. If the man is an only child and the woman is also an only child, that's a family that has to take care of four elderly people. Can they do it? They can't do it." This mother anticipated the growth of retirement homes in China.

Some children do indeed have the virtues that might translate into reciprocated care in the future, and their parents feel lucky because the effort to confer a competitive edge tends to overshadow everything else. Of course Chinese parents wish for their son or daughter to be a more caring person, but this value is fundamentally at odds with the contemporary values of independence and excellence (cf. Fong 2007). Some of the parents I came to know in Kunming, those who sometimes saw their child as not caring about others enough, expressed regret over paying so much more attention to school and special-talent education to the neglect of this aspect. But this was not a matter of choice as far as they were concerned.

The time-honored virtue of care for others and filiality has taken a backseat because parents see the future of their child as even less secure than their own. Wang Yan, who sometimes wished that her bright and talented daughter was a more caring person, felt satisfied, overall, especially when she saw other children experiencing academic difficulty. Wang Yan told me solemnly, "Actually, you know, us parents, we have jobs. We're working people. And then, food and clothing, we won't really lack anything. But the child's life, you know, she hasn't even walked much. Her life has just begun."

THE RULES OF LIFE

Because urban family life in post-Mao China has been so definitively shaped by political and global economic processes, a phenomenological approach to the lived experience of parenting is not immediately obvious. At the same time, the economic language one might be tempted to use in critically interpreting parental effort is not exactly far from experience either. Parents are well aware that education is being commercialized, that consumption is a form of investment, and that raising a high-quality child contributes to the national good. It might look from the outside as if all the effort mothers make is an internalization of ideological norms. But it is less accurate to say, "They do not know it, but they are doing it," than to say, "They know it, and they have no choice but to do it."

In this chapter, I have tried to warn against too quickly associating the competition craze and economic thinking with ideological mystification or with individualistic greed and materialism. The calculations going into creating *tiaojian* have a moral dimension. It is important for parents to feel that they have tried everything possible to ensure a fair chance for their only child. "*Property* and *propriety* are not etymologically so close by mere accident," Kenneth Burke says. "Morals and property are integrally related. They are obverse and reverse of the same coin. They both equip us for living" ([1935] 1954: 212). In contemporary China, the ethical and the economic are so closely intertwined that the economic becomes *the* cultural idiom in which moral experience gets articulated.

The popular television series *Snail House* is instructive. Based on a novel by Liu Liu (a penname), *Snail House* explores the troubles that young college-educated urbanites face in reconciling aspirations for home ownership with skyrocketing housing prices and poignantly captures the stress of coping with the economic realities and social pressures that go along with middle-class aspirations. In the very last episode of this thirty-three-episode series, Haiping makes a calculation of the cost of daily living in the context of a broader reflection on existence in urban China, as she sits with her sister Haizao, who is, by this point of the show, reeling from a personal tragedy (a hysterectomy that followed a miscarriage that followed a physical attack by the wife of her lover, a corrupt government official). It is the beginning of a much longer soliloquy:

> HAIPING. Every night, I sit in front of the window. Seeing the lights outside my window, I will start to think, this city sure is marvelous. There are as many varieties of lives as there are people. The lives of others I know nothing about. As for myself, a long string of numbers pop into my head as soon as I open my eyes in the morning: mortgage 6,000; food and clothing 2,500; Ran Ran's kindergarten 1,500; social expenditures 600; transportation 580; property management fees 340; cell phone bill 250; and 200 for utilities. That means that from the moment I take my first conscious breath I have to bring in 400 *kuai* every day. At least. That is the cost of my living in this city. These numbers force me to dare not be slack, not even for a day.

In this soliloquy, Haiping is both calculative and compelled by external forces—fulfilling, at the same time, the roles different social theorists have imagined for social actors. But she is by no means a rational actor competing for self-gain at the expense of others. Her calculations concern survival—not only of the economic kind but of the psychological and social kind. The numbers are invoked as a means for symbolizing and making concrete the intangible pressures of modern life. Such pressures exert a force that leaves little room for choice: one can only go along with the flow, even if that flow—as Haiping says later in the soliloquy—renders you invisible.

In making such an assertion about the nature of calculation and choice (or lack thereof), *Snail House* effectively crystallizes the sense of unease my informants often expressed. Both Teacher Wang and Mr. Deng have a lot to say about choice: that education and the power of choice are correlated, that parents have no choice but to make consumption choices, that there is no choice "but to cope with Chinese education," and that the choices faced are "really, really cruel."

Snail House also suggests that the urban Chinese economy of dignity is by no means a sphere of rational choice, because the system itself is irrational. Nor is it a system that depends on ordinary people's ignorance of their role in reproducing the system. Everyone knows that it is irrational, yet one has no choice but to participate in it, thereby reproducing it. This is suggested early on in the series when Haiping's husband (Suchun) and Haizao's boyfriend (Xiaobei) have a man-to-man talk about "what women want" shortly after Haiping and Suchun have an explosive argument over the financing of their home. Xiaobei, being the younger, unmarried man, tells Suchun that he has never understood why women want to purchase a home in the first place. Still naive about adult social pressures, he reasons that renting is much more "realistic" (*xianshi*) and less burdensome—invoking a word that could mean "utilitarian" in a different context. Suchun corrects him for his misunderstanding: "What you're talking about is not called realistic. It's called rational. What *realistic* refers to is not caring how high housing prices are, there will always be people who will do whatever they have to do to buy that one home." He goes on to point out, "Haiping is already in her thirties. People around her younger in age all have homes already. She does not. Just think how hard that is for her to bear."

Although *Snail House* is not a show about child rearing, it locates the pursuit of home ownership along a continuum of urban life pressures that includes child rearing. It is for this reason that I end with a brief discussion the show: *Snail House* was a hit because it "really nailed" some of the issues Chinese urbanites face.[13] Have a family, secure good schooling, buy a home—these are the inescapable rules of life, whether you like it or not. While the scene between Suchun and Xiaobei makes explicit the irrationality of home buying in the Chinese housing market, Mr. Deng, quite similarly, makes explicit the irrationality of participating in the tireless pursuit of endless education for children. Speaking for himself and friends and colleagues, he laments: "We all feel it's terrible. But it's useless to know, you still have to let your kid go and study. You know clearly that this is completely irrational, but you still have to execute."

Ordinary people in urban China are, sometimes, *acutely* aware of the arbitrary nature of the pressures that constrain them, but they also feel that participation is the only and best way in the present historical circumstance. Clear-eyed resignation to what one cannot control is, paradoxically, a modality of "existential control" (Jackson 1998). And it is in this context that the idioms invoked for the purpose of exercising personal efficacy over impersonal forces appear as instrumental when in fact they are ethical: to resign oneself is the same as not giving up.

SEVEN

Banking in Affects

ECONOMIC METAPHORS DO NOT NECESSARILY REVEAL how far
market logic has penetrated into noneconomic domains of life. They may
serve as ethical devices—for making sense of when, where, and how one
ought to act in the face of processes much larger than oneself. They may also
serve as cognitive devices—for articulating the principles behind such processes. In the case of the "human capital" metaphor, the logic of market capitalism is articulated. It is the principle that drives the processes awarding
investments and depleting resources. In another instance, the economic
metaphor concretizes the principle of affectivity—the power to affect and the
capacity to be affected.

"Banking in affects" (*qinggan yinhang*) is an expression that was spontaneously invented on the side of a famous lake in the context of a "summer camp"
trip I followed to Beijing. The expression comes from the teacher who led the
trip—a popular expert named Zhou Ting, a local Kunming person. Like the
experts discussed in earlier chapters, she takes issue with China's exam-
centric education system. However, rather than focus on overall quality,
appreciation (chapter 2), or economic planning (chapter 6), Zhou puts her
focus on *qinggan*—a term that refers to "emotion" in most contexts but
ought to be translated in the context of her theory as either "sensory emotion," or, more simply, "affect."

Zhou Ting is deeply engaged in the question of how children might be
educated differently to transform the fate of the nation. Though the aim of
her project is grand, she locates the source of potential change in the child's
body and its engagements with various material environments, both extraordinary and mundane. Her use of *qinggan* is best translated as "affect" because
she wishes to highlight the materiality of the sensed world and of the sensing

186

body, while also recognizing the embodiment of *qinggan* by nonhuman agents. Interestingly, the expression "banking in affects" shares with Western theorists of affect writing in the tradition of Deleuzian philosophy a certain ontological vision. It is a vision that understands the human body as porous— made and remade in relation to the various environments and things it gets assembled with. It is a vision that perceives the world as teeming with vitality—a world where continuities between the human and nonhuman worlds may be manipulated for human ends.

Thus the ethnographic material in this chapter will offer another version of the humanist antihumanist practice of disposition. Understanding the world in terms of affectivity takes the agencies of nonhuman forces and things seriously, but it may also, ironically, bring us into an area that seems to belong exclusively to humans: moral life. If there are various factors, forces, and agencies involved in any given situation, it is important for human actors to determine whether and where action is possible or required. Whatever that action may be, it is inseparable from the cultivation of sensitivity.

QINGGAN JIAOYU: CULTIVATING THE AFFECTIVE CHILD

For Zhou Ting, the education system in China is deeply worrisome. In the brochure advertising a mothering class she offered on Saturday nights, she states: "If the education of a child stresses only academic achievement, then the child will inevitably lose many developmental opportunities, because this age reserves a secure and happy life environment for children who have received an education of the heart-spirit and sensory emotions." When I met her in 2004, Zhou was trying to make sense of a multiple homicide that had taken place at Yunnan University, where she also teaches. Earlier that year, four students were found dead in a campus dormitory. They had been beaten with a blunt object, wrapped in newspapers, and stuffed into separate closets. Ma Jiajue, the culprit, was a fellow classmate and friend to the victims, a biotechnology student whom everyone else knew as a bit odd. The case stimulated a flurry of public discussions over what had driven him to crime: most commentators sympathized with Ma, a poor student from the countryside, while others argued that he should have personally taken more responsibility for his own mental health.

For Zhou Ting, Ma Jiajue was emblematic of an education system that continues to focus too much on academic achievement, despite ongoing efforts at reform. He was highly developed intellectually and earned good marks but was tragically underdeveloped with respect to his sensory emotions (*qinggan*). In her view, Ma Jiajue represents a hidden danger that lurks in an education system that overstresses academic achievement to the neglect of *qinggan* education. She does not identify herself as a *suzhi jiaoyu* advocate per se. Zhou advocates something called *qinggan jiaoyu,* or the education of sensory emotions, which she understands as filling the gap left behind by schools too intent on training test takers, too utilitarian in their goals. If *suzhi jiaoyu* advocates have the general concern that China's exam-centric system fails to liberate the potential of every child, Zhou Ting is especially worried that children in China have too few opportunities for accumulating sensory experiences (*tiyan*). This has implications for a child's capacity to relate and to connect with others. For Zhou, Ma Jiajue was a case in point. As a child in a poor farming family, Ma spent most of childhood staring at a wall while his parents toiled in the field, too busy to attend to his *qinggan* development.

Shortly after the murder, the State Council issued an official document titled "Regarding Suggestions for Another Step toward Strengthening and Improving the Construction of Young People's Morals" (2004). Zhou Ting was already engaged in school-based research projects on character development at the time but had been feeling dissatisfied with the scope of her efforts and thought she could easily get financial support for a more immersive research project with this official call to action. Her request was denied, however, so she decided to take matters into her own hands. In an interview with a newspaper reporter, she stated, "There's going to be another murder, for all we know. The upper levels want you to carry out moral education work, but people at the lower levels don't support you. How many people can I affect just teaching a mothering class?"

In this chapter, I discuss a "summer camp" trip Zhou Ting organized, where she explored her question of how sensory experience contributes to moral development in the practical context of guiding a group of children on a tour of Beijing that included visits to the Great Wall, the Forbidden City, the Imperial Gardens, Peking University, major museums, and less touristy but socially significant sites such as Peking Union Medical College Hospital. What I observed belongs to the larger context of the *suzhi jiaoyu* reform movement in that Zhou has been inspired by the celebrity experts who populate the national scene to develop her own approach to cultivating well-rounded children who will contribute to national strength. Although I have translated *qinggan* as "sensory emotion" up until this point, I will use the phrase "affective subject" to refer to the kind of human person Zhou Ting hopes to assemble into being, in a kind of theoretical translation. The phrase "affective subject" is meant to invoke the concept of affect, which is in no way synonymous with emotion but refers instead to a kind of circulatory energy—a charge of vitality that generates change. This way of conceptualizing affect requires a momentary detour through affect theory.

ON AFFECT

The concept of affect can be traced back to Baruch Spinoza, whose *Ethics* concerns the question of what a body can do. Here the body is defined not so much by its physical boundaries as by its power to affect and its capacity to be affected. This is a body to be grasped not in terms of its form, substance, or taxonomic name but rather in terms of the relations that it enters into (Deleuze 1992). For this reason, relations can also be called affects. For Deleuze and Guattari an affect can be a composition or assemblage of unlikely things: "For example, the Tick, attracted by the light, hoists itself up to the tip of a branch; it is sensitive to the smell of mammals, and lets itself fall when one passes beneath the branch; it digs into its skin, at the least hairy place it can find" ([1980] 1987: 257). The light and the tick, the tick and a smell, and finally, the tick nestled close to the body of a hairy terrestrial animal, these are "just three affects" (257). The body is defined by what it is capable of relative to what it assembles with, thus always "becoming" something else. Because a body could potentially enter into a relation with any number of things, it is hard to predict what a body can do.

Affect concerns change and transformation. One could even say that it refers to the animating principle behind *all* "natural" and "social" phenomena. Manuel De Landa (1992) finds support for this claim in the material world, where matter is forever undergoing transformative processes that involve creative solutions and new configurations in the balancing of physical forces. Drawing on nonlinear science and on the concept of phase transition especially—which would describe, for example, the transformation of a liquid into a crystal—De Landa argues that the "nonlinear flow of matter and energy" gives rise not only to solids, organisms, mountains, and planets but also to human bodies and to phenomena such as agriculture, irrigation, and civilization. You could say this is a reformulation of the scientific view of ecosystems as systems connected by flows of energy, matter, and information.

Importantly, De Landa's argument is in no way meant to be teleological. Just as there is nothing intrinsically better about a solid than a liquid, the same goes for "civilized" societies and hunter-gatherers (154). Moreover, theorizing this principle of transformation provides a recipe for how humans might facilitate change in the human world, made possible by setting the right "attractors" in place and by putting "bifurcations" in motion. For if mountains do become rocks and then pebbles once again, over time, so too can seemingly rigid social formations be unhardened (143).

While De Landa never uses the term *affect* in his essay "Nonorganic Life," he is certainly thinking of it. Among recent theorists, affect is understood as a kind of "preindividual" energy or vitality that circulates between bodies and environments, always on the move, never in residence (Ahmed 2004; Clough 2007; Wissinger 2007). If this sounds vague, it is because affect theory concerns something rather indeterminate and ineffable. This is not because the life of affect leaves too few traces but rather because it leaves *too many*. For this reason, theorists describe affect as a kind of intensity. As Brian Massumi points out, "Sensation is never simple" (2002: 13). Something as seemingly plain as an echo arises out of the complex patterning that forms by virtue of the movement of sound between two surfaces, which transforms surface distances into an "intensity."

This intensity constitutes a reserve of potential, a "pressing crowd of incipiencies and tendencies" (Massumi 2002: 30), from which the will and conscious thinking may selectively recognize in navigating the phenomenal world. For example, color perception involves the undifferentiated experience of the inseparability of color and light, but this integration is mostly experienced as a shadow, while "red," "blue," or "white" is extracted and named (162–65). In other words, the sensory stimuli that a human body encounters on a daily basis are simultaneously complex and undifferentiated. But because conscious life involves differentiating what is otherwise continuous and integrated, the uninterrupted flow of matter and energy remains a virtual phenomenon. What the body is capable of, meanwhile, is the "infolding" of impinging stimuli as affect.[1]

This relates directly to the core definition of affect, namely the body's power to affect and its capacity to be affected. Here I would like to quote Massumi's discussion of tactility at length:

Tactility is the sensibility of the skin as surface of contact between the perceiving subject and the perceived object. Proprioception folds tactility into the body, enveloping the skin's contact with the external world in a dimension of medium depth: between epidermis and viscera. The muscles and ligaments register as conditions of movement what the skin internalizes as qualities. . . . Proprioception translates the exertions and ease of the body's encounters with objects into a muscular memory of relationality. This is the cumulative memory of skill, habit, posture. At the same time as proprioception folds tactility in, it draws out the subject's reactions to the qualities of the objects it perceives through all five senses, bringing them into the motor realm of externalizable response. (58–59)

A body is best defined by its capacity to be affected—by its responsiveness to, say, the sensation of touch and movement, converted, by way of an accumulation of experience, into a muscular memory, which is then externalized into a habit, or a skill. What Massumi does not mention between these pages is how the capacity to be affected might be mobilized into a power to affect in a given historical context. A skill, a habit, a posture can have tremendous social and political significance, where a body's capacity to act, and to affect, may constitute a major focus of discursive concern and pedagogical intervention.

In China, the *suzhi jiaoyu* reform advocates have come to see the body of the child as a site where affective forces can be put into play in the changing of a nation's destiny. Although the understanding or formulation of *suzhi jiaoyu* varies between the official, school, and family domains, all of its advocates could agree on one thing: Chinese children are bereft of direct experience. Their bodies do not encounter much sensory stimuli, nor do they move much, as they sit for hours and hours behind a study desk, day after day. By 2000 this state of affairs had even become a cause for concern for then president Jiang Zemin, who urged in a speech, "We must not confine our youth in rooms and in books all day, and we must let them participate in some social practice, open their field of vision, and enlarge their social experience" (2001: 4). We could read this call to transform China's education system from one that emphasizes test taking to one that emphasizes direct experience as a call to "unharden" a system that has become too rigid—that is, to deterritorialize the stratified and sedimented and to set energies in motion. Because the child's body enters into too few relations, its capacity to act is diminished. For Zhou Ting, this has implications both small and grand— not only for China's quest for global strength but also for a child's moral development and his or her capacity to connect with his or her social, cultural, and natural environments.

A TRIP TO BEIJING: ASSEMBLING WITH CULTURAL ACCUMULATION

Early in July 2004, Zhou Ting signed up twenty-five children through her mothering class for a trip she would lead to Beijing. This trip to Beijing would be a convergence of her own research agenda with the willingness·of many middle-class Kunming parents to broaden their child's range of experience.[2] While the top of the registration form read "A trip to Beijing for 'children's *qinggan* experience of China's accumulated cultural achievements,'" at an info meeting Zhou introduced the trip as something that would allow participants to "read" Chinese history "right on site." Two kinds of experiences can educate *qinggan*, she explained: one is reading, the other is nature. The two are interrelated in that reading constitutes a kind of experience,[3] and only individuals who know how to sense, observe, and experience the world have the capacity to write.

In Zhou's advice to parents, "nature" is a loose concept that can refer to almost anything antithetical to home and school, while "the novel" refers to anything that a child has not already experienced directly. In one class, Zhou told the mothers sitting before her that some children truly have no idea what bamboo is, because they have never *seen* it. She attributes the difficulty children have with writing compositions to their lack of life experience, advising, "Let the child have a life they haven't lived before. Let your child come to know more concepts in more environments." China's children—who are confined either to a desk in a classroom or at home—do not know even the most basic things.

The trip to Beijing promised to expand the affective capacities of children by exposing them to "China's accumulated cultural achievements," which themselves are affective. "Chinese culture is of the *qinggan*," Zhou explained the day of registration, suggesting that China's historical and cultural monuments embody a certain energy and vitality. Foreshadowing Patricia Clough's (2007) characterization of affective economies as augmenting and expanding affect, Zhou advertised the trip as an opportunity to expand the participants' range of *qinggan* in the experience of Beijing, where she would "adjust," "expand," and "guide" *qinggan*s along the way. This promise was most explicitly realized the day the group visited the Summer Palace. The text below is a rendition of what my video camera recorded in prose.

Banking in Affects

It was the end of a muggy day in mid-July, and the weather had been stiflingly hot. The Summer Palace, former retreat of Empress Dowager Ci Xi, had been packed with visitors. Our group had already grown weary of all the unexpected hardships of the trip. For this reason, the *sudden fluctuation in weather* was significant for Zhou, who spontaneously stopped the children at the side of Kunming Lake on their way toward the exit. She wanted everyone to appreciate the view and the dramatic change in weather. It was suddenly much cooler, as the sun had retreated behind a blanket of clouds and a wind had begun to blow. Zhou asked the children if they could describe the kind of wind in the air. She suggested "gentle breeze." One child jokingly answered with "typhoon."

She instructed them to focus attention on their feeling (*ganshou*) and then directed their attention across the lake. "Please look at the little island and then at Seventeen-Arch Bridge from this angle," she said to them.

There was a pause. Most of the children gazed obediently while a few goofed off. Zhou continued, "At this moment, all of the natural conditions, weather, view, color, et cetera, how is this affecting your state of mind? Especially the things that your teacher wants you to do. It isn't that you cannot understand, it isn't that you cannot accept my instructions. Compare your state of mind at the time with what you are feeling now. If I were to ask you to do something now, would you be willing to do it, or would you be unwilling?"

A sixth-grade boy answered in a perfunctory and sing-song fashion, "Willing!" (*Yuanyi!*), poking fun at her exercise.

Zhou stated that she did not need an answer and began to give an improvised monologue. She spontaneously invented a novel idea. "This kind of beautiful, calm, and peaceful state of mind [*xinjing*], I'll tell you, you can't buy this with money, we have only these few minutes, here and now. If it were noon, under a scorching sun, and you were being drenched with sweat, you wouldn't even be in the mood for experiencing this nature. You'd be wiping sweat, drinking water, replacing water. How would your attention be on your state of mind? How would you have a good state of mind? That's why you are making deposits into your state-of-mind-bank [*xinqing yinhang*] right now."

Addressing the kids who were not paying attention, Zhou announced, "Some people have their doors open and could deposit bundles and bundles, but they're not willing, still busy with other business."

Zhou instructed the children to store the moment in their banks because it could influence them for the rest of their lives. She told them that Empress Dowager Ci Xi did not like to live in the Forbidden City and preferred to spend her time here for good reason. The empress came here to nourish her state of mind.

At this point, the just mentioned "state-of-mind bank" (*xinqing yinhang*) evolved into "*qinggan* bank." Teacher Zhou continued, "Open up your *qinggan* bank right now. The view right now is giving you bundles of *qinggan* banknotes [*chaopiao*] to store in your bank. The *renminbi* [China's currency] that you can really see is not valuable. What's valuable are your *qinggan* banknotes. Such a beautiful view, this is what you call valuable. Take it if you want it. But you have to use your heart, your *qinggan*s to make deposits."

A large crowd had gathered by this point. One mother-son pair not belonging to our group followed Teacher Zhou's instructions diligently, more so than some of the children in our group. Meanwhile, the wind began to pick up.

Integrating the moment at hand and what she knew about the Chinese curriculum in schools, Zhou instructed the children to "take a broad view. Look at how the water in front of you twinkles like jade. 'Ripples on the surface of the water,' those phrases, this is it, the image before your eyes. What's in your books, what you learned in your textbooks, still has to pass a [inaudible]. I'm telling you, why is it that some people cannot experience the most beautiful things described when they're learning literature? It's because they don't have this image in their *qinggan* bank."

Toward the end of her monologue, Teacher Zhou explained that deposits are made by opening the seven channels. Putting what the children were supposed to do in concrete terms, she instructed them to mind their sensory experience: "Your *qinggan* channels are your eyes, ears, nose, mouth, skin, your sense of movement. Including your sense of your insides. Most ordinary people rarely use these channels for making deposits into their *qinggan* banks."

Before concluding the lesson with a blast of her whistle and a wave of her yellow flag, Zhou instructed the group to remember this very moment and to store it in their "*qinggan* bank" so as to help them endure daily tasks, hardship, and the tedium of learning.

What are we to make of this odd expression—"banking in affects"?[4] This lakeside exercise seems to be a perfect example of the conversion of external wealth into cultural capital. These are middle-class children after all, whose parents paid a hefty sum to send them on this trip. The trip as a whole probably contributed to the well-rounded development of its participants in some way, shaping them as citizen-subjects that would embody the potential to deliver China to its destiny as a strong nation. The expansion of their affective capacity might raise their *suzhi*, actualizing national agendas for economic development pinned on turning China's population burden into a resource. Because mobility for leisure and cultural capital are highly correlated, the children at the side of Kunming Lake were quite literally acquiring or accumulating a noneconomic form of capital. The exercise legitimated parents' financial investments in the trip.[5]

Another possible reading might involve the notion of the affective economy, predicated on the observation that the current economic paradigm increasingly relies upon immaterial forms of labor, and on the assertion that life itself has become a domain of capital accumulation (Clough 2007: 20). In an affective economy, it is the manipulation of bodily capacities and the putting of indeterminate potentialities into play that produces value. Elizabeth Wissinger's work on the modeling industry is a case in point. Wissinger found the circulation and modulation of energy—between a model and environmental stimuli—to be more important than finding pretty girls and manufacturing beautiful images. Because what turns out to be most productive in the competition for consumers' attention is difficult to define, measure, and name, industry professionals remain characteristically vague about what gets a model work, while models themselves "work to be sensitive to the flow of affect by broadening their affective capacity so that stimulus easily produces affects in their bodies that might then translate into an external change" (2007: 237, 243). It is also the job of the assembled professionals to create an atmosphere in which the model could "get into the flow" with music, food, and some coddling and coaxing (242). The more relaxed a model, the more responsive she may be; the more variable her responses, the greater the potential for impact in a saturated marketplace.

One could argue that efforts to reform education in China reflect the logic of the affective economy. Speaking for the *suzhi jiaoyu* movement, one education minister located value-producing spontaneity in the human person:

"Humans are the most positive and lively element in productivity, they are the subject of its liberation and development" (Chen Zhili 2001: 4). What productive human capacities might be, however, is not always well articulated. In fact, advocates repudiate hard definitions, invoking, instead, the idea of potential.

If every child has potential, as the reform advocates claim to believe, the onus of responsibility is placed upon educators—parents and teachers—to create conditions (*tiaojian*) that could liberate that potential. Like Wissinger's industry professionals, educators are to create environments that stimulate affective flow. Parents especially ought to expose their child to as many life experiences as possible. The more opportunities presented, the more likely it is that a child's potential will find expression. The more experiences a child has, the more adaptable the child will be in a knowledge-based economy. The lakeside exercise, in this reading, is merely an instantiation of an economic logic that has subsumed all spheres of noneconomic life.

But let us for a moment stay close to the ethnographic material at hand. First, we may take this lakeside exercise as expressing a conception of the child's body as a composition of sensory surfaces that can convert distances into intensity. When Zhou encourages her participants to take note of the breeze, their feeling, the view, and the general "color" of the "natural" environment, she is effectively leading an exercise in the infolding of the external conditions so as to create a resonation—an echo, a complex pattern—that could possibly become something else. Massumi might call the child's body as she conceives it a transducer of qualitatively different forms of matter, "Like electricity into sound waves. Or heat into pain. Or light waves into vision. Or vision into imagination. Or noise in the ear into music in the heart. *Or outside coming in*" (2002: 135).

Or breeze, view, and color into compliance with a teacher, a good state of mind, and the capacity to appreciate literary phrases such as "ripples on the surface of the water." The issue of compliance here should not be understood in terms of power. That is to say, I am not interested in reducing the circulation of affect to the order of normalization. This is not simply about making pliable citizen-subjects who will obey the wishes of their teacher and ultimately the nation. Instead, these conversions may be seen as articulating with the same creative processes that animate change and transformation in the nonorganic, nonhuman world. In fact, the notion of accumulation, contained in the idea of a bank, is important here. Just as rocks form as a result of sedimentation (i.e., the accumulation of matter), historical monuments and literary phrases can also be understood in terms of sedimentation, as suggested by Zhou's name for this trip: "A trip to Beijing for 'children's *qinggan* experience of China's accumulated [*jidian*] cultural achievements.'" The notion of cultural accumulation is connected to the world of rocks, as *dian* alone means "to form sediment" and *dianji*—which reverses the characters in *jidian*—refers to geological sedimentation. Therefore, if sedimentation can flexibly refer to a process found in the human world (i.e., the accumulation of cultural achievements), then it is not a huge leap to infer such a process in subject formation, specifically the molding of virtue.

Importantly, the lakeside exercise was also a creative response to difficulties belonging to an irreducibly singular situation. This visit to the Summer Palace took place just a few days into the trip, when Teacher Zhou was already feeling overwhelmed. She had not prepared herself for all the heterogeneity that she would face. The day they departed Kunming for Beijing by train, Zhou suddenly found herself responsible for twenty-five children, more than she had planned to register, and many of whom she had never met before. In addition to narrating the trip (guiding, expanding, adjusting *qinggans*), managing her three assistants, and thinking about her research questions, she had to made sure that all the children ate enough, brushed their teeth, made their beds, and so on. Moreover, the trip was filled with unexpected hardship. Lacking the kind of facilities and means of transportation available to established summer camps, Zhou, her assistants, and the twenty-five children stayed in a tiny bungalow, took cold showers, used a public toilet, and traveled by public bus. Some children developed bloody blisters on their feet from walking; others had heat rashes from the humidity—something Kunming people are not used to. It was in preparation for a long bus ride back that Zhou asked her participants to take the moment seriously. At the very end of her monologue by the lake, Zhou promised that this kind of view, if stored properly, could treat hurt, hunger, thirst, and, most importantly, one's state of mind. Before concluding the lesson Zhou proclaimed, "Having seen all this, the next time you're in pain, think a little, and go into your *qinggan* bank right away and move these things out. Your state of mind will immediately return to the feeling you now have."

Zhou Ting's life project—"molding character" by way of stimulating the seven sensory channels—is affect theory applied. Zhou worries that China's children have been decapacitated. In her Saturday night mothering class, she reads from a book titled *If I Could Have Three Days of Light,* a collection of Helen Keller's writings (2004). In Zhou's view, China's children have a lot in common with the young Helen Keller. Lack of life experience disables children just as Keller was disabled by blindness and deafness. Because sensory experience is basic to moral development, in Zhou's view, the young Helen Keller and experience-deprived children are not predisposed to relate to others. Keller's inability to connect with the world around her resulted in wild temper tantrums, not unlike the tantrums that China's only children supposedly throw. In the book Zhou reads with her mothering class, Keller describes one particular tantrum she threw. Feeling confused over the words *cup* and *water,* she threw a porcelain doll that Sullivan had given her on the ground, shattering it to pieces. At the time, she felt neither shame nor remorse. Keller wrote, "In my dark and silent world, there was no gentleness nor empathy" (21). On this passage Zhou commented that it was only natural for Keller to be unable to experience such emotions, as "*qinggan*s are built from the seven channels."[6]

Like affect theorists, Zhou understands affect/*qinggan* as a singular principle of continuity—one that enters into the world as difference. After Keller destroyed her new porcelain doll, Sullivan swept the pieces to the side and took her pupil outdoors. She led Keller to a well house to clarify what water was. Putting her hand under a cold running stream, Sullivan spelled out *water* in the palm of Keller's other hand. This moment was transformative for Keller, who realized that what Sullivan had been doing on her palm was not merely a game. She recalls, "A mysterious feeling surged in my heart. I suddenly understood the mystery of language-words, knew 'water' was the cool and novel thing that was streaming over my hand" (21). Water too was alive with energy, carrying the power to affect. Its qualities were folded in through the skin of Keller's hand, drawing out a response at the same time. Back in the house, everything the young Keller touched suddenly teemed with vitality. She writes, "I thought about the doll that I destroyed, felt my way over to the stove, picked up the pieces. I wanted to put them back together again, but no matter how I tried I couldn't. Thinking about what I had done, I felt tremendous regret over what had already been done. My eyes filled with tears for the first time in my life" (21).

In this story, Keller not only learned that things have names. Her experience of water—cool to the touch, novel and streaming—expanded her affective capacity to the extent that she could feel empathy for the first time. It was, you could say, her first experience of interconnectedness. From that point on, the young Keller was transformed into a child who "eagerly antici-pated the next day," knowing that another lesson awaited (21).

If only China's children could have such enthusiasm, Zhou thinks. They just need to be catalyzed, not treated like ducks to be stuffed and machines to be trained. For many reform advocates, China's education system rewards students who "study to death and study dead books." To speak in the lan-guage of affect theory, it is devoid of vitality. Something like *qinggan jiaoyu* on the other hand, circulates affective flows, so that even "dead books" might be brought to life. In her commentary on the story of the well house, Zhou characterized Keller's newfound passion in terms of a blockage. Like the water that flowed out of the fountain, Keller's passion for learning was now gushing forth so vigorously you could not stop her even if you tried (*du dou du bu zhu*).

The exercise by Kunming Lake addressed not only the participants' capac-ity for enduring hardship but also their attitude toward learning. For many of them, the trip to Beijing was their first time encountering the national monuments described in textbooks. I would add that it was also their first time encountering the affectivity of sites such as the Summer Palace and Kunming Lake, which have inspired, it seems, phrases like "twinkling pieces of jade" and "ripples on the surface of the water." Set phrases linked to spe-cific places are commonly used in language instruction. For example, school-children learn to memorize the phrase "burning hot" for Gobi desert sand and "a sea of trees" for the Manchurian forest. Such instruction serves to insert schoolchildren into a language community rooted in classical Chinese. In promotional tourism literature, set phrases such as "lofty and awe-inspir-ing," "grand and fantastic," and "splendid and imposing" are chosen to invoke a familiar standard of writing.[7]

While such phrases may be taken as clichés, they are in fact rooted in a much deeper cultural history of circulating affective flows. Perhaps this is the reason why Zhou Ting asserts that Chinese culture is "of the *qinggan*." Both affect theory and indigenous Chinese thought posit a dynamic universe com-posed of fluid and transformative forces, leading to myriad change and dif-ferentiation. The affective quality brimming in nature may be in captured in language, art, and architecture. When Zhou refers to such phrases as "those phrases" and states, "This is it, the image before your eyes," she simultane-ously points to their canonical status and to the affectivity of the surface of the lake—its intensity—in the shortness of her language. Unlike Western travel traditions that emphasize the journey, adventure, and spontaneous encounters with nature and its wilderness, the premodern Chinese tradition—which never conceived of any nature/culture binary—emphasized affinity within a ritually enclosed and ordered nature. Ritual enclosure is effected in language—in the use of canonical phrases in travel writing and in literary inscriptions on rocks, and also in the performance of canonical views.[8]

Zhou's instructions on how to take in a view ("take a broad view"), what to look at ("the little island and then at Seventeen-Arch Bridge"), and from what angle ("this angle"), encouraged her participants to plug into the virtual, namely to history, and ultimately to a larger language community that includes modern and premodern persons, and historically significant landscapes. If media technologies aid in the circulation of affective flows in the case of Wissinger's modeling industry, achieving human contact in the space of the virtual, then it is the technology of architecture, particularly garden design, that puts affect into circulation in this case. Unlike media technologies however, garden technology is quite old. The Summer Palace, an imperial garden, plugs schoolchildren (and other tourists) into a virtuality that spans time rather than space. The performance of a canonical view connects them to the Empress Dowager Ci Xi, to whom this garden once belonged. It connects them to late Ming literati, who gazed at landscapes in ritualized sets of eight, ten, or more views. The enclosing and ordering of nature in ritualized language and performance could be considered an indigenous technology for assembling the human person by way of nonhuman agencies.

Just as travel in the neo-Confucian tradition was linked to self-cultivation, travel in the post-Mao period also constitutes a kind of moral pedagogy. Both involve plugging the human person into a larger order.[9] For the twenty-first-century child, exposing oneself to the circulation of affects, best achieved in direct experiences beyond the study desk, is key to enabling a citizen-subject who might contribute to the strengthening of the nation by first becoming an affective subject. For Zhou, such a project might begin in encounters with nonhuman agencies, like the lake, which could treat hurt, hunger, thirst, and one's state of mind if viewed correctly, in the right weather conditions. If her participants could allow themselves to be affected, they might develop moral emotions. If they could develop moral emotions, they might be able to bear the hardship of their trip. If they could bear the hardship of the trip, they might be able to bear the burden of learning. If they could bear the burden of learning, China as a nation just might have some hope after all—a hope that, for Zhou, had dimmed with the news of Ma Jiajue's crime.

Anthropologists primarily study two things: (1) hardened structures and (2) irreducible particulars. We are attuned to the tension between the given and the contingent, searching for stable patterns while following the flow. More often than not, the ethnographic materials we work with have both dimensions—both the quality of structured givenness and the quality of stubborn uniqueness. The *"qinggan* banknote" is no exception. It belongs to the context of China's marketization and the quest for global strength, which has involved not only an intensification of subjectivity but also the deployment of an affective economy that puts indeterminacy into play in the production of value. If capitalism feeds off affect, then the use of the banknote metaphor is no coincidence. To conceive of performing a canonical view in terms of making banknote deposits allows for the instantaneous capture of Kunming Lake's affectivity, to be circulated later in time.

Simultaneously, the lakeside exercise was irreducibly unique. Zhou's novel and spontaneous invention of the *qinggan* banknote feeds off one of capitalism's greatest inventions. It is a poaching of the medium that helped establish equivalence between dissimilar things, thereby making total subsumption possible, for a situation marked with singular qualities: this teacher, this hot day, these children, those blisters, that bus ride back. Playing on the children's familiarity with monetary value, Zhou effectively led an exercise in producing another kind of value by encouraging an accumulation of affects that, one day, would amount to good habits such as caring for people and for things. You could call it a surplus value of life.[10]

Today, the metaphor is the banknote. Tomorrow it will be something different.

On a different occasion during this trip, Teacher Zhou circulated the affectivity of the Roman Coliseum to manage the problem of too many shoes everywhere in the tiny bungalow where the group stayed, an image she encountered virtually by way of media technology. Setting out plastic washbasins, she asked the participants to stack their shoes in a circular fashion with the toe-side pointing downward, modeling how affectivity could be deployed in the management of life's many challenges. This example demonstrates that well-roundedness is more than a discursive ideal: it concerns becoming. The more one allows oneself to be affected, the more one can affect and therefore transform, rather than struggle against, difficult situations.

Did the participants of this trip, in fact, experience the personal transformation their parents and Teacher Zhou had hoped for? Was their capacity for connecting to others developed? Did they ever withdraw from their bank of affects?

I left Beijing prematurely because of other fieldwork obligations I had back in Kunming. When I reunited with one of the participants for the first time after the group's return, Wang Yan's then eight-year-old daughter Wu Linlin said to me, "Teacher Kuan, after you left a lot of unbelievable things happened." "Like what?" I asked. Wu Linlin replied, "You would be very sad if I told you." Because I had heard from another participant that one of the younger boys had nearly fallen into a river on one occasion, I asked Wu Linlin if this was what she was thinking of. She said no and then reported that Teacher Zhou and one of her assistants had gotten into an argument. "Teacher Hu even cried!" she exclaimed.

The question of how parents and children responded to this trip is a complicated matter, situated in the unexpected challenges everyone faced, and in parents' unease about the marketization of education. Back in Kunming, I learned that many parents, who had so eagerly sent their child on this trip because they thought it would be a good exercise (*duanlian*), had negative opinions about Zhou Ting. Their reasons were many. Some felt that she should not have carried out adult arguments in front of children. Some expressed discontent over not having been able to get in touch by phone. Some felt that Zhou had charged too much money considering the accommodations they had in Beijing and that subjecting children to cold showers endangered their health. One parent did not take issue with the conditions of the trip, "Eating-bitter education [*chiku jiaoyu*] is good. But," she added, "don't take so much of our money." This parent felt that education ought to be "voluntary" (*yiwu*).

That Zhou charged too much money was the biggest sticking point for parents, many of whom thought that education should not mix with business interests. One evening, months after the trip, Hu Qiuli, the assistant with whom Zhou had had a falling out, talked my ear off for a whole hour. We were sitting in the living room of a good friend of hers, Mrs. Du, who had sent her chubby seven-year-old on the trip—a boy who was throwing up every day for the first few days, from getting carsick on the bus. Hu Qiuli wanted to convince me that Zhou did not have love in her heart, unlike Wang Lingling, another local expert, who supposedly took phone calls at any hour free of charge. That Zhou had purchased *mantou* (plain buns) rather than *miantiao* (noodles) in the morning was just one of many ways money was poorly spent. Hu felt that her suggestions for managing the trip had fallen on deaf ears. Maybe Mrs. Du's son would not have gotten sick had Zhou listened to her suggestions. Worst of all, Hu said, Zhou would check on her own son, who was also on the trip, the first thing every morning. The implication was that a teacher ought to be utterly fair.

Mrs. Du, meanwhile, kept chiming in, calling the bungalow they had stayed in a prison and Teacher Zhou a cheat.

The participants certainly had their complaints too. The public toilet was foul, they felt exhausted, the teenagers hated having to wear matching baseball caps for ease of identification, and though no one explicitly complained about this to me, I knew from their body language that Zhou's knack for verbal expression could really wear her students out. (A teenager who knew her from a different context characterized her as someone who had ten things to say for every one thing you wanted to say. "It's intolerable!")

Deng Siwen, who was eight years old at the time, had his own grudge against Teacher Zhou. "I most especially dislike her," he said at a lunch we had with his parents after the trip—which his mother translated as "He's really afraid of her." He added the complaint that "we ate out every day and never ate at home."

Deng Siwen became acutely homesick the morning of our visit to the Forbidden City. As the group waited for Teacher Zhou to return with the entrance tickets, Deng Siwen wandered right into a rushing flow of human traffic before one of the older boys picked him up by the handle of his backpack and threw him into a safer area, scolding him as he did so. This caused him to feel very upset, and, having witnessed the incident myself, I tried to console him as his tears began to well.

Teacher Zhou later lectured Deng Siwen about this incident, inviting him to reflect on what she saw as his wrongdoing by asking him a series of rhetorical questions. She wanted him to understand that what had happened to him was at least better than getting trampled. Perhaps this only added insult to injury, because after that Deng Siwen wanted to go home very badly. His complaint about eating out was inaccurate because many of our dinners were eaten back at the bungalow, cooked by two of the assistants with spices and sauces brought from Kunming. Obviously, the metaphor of food allowed Deng Siwen to express his discontent.

I also heard and observed contradictory things. Some parents were happy to report changes in their children, especially improved daily habits. Zhou had maintained a tight morning schedule so as to get twenty-five participants washed up and ready to go each day, which required everyone to be as efficient as they possibly could. A seven-year-old girl named Ye Kexin had a certain habit that changed by the end of the trip: she ate only a single grain of rice for every bite she took.

Some seemed to have integrated Zhou's favorite words, such as *heart-spirit* (*xinling*) and *celebrity* (*mingliu*), into their own personal vocabulary.[11] Meanwhile, Deng Siwen seemed to have integrated our visit to the China Science and Technology Museum into his repertoire of knowledge. He once tested me on my knowledge of China's four great inventions, in a gamelike fashion. He had spent a lot of time on the premodern science and technology floor the day we visited that museum, in the company of a couple of teenagers who were very kind and gentle with him.

Some parents reported that their child did not feel he or she had "suffered," as parents had worried, and that the child had found the trip a lot of fun (*hao wan*). Indeed, I had observed among the participants the kind of intense companionship that comes with living and traveling with peers. Self-directed play had been most obvious back at the bungalow at a day's end. The younger kids especially would go wild once Zhou left for an evening foot massage. When I commented on how lively everyone was one night, one of the teenagers tried to persuade me to stay with them despite their crammed living quarters. Why would I want to go back to a lonely hotel room when I could be having fun with them, she thought.

While opinions and responses were mixed, Zhou had something very important working in her favor that year: her two sons—one of her own (a preteen) and one from a marriage (a teenager). In a conversation I observed between a group of parents, one parent marveled at what great problem solvers they were. This young mother had participated in a local hiking trip Zhou had organized for families with small children. She described how Zhou's sons had swashbuckled their way through unpaved paths, pushed away fallen trees, and helped the kids make their way through the forest. When dusk fell, and many hikers were blistering from poisonous plants, parents had been grateful to have Zhou's two sons around as they made their way back through the semidarkness. This is important, for popular recognition of authority on matters of parenting heavily depends on that expert's personal success.

A Formula for Living

This ethnographic account of the human dramas surrounding the lakeside exercise pulls us into the mundane world of interpersonal conflict and pecuniary disagreements, a world far from the one invoked by Kunming Lake—the heavenly world of the former empress who had an expansive garden to take rest in. But it is precisely the mundaneness of skin blisters, nauseating bus rides, overcrowded living quarters, and adult arguments that made the lakeside exercise so significant. Whatever one's opinion about the purity of Zhou Ting's intentions, her invention of the "*qinggan* bank," and smaller lessons in how to put shoes away, were utterly sincere attempts in conveying the skills of artful disposition. Grander lessons concerned how to deploy the affectivity of the material environment for human ends—in this case, the contagious vitality of water, artfully captured by architectural design. Smaller practical lessons concerned how to best distribute human effort in the management of everyday tasks.

This was a lesson I learned rather uncomfortably the day I was given the task of washing cucumbers for the entire group, the one time I was given an actual task. Not only did I forget to do a soak before I washed them, so as to remove pesticides, but I was so slow that one of the assistants had to finish the wash for me. (His hand movements were very brisk.) Most embarrassing of all, Zhou spotted me carrying a full plastic bag of cucumbers just before our departure for the day's destination, struggling to double up on the bagging to support the weight. "One person should not have to bear this kind of burden," she said to me as she began to redistribute cucumbers into the lunch bags all the kids were already carrying themselves. I apologized for putting her in the situation of having to manage something as trivial as this.

The art of disposition can in fact involve something as simple as material rearrangement. But the logic behind this mundane technique is also the logic behind the metatheory for identifying the boundary between human and nonhuman agency and constraint in the midst of living a life. That we had to pack cucumbers was a response to the material constraint of hot summer weather and the possibility of dehydration, a response to forces with their own agency. That I could redistribute all the cucumbers was a mode of possible action I failed to discern in my morning daze, a failure that was not only technical but ethical as well. I was not fully present in the moment, which made a difference—though minute—to the people around me: one more thing for Zhou to manage.

Given all the irreducible particulars that surrounded the "banking in affects" exercise, reducing this invention to the order of biopolitics would be grossly inappropriate. Indeed there is a structured givenness to the *suzhi jiaoyu* movement, the larger context in which Zhou's efforts are situated, itself situated in the larger context of official development policies. But how various experts have responded to the perceived disjuncture between the demands of global competition and the education system's capacity for cultivating the right kind of human subject is as variable as the shapes and colors of a handful of pebbles. Zhou's emphasis on the sensing body and its attunement to environmental opportunities is quite different from Wang Lingling's pragmatism (chapter 6) and from the emphasis many other experts put on psychological interiority (chapters 2 and 3).[12] And the lakeside exercise was a contingent response to the unexpected challenges of the trip.

When we consider the interface between Zhou Ting herself and the participants, we have once again the tension between what is hardened and that which flows, unfolding at a different scale. In this context, it is the teacher's authority that constitutes the given, and the heterogeneity of all the participants' ages, temperament, habits, and quirks that constitutes the contingent. To what extent the lakeside exercise, and Zhou's lessons more generally, have "made an impact" is a difficult question to answer, considering the virtual nature of affect itself. Affect is indeterminate and ineffable. The multiple traces left on an individual body by the life of affect accumulate in a reserve of potential, a "pressing crowd of incipiencies and tendencies" (Massumi 2002: 30). The Chinese expression "imperceptible change" (*qianyi mohua*) articulates a similar idea. It is the principle behind the enduring practice of asking young children to memorize Tang dynasty poems: whether they understand them is irrelevant. Simply reciting the words is a process of bodily incorporation.

In this section, I have reported the effects I was able to directly observe, in action and in speech. But it is important to note that what I have collected are only fragments of a much larger crowd. Consciousness is subtractive, while experience is undifferentiated and indeterminate. What interlocutors reveal in our ethnographic engagements, what friends and family members reveal to one another in the course of living out lives together, is merely a fraction of a much greater number of potential revelations. Even literature, which can plumb the depths of human experience like no other form of representation, expresses "but a fraction of the crowded consciousness" of the moral agent (Nussbaum 1990: 185).

Perhaps I am too hopeful that the lakeside exercise meant as much to the children as it meant to me. But it is a hope I share with Zhou Ting, who expresses a vision of the world that is worth learning from: the condition of affectivity and human ethics are mutually implicated. Human actors are enmeshed within relational webs made of various ideas, people, and things. Through the art of disposition, it is possible to manipulate reality not by changing a given condition itself but by deploying the energy contained within a dynamic relationship and by partnering with the fluctuations of reality. In the case of the lakeside exercise, it was a sudden fluctuation in weather that was deployed. The lesson intended to demonstrate how the world teems with contagious vitality, thereby presenting multiple opportunities for stimulation and education. One need only be exposed to a given environment and encounter it with sensitivity, and change will follow as a matter of course. Although humans have limited control of their external circumstances, the moral agent in pursuit of self-cultivation may sometimes make choices about what to be exposed to.

Conclusion

WHEN I THINK ABOUT MY OWN CHILDHOOD, growing up in a laid-back, multiethnic suburb on the edge of Los Angeles County, I remember the roly-polys. I loved watching them curl, and I would collect them in the used Danish butter cookie tins my mom used to buy. I think about how my brother and I would collect every pencil and pen in the house to create imaginary streets and highways for racing our Hot Wheels cars around. I remember our biggest accomplishment being a fully assembled motorized Lego racecar, and I remember how my best friend and I assembled homemade pizzas for a backyard picnic once, only to have them eaten by my dog. I remember how much I worshipped my older teenage sister, and how I would sit in her room when she had friends over, watching their conversation as one would watch a tennis match—the head did not tire of the back and forth. I remember the feeling of summer and the overwhelming sadness nightfall would give me, when all of us "neighborhood kids" would have to climb off our bike seats and each other's handlebars to return home for dinner. Knowing that there is always tomorrow is no consolation when the fun has to end. You are sad all the same.

Although I went to various dance classes at the neighborhood parks, took piano lessons with Mrs. Taylor just a few blocks away, and had negligible amounts of homework to complete on a daily basis, my childhood was relatively carefree. In a different time or a different place, things would have been different, as the anxious government of childhood has become the norm in certain corners of the world. Born around the 1950s and 1960s, middle-class parents in both Annette Lareau's study and the CELF study remember their own childhoods as being less busy and less structured.[1] Meanwhile, other research has shown a dramatic increase, between the 1980s and 1990s, in the amount of homework students were doing.[2] Needless to say, the Kunming parents I came to know had had radically different childhoods from those of their own children. They had been born between the late 1960s and early 1970s, when educational achievement and the accumulation of cultural capital had not yet come to define the purpose of life, as China was in the final years of its socialist experiment. Their own parents had too many children and too many other concerns to be fretting over whether they were being "good parents."

In this book, I have focused on the ethical and existential consequences of a major political project for ordinary parents raising school-age children—the project of modernizing China by "modernizing" subjectivity. In this context, middle-class parents, especially mothers, have been put in the position of having to reconcile the contradictions of this national project, as stewards of a generation carrying the hope of national revitalization. Indeed, the life problems of the people I came to know pale in comparison to the suffering of migrant workers, villagers living with industrial pollution, the displaced, the marginal, and the unemployed. But contemporary problems come in many forms. The popular saying "You don't want to lose at the starting line" points to a problematic sorting system that appears to reward the few while eliminating the rest. The parents I came to know lived with the hope that the hyperpursuit of education would confer life security over the long term. But they also lived with a nagging sense that academic success was subject to many contingencies, forces beyond any individual's personal control.[3]

Is it a coincidence that my study found parents feeling confusion and ambivalence over the right amount of intensity, while the CELF study found a family sending their fifth-grade son to an SAT review course, even while recognizing that "it's kind of sick" (Kremer-Sadlik and Gutiérrez 2013: 139)? Why are clocks and calendars so central to middle-class family life (Graesch 2013: 41)? Why is it that parents in Hong Kong, my new (old) home, will line up a few days before an admissions talk to increase a child's chances for admission into a coveted primary school?[4] Why do some parents in mainland China propitiate at local temples around the time of the college entrance exam, taking time off work to orbit around a test taker? Why would a younger parent like Chen Jialing press her daughter to learn the violin when Precious was already exhibiting school-related anxiety as early as the first grade, waking up in the middle of the night to check that her backpack was packed for the next day?

Citing a nationwide survey conducted in 1990, at the end of Japan's growth period, Norma Field (1995) argued that the rising incidence of adult diseases such as stress-related baldness and high blood pressure indicates that Japanese children suffer from "soft violence." Of course, children living in developed countries are privileged to have access to formal schooling and freedom from the terrors of war, disease, and malnutrition. And of course middle-class children in both developing and developed countries have better life chances than their age counterparts in the countryside and inner city. But the normalized suffering of children in peace and material comfort is, Field insists, "a different display of capitalist contradictions." Japanese children have been harnessed to "the logic of acceleration and expansion," enslaved to an "overdetermined future" the moment they are born (70).

Chinese childhoods at the turn of the twenty-first century are geared not so much to the production of a homogeneous, disciplined workforce, as was the case in prerecessionary Japan, as to a regime of human capital accumulation and intense competition. Here too, we find an organization of human energy by the logic of acceleration, and also efficiency, calculability, and productivity. It is the logic behind the kind of exhortation a parent might shout over the most mundane of tasks—"Hurry up!" "*Dongzuo kuaidian!*"—for the use of time and effort should be directed toward optimum outcomes, constantly. In a world where everyone and everything is in competition, students against students, teachers against teachers, applicants against applicants, schools against schools, and countries against countries, there is no room for slack. Of course, the parents I came to know *wanted* to do what the experts recommend—to be more humane and to attend to a child's psychological needs. But they saw a threat to promoting their child's subjectivity, namely self-esteem and self-confidence, not so much in their own bad parental behavior as in the market economy their child would have to face one day.

In this book, I have tried to challenge the image of middle-class mothers as being excessively ambitious for their children, obsessed with perfection and the social status that a good education will bring. I have tried to bring the ethical dimension of "mindless" middle-class life to light, though some may see this ethnography as having little anthropological value.[5] I have tried to go beyond the tired dichotomies of power versus agency, reproduction versus resistance, by focusing on moral experience and by locating the art of disposition in everyday life. I began with the obvious premise that all human activity is enmeshed within relational webs, while recognizing that all actors participate in vital chains of causality, generating worldly differences—large or small—by virtue of activity itself.

This approach to interpreting something as mundane and banal as middle-class child rearing has, I hope, revealed how wisdom can be found in the most surprising of places. The art of disposition offers an alternative metatheory about the nature of reality and human purpose—one that avoids the mistake of erring too far on the side of determinism or too far on the side of human mastery and control. The capacity for discernment and disposition is an ethical and philosophical problem that, to borrow from Gregory Bateson, "concerns only the widest universe and the deepest psychological levels" (2000: 336). Is it a coincidence that the *tiaojian* discourse of middle-class mothers resonates with the famous "Serenity Prayer" associated with Alcoholics Anonymous? "God grant us the serenity to accept the things we cannot change, courage to change the things we can, and wisdom to know the difference."[6] Bateson found in the theology of Alcoholics Anonymous an ethos of humility and submission—and an alternative to the "strange dualistic epistemology characteristic of Occidental civilization" (2000: 321). There are powers greater than the "self."

To recognize antihumanist realities does not require giving up humanist aspirations. Wisdom is required for judging the difference between what can and cannot be controlled. If and when the skill of discernment is well cultivated, it can provide some much-needed serenity amid the many troubles of contemporary life—a serenity that is by no means defined only by passivity and acceptance. Knowing the difference between what is and what is not within one's sphere of influence, cultivating sensitivity, and having a sense of timing give rise to responsiveness and courage—the courage to do what can and must be done.

NOTES

INTRODUCTION

1. The doctor was probably referring to "systemic family therapy," which is a specific school of family therapy rather than a description of the therapy itself.

2. See also Kleinman et al. (2011) and J. Yang (2012, 2014).

3. Interestingly, the policy document "Some Recommendations for Strengthening Psychological Health Education in Primary and Middle School" warns against medicalizing, and moralizing, the issue of psychological health: "[We] must not simply sum up students' psychological issues as moral issues. [We] must guard against the trend of the medicalization [*yixue hua*] of psychological health education and keep psychological health education from becoming an academic discipline [*xueke hua*]" (Ministry of Education 1999, VI.2).

4. There are many resonating themes between Chinese discourses of the psychological child and the psychological "soft individualism" Kusserow found in upper-middle-class families in New York (2004).

5. For a look at how the discourse of freedom has appeared in other domains, see Hoffman (2006, 2010).

6. My understanding of "actor" is informed by neo-Aristotelian philosophy (Arendt [1958] 1998; Mattingly 2010, 2012, 2014; Nussbaum 1990, [1986] 2001; Williams 1981), actor-network-theory (ANT) (Bray 2013; Laidlaw 2010; Latour 2005), and Gregory Bateson's cybernetic theory of self ([1972] 2000). Following Bateson especially, I understand the actor to potentially be a composite of many subsystems. A single actor, meanwhile, may be a mere constituent of other larger systems. For example, my ability to write this sentence relates to my digestive system, which has allowed me to transform food energy from breakfast this morning into words on a page. These words will go on to act in other systems unrelated to digestion. How an actor is defined, where one actor ends and another begins, depends on focus. In anthropology, we tend to talk about human actors. Following ANT, an actor may be considered as nothing more than one node within larger networks of activity.

7. My understanding of affectivity is informed by the resonance I have found between the recent "affective turn" in social theory, to be discussed in chapter 7, and Chinese thought—namely Daoist philosophy. In affect theory, *affect* generally refers to the "power to affect and the capacity to be affected." A similar idea is rendered as "influence" in Chinese thinking, a translation that captures attunement to flow. For my own purposes, both *affect* and *influence* are useful terms. While *affect* invokes causality—that is, cause and effect—*influence* invokes a breathlike vitality.

8. See the collection *Privatizing China* for a picture of how the "powers of the self" have been unleashed within the context of state regulation (Ong and Zhang 2008).

9. In her research with elite university students in Beijing, Susanne Bregnbæk also found major contradictions in the *suzhi jiaoyu* project. University students struggle to balance the coexisting social imperatives of self-sacrifice and self-actualization, thereby living in an existential double-bind (2010, 2011).

10. See Foucault ([1976] 1990: 105, 141); Greenhalgh (2011); Greenhalgh and Winckler (2005).

11. To be fair, Allison gives some nuance to her interpretation by suggesting that there are opportunities for creative play in preparing *obentō,* but her argument ultimately favors the work of ideology.

12. The voice of Althusser is still around, however, as demonstrated by Harriet Evans finding a "hailing" of female subjectivity in post-Mao discourses celebrating the emotional capacities of women (2012: 134). This is true also of anthropology more generally, as when the introduction to the volume *The Global Middle Classes* notes an "increasingly common subject/citizenry [the middle class] hailed by political and corporate leaders" (Heiman, Liechty, and Freeman 2012: 7).

13. Another version of this picture goes something like this: Chinese parents, locked in a Confucianist mind-set, find comfort in the authority that comes with being a parent and, in accordance with the Confucianist logic of hierarchy, impose their artificial wishes on children.

14. See also Anagnost (2008) for an interpretation of child rearing in economic terms. Anagnost notes that the management of childhood "entails an obsessive commodity fetishism" (63), while a recognition of "real psychological pain" is brief (71).

15. For an early example from the nineteenth century, see Edward Tylor's classic essay "The Science of Culture" ([1873] 2010: 30–31). For a discussion of this worry in the contemporary literature, see Sherry Ortner's *Anthropology and Social Theory* (2006), especially 127 and 131.

16. Expectations exist for both men and women, but women especially "must sparkle and shine" (Wikan 1990: 24).

17. See Robbins (2012).

18. Interestingly, contributions to the study of ordinary ethics by China anthropologists have focused on judgment (Stafford 2013). For example, Ellen Oxfeld's (2010) research shows how judgments about other people's capacity to remember their social debts pervade the life of one agricultural community in Guangdong Province.

19. Once, in between asking me about what Disneyland had to offer, Precious asked me a slew of questions about my own childhood and what primary school was

like: How much homework did you have? When were you dismissed? When did you have to be at school by? What about high school? Were your teachers strict? Did they scold you? Are American teachers more strict or are Chinese teachers more strict? Do you think America is more fun or is China more fun? Did you like school? She interviewed me better than I could interview her.

20. This discussion is based on research published in Kipnis and Li (2010) and Kipnis (2011: 64).

21. I thank Yunxiang Yan for alerting me to these sayings.

22. For example, those rebelling against an authoritarian state at the height of its power will only be "broken by it," while those who can wait until the "impractical" falls apart "of its own accord" can profit tremendously (quoted in Jullien [1992] 1995: 200).

23. What Saba Mahmood describes, the daily practices to which a group of pious Egyptian women subject themselves, could also be understood as enacting a kind of participatory agency (2005).

24. To give an illustration: one informant related an incident concerning her husband's father, who had been visiting from out of town. He secretly gave her twelve-year-old son 500 RMB. She happened to catch her son putting a bundle of cash away, so she persuaded him to return the money. Her son obeyed, but his grandfather refused to take it, putting her in an awkward position of having to refuse a gift. She had to explain to her father-in-law about the kind of "opportunities" (*jihui*) this bundle of money implied, having in mind the "disorderly" (*fuza*) environment surrounding her son's school. But the two were not able to see eye to eye. She worried about whether she was being too direct and lacking in human feeling (*renqing*) but then decided that she had to persist in reasoning with him. When she related this incident to me, she was uncertain as to whether he would eventually understand.

25. Cf. Arendt ([1958] 1998: 8).

I. THE POLITICS OF CHILDHOOD

1. Huang's books belong to a broader genre of books about life abroad. See Woronov (2007) for an in-depth analysis of Huang's books.

2. Chinese intellectuals took great interest in eugenics beginning in the late nineteenth century. See Sakamoto (2004) and Dikötter (1998).

3. See Milwertz (1997: 131); Dikötter (1998: 128, 132–33).

4. My copy of *Harvard Girl* was printed October 2004. It was the sixty-fourth printing, putting the book's circulation number at 1,770,000 copies. According to the *China Book Business Report*, *Harvard Girl* was a top-ten national best seller in 2000 and 2001. See "The Hottest Best-Sellers of a Ten-Year Period," *China Book Business Report*, January 21, 2005, www.cbbr.com.cn/info_893_1.htm.

5. Greenhalgh and Winckler (2005) and Greenhalgh (2011) give excellent discussions of governmental shifts.

6. See especially Woronov (2003: 5–57) and Yan (2003).

7. Many China scholars have analyzed *suzhi* discourse. See D. Davies (2007), Friedman (2004), Hsu (2007), Kipnis (2006, 2007), Murphy (2004), W. Sun (2012), Yan (2003), and L. Zhang (2001).

8. One could argue that this is all empty political jargon. But if slogan making has been found to have "social and political effects that matter" (Greenhalgh 2011: 90), then these verbs play an important role in orienting and endorsing a set of reform measures. The notion of "steely quality" is borrowed from Latour (2005).

9. "Xu Guanhua: The Government Cannot Make a Steve Jobs," *Xinjing Bao*, March 7, 2012, http://scitech.people.com.cn/GB/17312132.html.

10. The preschool training class is the third in a series of required training. The first is required for a marriage certificate (*hunyin zheng*), the second for a certificate to give birth (*shengyu zheng*).

11. The "1990s Outline" was written in response to a United Nations charter on the rights of children. The issues addressed are broad and include reproductive health, maternal and child health, food and water safety, and the elimination of illiteracy. The issue of disseminating family education knowledge does not come up until later in the document.

12. Anne Behnke Kinney reminds us, "Although the Han preserved much of the apparatus of the Legalist Qin state, Confucian thinkers believed that moral education would serve as a more effective deterrent to crime than the strict laws and punishments of the Qin regime" (2004: 16). In this context of changing political reason, educational institutions were established throughout the empire, and canonical texts were identified and officially endorsed (14). Importantly, one of these texts, the Book of Rites, would continue to serve as an authoritative source for educational theory and practice for the next two thousand years (Bai 2005: 16). It discusses the different stages of childhood and what adults can expect or begin to teach.

At this time pre-Han ideas concerning "fetal education" were also further developed, relating the notion of embryonic development to dynastic fate, and the education of children to the practical need for staffing an expanding bureaucracy. Liu Xiang's "Traditions of Matronly Deportment," a chapter in his *Traditions of Exemplary Women*, broke with earlier ideas concerning the moral instruction of young children in pushing back the age for education and in granting mothers an important role: their responsibility for a child's moral development began in utero. In "a concern for auspicious beginnings and ritual correctness," a mother was supposed to not only be careful about what she saw, ate, heard, and said but also govern her own deportment (Kinney 2004: 21). After a child was born, a mother was to continue vigilant watch over a child's environment up to the adolescent period, as part of a program claimed to be "uniformly efficacious" (25).

13. I thank Andrew Kipnis for pointing this out to me.

14. Kipnis describes the effort to make vocational education appealing to families, who nonetheless continue to see it as a last resort (2011).

15. Howard Gardner is a prolific author based at the Harvard Graduate School of Education. His theory was first elaborated in a 1983 book *Frames of Mind: The Theory of Multiple Intelligences*.

16. The notion of well-rounded development goes back to the late nineteenth century and to the influence of Herbert Spencer on Chinese intellectuals. The definition of well-rounded development in relation to moral, intellectual, and physical development persisted in educational policies through the Maoist era up to the present (Woronov 2003:52–54). Other components are sometimes added to this tripartite formulation, such as aesthetic development, added by Cai Yuanpei, and psychological *suzhi,* added in the post-Mao era. But most importantly, the contemporary *suzhi jiaoyu* fever harks back to a rather old saying: "joys of the literati"— music, chess, calligraphy, and painting (*qin qi shu hua*).

17. These figures refer to the mid-2000s.

18. Disparities between schools in China are rooted in the "key school" policy, which channels state support to designated "key-point" schools according to broader state plans (D. Yang 2006).

19. These statistics come from a report written by Bai (2006: 128–29).

20. A hundred-plus universities are officially designated as "211" institutions, which means they have been selected for government support as part of the 211 Project for strengthening research universities. Yunnan University is a 211 university. The approximately forty "985" universities are even more elite, earmarked for government support with the goal of becoming "world class." Job applicants are stratified according to the status of the university from which they have graduated (Chan 2012).

21. For more discussion of these various factors, see Bai (2006); Chan (2012); Ding ([2003] 2005); Fong (2004, 2011); X. Wang and Liu (2011). See also Ted Plafker, "As China Churns Out Graduates, Job Prospects Are Dicey," *New York Times,* February 17, 2004.

22. Quoted by Lillian Lin, "China's Graduates Face Glut," *Wall Street Journal,* August 22, 2012.

23. This is precisely why cultural capital works the way it does. Small things make a big difference in the long run. Or, to put it another way, the seemingly insignificant things that happen in childhood install "durable dispositions" that produce and reinforce class distinctions. For Bourdieu, the process takes place completely outside the awareness of the bourgeoisie, creating a kinship between the sociology of taste and psychoanalysis: both study "denial" (1984: 11). But Bourdieu's analysis has its limits where contemporary Chinese society is concerned. My informants were hardly unaware social actors. It was as if their child-rearing strategies assumed a theory of class formation.

2. THE HORRIFIC AND THE EXEMPLARY

1. The presentation of models is found in official histories, in the biographical tradition, in popular sayings, and—in socialist China—in mass celebrations and state-bestowed honorific titles given to individuals, households, and cities (Anagnost 1997b; Bakken 2000; Furth 2007; Kipnis 2011; J. Li 2001; Munro 1977). It aims

to promote good conduct, even when no one is looking, through inspiration rather than the imposition of law from above (Munro 1977: 137).

2. Discussant comments that Cheryl Mattingly gave at the 2004 AAA meeting helped me to see the theoretical significance of horror stories.

3. This reading is informed by Goodman (2005).

4. This differs from the Shōnen A case that Arai (2000) describes in "The 'Wild Child' of 1990s Japan," and from media coverage of school shootings in the United States, where a child's hidden disturbances are revealed.

5. Less school did not mean less learning. There was to be a qualitative reorientation of what constituted learning. For the quantitative and qualitative aspects of the *jianfu* movement, see Woronov (2003: 111, 144).

6. This observation is inspired by Ann Anagnost's reading of a story, published in the newspaper *Peasant Gazette,* that tells of one horoscope peddler's surprising win of a "law-abiding household" plaque. The horoscope peddler traverses an opposition between spontaneity and socialist propriety in a series of events that led up to his winning of the plaque. Anagnost identifies this as a classic structuring device in socialist realism, one that opposes political consciousness to the prepolitical body that easily falls prey to pleasures outside the domain of political rationality (1997b: 104–5).

7. See Anagnost (1997b: 29).

8. See Hung and Chiu (2003).

9. See D. Davies (2007); Anagnost (2004).

10. This phrase comes from Anagnost (2004: 195). Such "fables" also partake in a celebration of the individual in their biographical or autobiographical modes, a related genre that, like success literature, emerged only in the post-Mao era. See Farquhar (1996, 2002).

11. On Deng Pufang, see Kohrman (2005).

12. As an adjective, *xing* means "capable" or "competent." As a verb, *xing* can indicate "to walk" or "to go." But the term has a much broader meaning for Zhou Hong.

13. This interpretation borrows from Nussbaum ([2001] 2006: 240–46).

14. Unlike most Chinese city dwellers, who live in apartments, Mrs. Lan and her family lived in a nice villa.

3. "THE HEART SAYS ONE THING BUT THE HAND DOES ANOTHER"

1. This approach to analyzing subjectivity is inspired by Biehl, Good, and Kleinman (2007).

2. Harriet Evans observes that there is now a wider diversity of topics, as the "representational terrain" has expanded (1995: 389). Lisa Rofel, meanwhile, notes something she calls the "allegory of postsocialist modernity." According to this allegory, the Maoist regime repressed natural difference in promoting gender equal-

ity and androgyny, suggesting a stronger break in history than has been the case (1999: 217–56; 2007: 65–83).

3. See Croll (1978: 247); Davin (1976); Evans (2008: 107); Manning (2006: 577).

4. See Susan Glosser's discussion of New Culture intellectual Liao Shuan's vision for the companionate marriage, and also of entrepreneur You Huaigao's vision for how labor ought to be divided within the *xiao jiating* (2003: 44–46, 159–65). In the interest of space, I limit my discussion to the PRC.

5. It is not unique to China, though Chinese gender inequality can be traced to certain sources. For example, the devoted mother is a common figure in cultural texts, most common in tales of famous men (Stafford 1995: 71–78). These are mothers who attend to every minor detail and do whatever it takes to set a child on the right path. Hu Shi's laudatory description of waking up to his mother licking his eyeballs on one occasion, in the belief that his eye infection could be licked away, is especially striking (76). In Shandong, sixth-grade students memorize the Tang dynasty poem "Youzi Yin," which tells of "an old mother sewing clothes for her son by candlelight so that he can spend all of his time studying and become an official in a faraway place" (Kipnis 2011: 145).

6. Fathers in the CELF study got to have more "me" time in comparison to CELF mothers (Graesch 2013). Moreover, percentages for time spent with children in the three categories of leisure, communication, and child care were inversely proportional. While mothers spent more time engaged in nonleisure activities with children, it was the opposite for fathers. Graesch notes, however, that this finding reflects averages. There was actually a high degree of variability between families (38).

7. In a Toraja community Douglas Hollan lived in, anger is thought to be disruptive to human relationships and to relationships between humans and the supernatural world. They have a number of informal strategies for "cooling" their anger, thereby creating the public appearance of a "warm, friendly, and hospitable" community (Hollan 1988: 56). The Utku have strong sanctions against anger and volatility, so antithetical to their central value of care (Briggs 1970). They practice emotional control by releasing tension with joking and laughter, blending criticism with warmth and cheer, and they dispel the anger of others with expressions of care. Urapmin Christians place great value on peaceful hearts and good thinking. They work with anger in confession and anger-removal rituals, or they avoid situations that predispose a person to willfulness, which is associated with anger. While anger is problematic for all members of the community in the first two cases (Hollan 1998: 69 n. 16; Briggs 1970: 333), with exceptions extended to children in the case of the Utku, in the Urapmin case big men must exercise anger to accomplish things, thereby taking moral risks on behalf of their followers (Robbins 2005: 199–200). For further examples of cultural directives for emotional control, see Wikan's discussion on the expectation that women be cheerful and "bright" (1990), and Throop's discussion of the value of selective expression in Yapese morality (2010: 102–5, 138–41). Interestingly, Augusten Burroughs, in his 2002 memoir *Running with Scissors*, describes how his mother's therapist encouraged him to express anger

as often as possible. Although expressivity is quite the opposite of control, rules are just as active in cultures that value expression.

8. In China there is a long history of textual constructions of maternal responsibility for emotional regulation, but this responsibility concerned pregnant and nursing women specifically. Fetal education required mothers to monitor what they were affected by. Han dynasty thinker Liu Xiang claimed that "if a woman was affected [*gan*] by good things, her child would be good, and if by bad things, the child would be bad" (quoted in Kinney 2004: 21). Ming-Qing doctors expressed concerns not so much over the moral development of the fetus as over infant diseases. Charlotte Furth tells us, "To be moved by emotions, especially passion or anger, to give way to lust, or to indulge in rich food or drink was to risk pathological fire within, endangering the child's health and well-being in utero and making it susceptible to disease in infancy" (1995: 171). Responsibility for emotional regulation continued after the birth of a child, as a mother's emotional state was believed to influence the quality of breast milk. A Ming dynasty medical text titled *Precious Guide for Saving the Young* lists ten kinds of illness causing breast milk problems, of which four are related to a mother's emotional state: exhilarated milk, angry milk, exasperated milk, and licentious milk (Hsiung 2005: 81–82).

9. Yao (2002a: 265–68). See also Brown (1987), Keenan (1977), and Yao (2002b).

10. The Working Committee for Caring about the Next Generation is a state initiative that specifically focuses on developing research and organizing activities that promote "healthy development"(*jiankang chengzhang*) in youth. Drug and Internet addiction and a general "pollution" of society constitute some of the challenges this initiative aims to address.

11. According to Tang dynasty *nüxue,* the Confucian woman had the same capacity for exemplary virtue as a man through bodily education and emotional mastery in the inner realm. See Woo (2002, 2009).

12. Cf. Kipnis (2006, 2007).

13. One example of cultural media would be classical poetry. Gloria Davies's discussion of how Qu Yuan and his poem "Encountering Sorrow" have inspired twentieth-century thought is illuminating. She points out that while intellectuals have rejected Confucian society, "the Confucian *program* of self-cultivation and constant self-inspection has thrived" (2008). In her study on *qing,* Haiyan Lee (2007) shows how discourses on virtuous emotions have formed around different concerns in the twentieth century, discourses that drew upon preexisting "languages" in new ways.

14. Chodorow (1999); Levy (1984); Lutz (1988); M. Rosaldo (1984); Shweder (2003).

15. Naftali interprets the ambivalence of her Shanghai informants in terms of mothers' desire to "associate themselves with a global, 'middle-class' modernity," and "deep-seated notions of the correct way of handling children" (2009: 100–101).

16. The term *shorthand* is borrowed from Burke ([1935] 1954: 221).

17. Fong argues that the cultural models behind these values get lost in "transmission" and attributes the tension between parents and teenagers to a "mismatch

between parents' and children's cultural models" (2007: 115), differing strategies for reconciling conflicting models, and an "illusion of wholeness" that "prevented parents from emphasizing the context sensitive quality of valued practices" (113). According to Fong, the cultural models parents hold in mind are complex and context-sensitive, but parents speak of values in simple and seemingly inflexible terms. She writes, "The parents I knew in Dalian talked as if they always lived by the same set of values, even though they actually followed different, often contradictory principles in different contexts. Parents' tendency to claim wholeness and integration despite the contradictions and fragmentation in their child socialization practices resulted in inconsistencies that children found frustrating" (112).

18. Chinese translations of the *Chicken Soup for the Soul* book series use *xinling* as a translation for "soul."

19. These metaphors resonate with a key metaphor Kusserow (2004) discovered in her work with upper-middle-class families in Manhattan. Child rearing among these families was guided by an image of the child as delicate flower. Parents believed that by providing an encouraging environment, a child's "true self" would unfold and blossom.

20. *Yaohao* literally means "to throw dice, to gamble."

21. Liu Chao, "Fen bugou, ju shuoqing: Jiazhang kutan zexiao fei, xiaozhang wunai guan shouji" [Not enough points, pleas are refused: Parents bitterly sigh over school-selecting fees, principals have no choice but to turn off their mobiles], *Chuncheng Wanbao* [Spring City Evening News], July 27, 2010, A09.

22. The phrase *virtual knowing* comes from William James (quoted in Massumi 2002: 296 n. 29).

4. CREATING *TIAOJIAN*, OR, THE ART OF DISPOSITION

1. *Jieceng* can be differentiated into "salary/wage-based stratum" (*gongxin jieceng*), "middle-propertied stratum" (*zhongchan jieceng*), "elite stratum" (*jingyin jieceng*), and so on. (See L. Zhang [2010] for more discussion on *jieceng* versus *jiejie*.)

2. "Help Children Overcome Their Sick-of-Learning Mind-Sets," *Family Education Digest*, March 6, 2004.

3. In her study of primers for children, Limin Bai observes the use of this story in a Tang dynasty village school primer *Mengqiu* (2005: 29–30).

4. See Bai (2005: 11–15) for a rich discussion.

5. In *Moral Luck* (1981), Williams distinguishes between two kinds of regret. Regret in general involves the thought "How much better if it had been otherwise" with regard to a state of affairs. General regret can be felt by anyone who knows about a particular state of affairs (1981: 28). The second kind of regret Williams calls agent-regret, "which a person can feel only towards his own past actions (or, at most, actions in which he regards himself as a participant)" (28). So, general regret and agent-regret differ in that the latter is experienced from a first-person perspective, containing psychological content not found in general regret.

6. Known in Chinese as *bamaodui:* gangs that bully for money.

7. Linda was saddened that her homeroom teacher, the teacher who had threatened her with expulsion, did not care to ask about her well-being when she returned to school after some time away. While her other teachers wanted to know why she had been gone and if she was okay, her homeroom teacher spoke to her only about practical matters such as whether she had handed in a required fee for something.

8. Subjunctivity is a defining feature of narrative. "The historian speaks of what has happened, the poet of the kind of thing that *can* happen" (Aristotle 1970: 32–33). Good stories subjunctivize reality, "trafficking in human possibilities rather than in settled certainties" (Bruner 1986: 26). They succeed by "exploring the indeterminacy of reality and stimulating such exploration in the reader" (Good 1994: 153). For in the act of reading, readers must continually revise their expectations as they wander through a text (Iser 1978). And as in reading, so in life (Mattingly 1998a, 2006). This is because the relationship between narrative and life-as-lived is not as discontinuous as some might argue. Surely life is not tidy like a story, David Carr argues, and "things do not always work out as planned, but this only adds an element of the same contingency and suspense to life that we find in stories" (1997: 13).

9. The problem of overproduction is a consequence of the 1999 decision to expand higher education, which had the shortsighted goal of stimulating domestic consumption in the absence of long-term planning. Many observers have noted the structural mismatch between the expansion of higher education and manpower needs (Bai 2006; Chan 2012; Di [1999] 2000; X. Wang and Liu 2011). See also Lillian Lin, "China's Graduates Face Glut," *Wall Street Journal,* August 22, 2012.

10. Arendt ([1958] 1998); Jackson (1989, 1996, 1998); Massumi (2002); Mattingly (2014); Soper (1986).

11. I borrow this phrasing from Jullien ([1992] 1995: 204).

12. Quoted in Rappaport (1999: 109).

5. THE DEFEAT OF MATERNAL LOGIC IN TELEVISUAL SPACE

1. Gao Xuan and Ren Baoru, "Exclusive News: Screenwriting Diary 1—The Origin of *Youth,*" Sohu Entertainment, April 12, 2009, http://yule.sohu.com/20090412/n263339408.shtml. "Idol dramas" are essentially soap operas. What makes them different from American soaps is the cast, which always consists of pop stars who have enormous followings of obsessed fans. They are famous not because of their talent but because of their good looks. "Idol dramas" are an East Asian phenomenon, much as Bollywood is an Indian phenomenon.

2. The men in this fictional family are either dead or feckless. *Who Shall Decide My Youth?* is a female-centered story where men are evaluated in terms of whether or not they can provide material security and comfort. The male characters do not have much of a story apart from the usefulness they are able to demonstrate to their girlfriends and their families. But it would be difficult to fully assess the gender

implications of this show without seeing the first and the last drama in Zhao Baogang's trilogy. Therefore, I make only this brief mention of gender.

3. The comments and posts I collected came from all over the country, though usually from a capital city or a prefecture-level city. According to a survey conducted in 2004 by China Internet Network Information Center, "The majority of Chinese internet users are young people. Among all the users, 54.1% are under 24 and 70% are under 30 years old" (Bu Wei 2006: 215). Meanwhile, Bu Wei's study—conducted in the cities of Beijing, Shanghai, Guangzhou, Chengdu, Changsha, Xining, and Huhehot—showed that Internet use among youth was generally highest in the most developed cities. But it was Changsha, a midrange city, that had the highest percentage of all. Guangzhou came in second (219).

4. See Ang (2004); Hu (2008); Lukács (2010).

5. Posted May 8, 2009, on *Sohu*.

6. Hou Jiang, "Beijing Evening News: Who Says You Get to Be Someone Else's Master?" posted on *Sina*, April 30, 2009, http://ent.sina.com.cn/r/m/2009–04–30/21252499336.shtml.

7. Posted April 22, 2009, on *Sohu*.

8. Posted May 12, 2009, on *NetEase* by a netizen from Hechi City, Guangxi Province.

9. Posted May 4, 2009, on *Sohu* by a netizen from Lanzhou City, Gansu Province.

10. Posted April 17, 2009, on *Sohu* by a netizen from Shijiazhuang City, Hebei Province.

11. Posted April 10, 2009, on *Sina*, http://video.sina.com.cn/ent/v/m/2009–04–10/012538934.shtml.

12. Episode 4.

13. The valorization of intergenerational communication is a post-Mao era phenomenon, and it is gendered (Evans 2008).

14. "Counts as an Album for Our Youth, Counts as a Family Manual for Parents," posted May 27, 2009, on *Sina*, http://blog.sina.com.cn/s/blog_53303d780100cl65.html.

15. Posted April 25, 2009, on *NetEase* by a netizen from Shunde district, Foshan City, Guangdong Province, http://comment.ent.163.com/ent_bbs/57LCSDA500031H2L.html, 1.

16. Posted on April 25, 2009,on *NetEase* by a netizen from Liuzhou City, Guangxi Province; posted on April 26, 2009, on *NetEase* by a netizen from Shenyang City, Liaoning Province.

17. Posted April 24, 2009, on *NetEase* by a netizen from Shanghai.

18. That the social and the economic are mutually interdependent is a well-established fact in anthropology.

19. Kipnis (2011: 144–45); Stafford (1995: 80).

20. I put "better" in quotes to honor those viewers who took offense at the suggestion that Beijing was superior to Chinese cities such as Yinchuan.

21. Episode 23.

22. Episode 14.

23. Episode 29.

24. Posted April 27, 2009, on *Sina* by cityofangell, a "high-level member," http://club.ent.sina.com.cn/thread-365463-1-1.html.

25. Posted April 25, 2009, on *NetEase* by a netizen from Shaoxing City, Zhejiang Province.

26. Northrup Frye quoted in Geertz (1973: 450).

27. Raymond Zhou, "Why 'Desperate Housewives' Flopped in China," *China Daily,* December 31, 2005, www.chinadaily.com.cn/opinion/2005–12/31/content_536993.htm.

6. INVESTING IN HUMAN CAPITAL, CONSERVING LIFE ENERGIES

1. See, for example, Allison (1996); Field (1995); Rothman (1994, 2004).

2. For more discussion, see Champagne (1992); Gottschang (2000, 2001); Woronov (2003).

3. To be fair, Anagnost's argument is more complex than I portray it to be here. She is sensitive to the lived problem of uncertainty and does suggest that fetishism serves as a strategy for managing uncertainty. But she does not develop this argument, something I intend to do in this chapter.

4. *Rusticated youth* refers to the generation of urban youth that Mao Zedong sent down to the countryside to help modernize the nation, a generation also known as the "lost generation" for having lived through the suspension of higher education during the Cultural Revolution. The admiration expressed here may be the result of official depictions of "this generation as having been steeled in the furnace of the Chinese countryside" (Sausmikat 2002: 278).

5. Ma Jiajue was a Yunnan University student who was executed for a multiple homicide. Liu Haiyang, also a university student, threw acid on bears in a zoo. The reasons for their crimes have been hotly debated.

6. Cultural capital differs from human capital in that the notion of human capital is a product of economic theory and is correlated with the acquisition of education and knowledge. Cultural capital on the other hand is a critical concept describing a form of capital that is transmitted and acquired unconsciously, usually within the domain of the family (Bourdieu 1986). That human capital has been the focus of this chapter bears directly on the argument I am trying to make: we have not paid sufficient attention to the ways in which the people we study are more aware of social relations than we give them credit for.

7. Developing the child's social virtues includes "letting the child have a good personality," "creating experiences of caring about others," creating a "capacity for working with peers," and helping the child "[learn] how to interact with adults" (Wang Lingling 2004: 77–79).

8. See Rosen (1999) for a discussion.

9. Why mothers have more parental intensity than fathers may have something to do with gendered differences in career development—differences that intersect with age and life course (Andrew Kipnis, e-mail, September 4, 2013). Because I do not sufficiently understand the relationship between gender disparities in career advancement on the one hand, and parenting strategies on the other, I can only note this as a worthy issue for future research.

10. In the 1996 edition of the *Xiandai Hanyu Cidian* [Modern Chinese Dictionary] *touzhi* had a three-part definition. In the 2005 edition, a fourth definition was added: "a metaphor for the overexpenditure of energy [*jingshen*] and physical strength" (Ning Yu, e-mail, September 7, 2007).

11. Metaphor is a mode of thought that conceives of "one thing in terms of another" (Lakoff and Johnson 1980: 36); it is a process by which distant things or ideas appear close (Ricoeur 1979: 145); it is the "application of the name of a thing to something else" (Aristotle 1970); and it creates new links between incongruous things (Burke [1935] 1954).

12. It may seem contradictory to argue that the metaphors in this chapter both have a structure of transference and reiterate immanent connections. But I would argue that one does not necessarily cancel out the other, as the incongruity between target and source domain is often only a superficial incongruity, obscuring what may otherwise be an immanent connection. This is precisely the kind of corrective that non-Western thinking offers to the advancement of social theory: the world is not as compartmentalized as we tend to think.

13. "Hit TV Series Strikes Chord with China's 'House Slaves,'" *Wall Street Journal,* November 26, 2009, http://blogs.wsj.com/chinarealtime/2009/11/26/hit-tv-series-strikes-chord-with-chinas-house-slaves/; "The Soap Opera of China's housing boom," *Financial Times,* January 6, 2010, www.ft.com/intl/cms/s/0/dc8393f4-fafa-11de-94d8-00144feab49a.html#axzz1xbnJmoFa; "Chinese Soap Highlights Housing Issue," *Marketplace,* January 19, 2010, www.marketplace.org/topics/world/chinese-soap-highlights-housing-issue?refid=0&utm_source=feedburner&utm_medium=feed&utm_campaign=Feed%253A+APM_Marketplace+%2528APM%253A+Marketplace%2529.

7. BANKING IN AFFECTS

1. As Eric Shouse puts it, "The body *responds* by infolding them all at once and registering them as an intensity" (2005: 9, my emphasis).

2. Zhou Ting is not a pseudonym. Teacher Zhou consented to my using her real name in the hope that I could help circulate her ideas. My landlord, a university professor who often gave me advice, provided the introduction. Teacher Zhou allowed me to observe and tape-record her Saturday night mothering classes and invited me onto this trip. Although I had separate accommodations, I followed the group on a daily basis, returning to Kunming earlier because of other fieldwork obligations. Teacher Zhou referred to me as a collaborator and often sought my

input on her pedagogy, even though I usually had little to say. The children on the trip addressed me as Teacher Kuan, although I did nothing more than observe and follow, often recording with my video camera. Interestingly, a feature published by the *Yunnan Daily* on April 15, 2005, reported that Zhou Ting had "attracted the strong interest and deep investigation of a University of Southern California doctorate" and that "[Zhou's] courage and creativity [will] forever change [*congci gaixie*] perceptions of Chinese child-rearing practices in the West." See www.yndaily.com/html/20050415/news_84_193540.html.

3. Zhou sometimes uses "to read" (*yuedu*) and "to experience" (*ganshou*) interchangeably.

4. The question of how to "treasure" an "odd way of speaking" is raised by Latour (2005: 48).

5. The trip cost approximately 6,000 RMB for over three weeks of travel.

6. July 3, 2004, class.

7. Woronov (2003: 246); Nyíri (2006: 53).

8. See Brook (1998); Nyíri (2006); Strassberg (1993).

9. For premodern literati, "The comprehension of universal principles in the world and in the mind through a combination of empirical inquiry and self-scrutiny," best achieved in nature, "was the key to perfecting the Noble Man and his ability to create social and political order" (Strassberg 1993: 46).

10. In his discussant comments on a shorter version of this paper, presented at the 2011 AAA meeting in Montreal, Massumi noted a surplus of effect over cause. I thank him for pointing out the creation of a "surplus value of life" here and for helping me better understanding the idea that continuity comes in as difference.

11. Zhou named the trip "Heart-Spirit Pillar" (*Xinling zhu*) to give it a child-friendly narrative frame. In her explanation to the participants, the heart-spirit is located within a structure of planks covered by rock, mud, and sand. As a child grows up and receives education, rock, mud, and sand begin to fall away. "Character education," "heart-spirit education," and "*qinggan* education" help to install windows in the structure. Each window has its own name, such as "tolerance" (*kuanrong*) or "care" (*aixin*). Children who do not have windows are selfish and weak. Stimulating the seven senses is the first step in clearing the way for windows.

Zhou used the term *celebrity* in a meeting with her participants back in Kunming, where she reviewed a lesson she had taught earlier about the bigger significance of their trip. She stated, "You are all the celebrities of the future. But I'm not talking about being a pop star. I'm talking about someone who plays a big role in pushing the development of society, in advancing humanity, a talent [*rencai*] who plays a definite role." Then she asked her group, "So tell me again, children, what will we become?" They exclaimed in unison, "Celebrities!"

12. While many experts focus on the child's *xinli*, often symbolized by *xinling*, Zhou takes interest primarily in *qinggan*, *ganshou*, and *tiyan*. But of course there are many instances of overlap; the distinction I make pertains only to emphasis.

1. Lareau (2011: 246); Kremer-Sadlik and Gutiérrez (2013: 148).

2. Cited in Kremer-Sadlik and Gutiérrez (2013: 134).

3. Those who have the opportunity to send a child abroad will do so, because study abroad is seen as offering an escape. For an excellent study of the phenomenon of young Chinese studying abroad, see Fong (2011).

4. I thank Helen Hei Man Kwan, a former undergraduate supervisee of mine, for this example.

5. The putative "mindlessness" of the middle class is mentioned and challenged by Miller (2004) and Ochs and Kremer-Sadlik (2013). To focus on the middle class as a China anthropologist is especially tricky. How could I justify such a focus when the middle class already has a voice (Sun 2012)? The introduction to the volume *The Global Middle Classes* has rightly noted that anthropology "as a whole has traditionally privileged the powerless ethnographic subject as indicative of a more purposeful, 'morally engaged' scholarship" (Heiman, Liechty, and Freeman 2012).

6. This version is quoted in Bateson's essay "The Cybernetics of 'Self'" ([1972] 2000: 334).

BIBLIOGRAPHY

Ahmed, Sara. 2004. "Affective Economies." *Social Text* 22 (2): 117–39.

Allison, Anne. 1996. "Producing Mothers." In *Permitted and Prohibited Desires: Mothers, Comics, and Censorship in Japan*, 105–22. Boulder, CO: Westview Press.

Anagnost, Ann. 1995. "A Surfeit of Bodies: Population and the Rationality of the State in Post-Mao China." In *Conceiving the New World Order: The Global Politics of Reproduction*, edited by Faye D. Ginsburg and Rayna Rapp, 22–39. Berkeley: University of California Press.

———. 1997a. "Children and National Transcendence in China." In *Constructing China: The Interaction of Culture and Economics*, edited by Kenneth G. Lieberthal, Shuen-fu Lin, and Ernest P. Young, 195–22. Ann Arbor: Center for Chinese Studies, University of Michigan.

———. 1997b. *National Past-Times: Narrative, Representation, and Power in Modern China*. Durham, NC: Duke University Press.

———. 2004. "The Corporeal Politics of Quality (Suzhi)." *Public Culture* 16 (2): 189–208.

———. 2008. "Imagining Global Futures in China: The Child as a Sign of Value." In *Figuring the Future: Globalization and the Temporalities of Children and Youth*, edited by Jennifer Cole and Deborah Durham, 49–72. Sante Fe, NM: School for Advanced Research Press.

———. 2013. "Introduction: Life-Making in Neoliberal Times." In *Global Futures in East Asia: Youth, Nation, and the New Economy in Uncertain Times*, edited by Ann Anagnost, Andrea Arai, and Hai Ren, 1–27. Stanford: Stanford University Press.

Anderson, Marston. 1990. *The Limits of Realism: Chinese Fiction in the Revolutionary Period*. Berkeley: University of California Press.

Ang, Ien. 2004. "The Cultural Intimacy of TV Drama." In *Feeling Asian Modernities: Transnational Consumption of Japanese TV Dramas*, edited by Koichi Iwabuchi, 303–10. Hong Kong: Hong Kong University Press.

Arai, Andrea G. 2000. "The 'Wild Child' of 1990s Japan." *South Atlantic Quarterly* 99 (4): 841–63.

Arendt, Hannah. [1958] 1998. *The Human Condition*. Chicago: University of Chicago Press.

Aristotle. 1967. *Poetics*. Translated by Gerald F. Else. Ann Arbor: University of Michigan Press.

Bai, Limin. 2005. *Shaping the Ideal Child: Children and Their Primers in Late Imperial China*. Hong Kong: Chinese University Press.

———. 2006. "Graduate Unemployment: Dilemmas and Challenges in China's Move to Mass Higher Education." *China Quarterly* 185:128–44.

Bakken, Børge. 2000. *The Exemplary Society: Human Improvement, Social Control, and the Dangers of Modernity in China*. Oxford: Oxford University Press.

Barlow, Tani E. 1994. "Theorizing Woman: *Funü, Guojia, Jiating* (Chinese Woman, Chinese State, Chinese Family)." In *Body, Subject and Power in China*, edited by Angela Zito and Tani E. Barlow, 253–89. Chicago: University of Chicago Press.

Bateson, Gregory. [1972] 2000. "The Cybernetics of 'Self': A Theory of Alcoholism." In *Steps to an Ecology of Mind: Collected Essays in Anthropology, Psychiatry, Evolution, and Epistemology*, 309–37. Chicago: University of Chicago Press.

Biehl, João, Byron Good, and Arthur Kleinman. 2007. "Introduction: Rethinking Subjectivity." In *Subjectivity: Ethnographic Investigations*, edited by João Biehl, Byron Good, and Arthur Kleinman, 1–23. Berkeley: University of California Press.

Bourdieu, Pierre. 1984. *Distinction: A Social Critique of the Judgment of Taste*. Translated by Richard Nice. Cambridge, MA: Harvard University Press.

———. 1986. "The Forms of Capital." In *Handbook of Theory and Research for the Sociology of Education*, edited by John G. Richardson, 241–58. New York: Greenwood Press.

Bray, Francesca. 2013. "Tools for Virtuous Action: Technology, Skills and Ordinary Ethics." In *Ordinary Ethics in China*, edited by Charles Stafford, 175–93. London: Bloomsbury Press.

Bregnbæk, Susanne. 2010. "Family, State and the Quandaries of Education: The Tension between Self-Sacrifice and Self-Actualization among University Students in Beijing." PhD diss., Institute of Anthropology, University of Copenhagen.

———. 2011. "A Public Secret: 'Education for Quality' and Suicide among Chinese Elite University Students." *Learning and Teaching* 4 (3): 18–36.

Briggs, Jean. 1970. *Never in Anger: Portrait of an Eskimo Family*. Cambridge, MA: Harvard University Press.

Brindley, Erica Fox. 2010. *Individualism in Early China: Human Agency and the Self in Thought and Politics*. Honolulu: University of Hawai'i Press.

Brook, Timothy. 1998. *The Confusions of Pleasure: Commerce and Culture in Ming China*. Berkeley: University of California Press.

Brown, Hubert O. 1987. "American Progressivism in Chinese Education: The Case of Tao Xingzhi." In *China's Education and the Industrialized World: Studies in Cultural Transfer*, edited by Ruth Hayhoe and Marianne Bastid, 120–38. Armonk, NY: M. E. Sharpe.

Bruner, Jerome. 1986. *Actual Minds, Possible Worlds*. Cambridge, MA: Harvard University Press.

Bruya, Brian J. 2010. "The Rehabilitation of Spontaneity: A New Approach in Philosophy of Action." *Philosophy East and West* 60 (2): 207–50.

Burke, Kenneth. [1935] 1954. *Permanence and Change: An Anatomy of Purpose*. Los Altos, CA: Hermes Publications.

Bu Wei. 2006. "Internet Use among Chinese Youth." In *Chinese Youth in Transition*, edited by Jieying Yi, Yunxiao Sun, and Jing Jian Xiao and translated by Qingling Liu, Zhufen Chen, and Caixia Ma, 215–32. Hampshire: Ashgate.

Carr, David. 1997. "Narrative and the Real World: An Argument for Continuity." In *Memory, Identity, Community: The Idea of Narrative in the Human Sciences*, edited by Lewis P. Hinchman and Sandra K. Hinchman, 7–25. Albany: State University of New York Press.

Champagne, Susan. 1992. "Producing the Intelligent Child: Intelligence and the Child Rearing Discourse in the People's Republic of China." PhD diss., School of Education, Stanford University.

Chan, Wing Kit. 2012. "Employability Does Not Necessarily Lead to Competitiveness." *Chinese Education and Society* 45 (2): 21–37.

Chen Shanyuan and Jianli Zhang. 2003. "Fumu de cuo zai nali" [Where parents are making mistakes]. In *Shisi sui de nühai xiang lijia* [A fourteen-year-old girl wants to run away from home], edited by Shi Daping and Le Fu, 241–52. Shanghai: Hanyu Dacidian chubanshe.

Chen Zhili. 2001. "Yi Jiang Zeming tongzhi 'tanhua' jingshen wei zhidao nuli kaichuang 'shiwu' qijian jiaoyu gongzuo xin jumian" [Under the guidance of the spirit of Comrade Jiang Zemin's "discussion," initiate with effort a new phase in education work in the tenth five-year period]. In *Suzhi jiaoyu de huhuan: Shuo "jianfu," tan gaige* [The call for education for quality: Say "reduce," discuss reform], edited by Li Peng and Chen Li, 1–10. Beijing: Xinhua chubanshe.

Chodorow, Nancy J. 1999. *The Power of Feelings: Personal Meaning in Psychoanalysis, Gender, and Culture*. New Haven, CT: Yale University Press.

Clough, Patricia Ticineto. 2007. Introduction to *The Affective Turn: Theorizing the Social*, edited by Patricia Ticineto Clough with Jean Halley, 1–33. Durham, NC: Duke University Press.

Croll, Elisabeth. 1978. *Feminism and Socialism in China*. London: Routledge and Kegan Paul.

———. 1995. *Changing Identities of Chinese Women: Rhetoric, Experience and Self-Perception in Twentieth-Century China*. London: Hong Kong University Press.

Das, Veena. 2012. "Ordinary Ethics." In *A Companion to Moral Anthropology*, edited by Didier Fassin, 133–49. Malden, MA: Wiley-Blackwell.

Davies, David. 2007. "Wal-Mao: The Discipline of Corporate Culture and Studying Success at Wal-Mart China." *China Journal* 58:1–27.

Davies, Gloria. 2008. "Moral Emotions and Chinese Thought." *Michigan Quarterly Review* 47 (2): 221–44.

Davin, Delia. 1976. *Woman-Work: Women and the Party in Revolutionary China*. Oxford: Clarendon Press.

De Landa, Manuel. 1992. "Nonorganic Life." In *Incorporations*, edited by Jonathan Crary and Sanford Kwinter, 129–67. New York: Zone.

Deleuze, Gilles. 1992. "Ethology: Spinoza and Us." In *Incorporations*, edited by Jonathan Crary and Sanford Kwinter, 625–33. New York: Zone.

Deleuze, Gilles, and Félix Guattari. [1980] 1987. *A Thousand Plateaus: Capitalism and Schizophrenia*. Translated by Brian Massumi. Minneapolis: University of Minnesota Press.

Di Feng. [1999] 2000. "Will There Be Much Difficulty in Finding Employment for 1999 College Students?" *Chinese Education and Society* 35 (1): 28–36.

Dikötter, Frank. 1998. *Imperfect Conceptions: Medical Knowledge, Birth Defects, and Eugenics in China*. New York: Columbia University Press.

Ding Wei. [2003] 2005. "University Student Employment: Insights Gained under Pressure." *Chinese Education and Society* 38 (4): 77–81.

Douglas, Mary. [1966] 1994. "Magic and Miracle." In *Purity and Danger*, 59–73. New York: Routledge.

Elman, Benjamin A. 1991. "Political, Social, and Cultural Reproduction via Civil Service Examinations in Late Imperial China." *Journal of Asian Studies* 50 (1): 7–28.

———. 2000. *A Cultural History of Civil Examinations in Late Imperial China*. Berkeley: University of California Press.

Evans, Harriet. 1995. "Defining Difference: The 'Scientific' Construction of Sexuality and Gender in the People's Republic of China." *Signs* 20 (21): 357–90.

———. 2008. *The Subject of Gender: Daughters and Mothers in Urban China*. Lanham, MD: Rowman and Littlefield.

———. 2012. "The Intimate Individual: Perspectives from the Mother-Daughter Relationship in Urban China." In *Chinese Modernity and the Individual Psyche*, edited by Andrew Kipnis, 119–47. New York: Palgrave Macmillan.

Evans-Pritchard, E. E. 1976. *Witchcraft, Oracles, and Magic among the Azande*. Oxford: Oxford University Press.

Farquhar, Judith. 1996. "Market Magic: Getting Rich and Getting Personal in Medicine after Mao." *American Ethnologist* 23 (2): 239–57.

———. 2002. "Writing the Self: The Romance of the Personal." In *Appetites: Food and Sex in Postsocialist China*, 175–209. Durham, NC: Duke University Press.

Farquhar, Judith, and Qicheng Zhang. 2005. "Biopolitical Beijing: Pleasure, Sovereignty, and Self-Cultivation in China's Capital." *Cultural Anthropology* 20 (3): 303–27.

Field, Norma. 1995. "The Child as Laborer and Consumer: The Disappearance of Childhood in Contemporary Japan." In *Children and the Politics of Culture*, edited by Sharon Stephens, 51–78. Princeton, NJ: Princeton University Press.

Fong, Vanessa L. 2004. *Only Hope: Coming of Age under China's One-Child Policy*. Stanford, CA: Stanford University Press.

———. 2007. "Parent-Child Communication Problems and the Perceived Inadequacies of Chinese Only Children." *Ethos* 35 (1): 85–127.

———. 2011. *Paradise Redefined: Transnational Chinese Students and the Quest for Flexible Citizenship in the Developed World.* Stanford, CA: Stanford University Press.

Foucault, Michel. [1976] 1990. *The History of Sexuality.* Vol. 1. *An Introduction.* Translated by Robert Hurley. New York: Vintage Books.

———. 1977. "Panopticism." *In Discipline and Punish: The Birth of the Prison*, translated by Alan Sheridan, 195–228. New York: Vintage Books.

———. 1991. "Governmentality." In *The Foucault Effect: Studies in Government Rationality*, edited by Graham Burchell, Colin Gordon, and Peter Miller, 87–104. Chicago: University of Chicago Press.

———. [1994] 1997. "The Birth of Biopolitics." In *Ethics: Subjectivity and Truth*, edited by Paul Rabinow, translated by Robert Hurley, 73–79. New York: New Press.

Friedman, Sara. 2004. "Embodying Civility: Civilizing Processes and Symbolic Citizenship in Southeastern China." *Journal of Asian Studies* 63 (3): 687–718.

Fu Kejun. 2005. *Zhongguo jiazhang xinli de tong: Dangdai dalu jiaoyu fansi* [The pain in the hearts of Chinese parents: Contemporary rethinking of mainland education]. Shenzhen: Haitian chubanshe.

Furth, Charlotte. 1995. "From Birth to Birth: The Growing Body in Chinese Medicine." In *Chinese Views of Childhood*, edited by Anne Behnke Kinney, 157–92. Honolulu: University of Hawai'i Press.

———. 2007. "Introduction: Thinking with Cases." In *Thinking with Cases: Specialist Knowledge in Chinese Cultural History*, edited by Charlotte Furth, Judith T. Zeitlin, and Ping-chen Hsiung, 1–27. Honolulu: University of Hawai'i Press.

Garcia, Angela. 2010. *The Pastoral Clinic: Addiction and Dispossession along the Rio Grande.* Berkeley: University of California Press.

Geertz, Clifford. 1973. "Deep Play: Notes on the Balinese Cockfight." In *The Interpretation of Cultures*, 412–53. New York: Basic Books.

Gleason, Mona. 1999. *Normalizing the Ideal: Psychology, Schooling, and the Family in Postwar Canada.* Toronto: University of Toronto Press.

Glosser, Susan L. 2003. *Chinese Visions of Family and State, 1915–1953.* Berkeley: University of California Press.

Goh, Esther C. L. 2011. *Child's One-Child Policy and Multiple Caregiving: Raising Little Suns in Xiamen.* London: Routledge.

Good, Byron. 1994. *Medicine, Rationality, and Experience: An Anthropological Perspective.* Cambridge: Cambridge University Press.

Goodman, Bryna. 2005. "The New Woman Commits Suicide: The Press, Cultural Memory, and the New Republic." *Journal of Asian Studies* 64 (1): 67–101.

Gottschang, Suzanne K. 2000. "A Baby-Friendly Hospital and the Science of Infant Feeding." In *Feeding China's Little Emperors: Food, Children, and Social Change*, edited by Jun Jing, 160–84. Stanford, CA: Stanford University Press.

———. 2001. "The Consuming Mother: Infant Feeding and the Feminine Body in Urban China." In *China Urban: Ethnographies of Contemporary Culture*, edited by Nancy N. Chen, Constance D. Clark, Suzanne Z. Gottschang, and Lyn Jeffrey, 89–103. Durham, NC: Duke University Press.

Graesch, Anthony P. 2013. "At Home." In *Fast-Forward Family: Home, Work, and Relationships in Middle-Class America*, edited by Elinor Ochs and Tamar Kremer-Sadlik, 27–47. Berkeley: University of California Press.

Grant, Julia. 1998. *Raising Baby by the Book: The Education of American Mothers*. New Haven, CT: Yale University Press.

Greenhalgh, Susan. 2003. "Science, Modernity, and the Making of China's One-Child Policy." *Population and Development Review* 29 (2): 163–96.

———. 2011. *Cultivating Global Citizens: Population in the Rise of China*. Cambridge, MA: Harvard University Press.

Greenhalgh, Susan, and Edwin A. Winckler. 2005. *Governing China's Population: From Leninist to Neoliberal Biopolitics*. Stanford: Stanford University Press.

Guo Jinhua and Arthur Kleinman. 2011. "Stigma: HIV/AIDS, Mental Illness, and China's Nonpersons." In *Deep China: The Moral Life of the Person, What Anthropology and Psychiatry Tell Us about China Today*, edited by Arthur Kleinman, Yunxiang Yan, Jing Jun, Sing Lee, Everett Zhang, Pan Tianshu, Wu Fei, and Guo Jinhua, 237–62. Berkeley: University of California Press.

Hardt, Michael. 1999. "Affective Labor." *boundary 2* 26 (2): 89–100.

Heiman, Rachel, Mark Liechty, and Carla Freeman. 2012. "Introduction: Charting an Anthropology of the Middle Classes." In *The Global Middle Classes: Theorizing through Ethnography*, edited by Rachel Heiman, Mark Liechty, and Carla Freeman, 3–29. Santa Fe, NM: School for Advanced Research Press.

Hochschild, Arlie Russell. 1983. *The Managed Heart: Commercialization of Human Feeling*. Berkeley: University of California Press.

Hoffman, Lisa. 2006. "Autonomous Choices and Patriotic Professionalism: On Governmentality in Late-Socialist China." *Economy and Society* 35 (4): 550–70.

———. 2010. *Patriotic Professionalism in Urban China: Fostering Talent*. Philadelphia: Temple University Press.

Hollan, Douglas. 1988. "Staying 'Cool' in Toraja: Informal Strategies for the Management of Anger and Hostility in a Nonviolent Society." *Ethos* 16 (1): 52–72.

Honig, Emily, and Gail Hershatter. 1988. *Personal Voices: Chinese Women in the 1980s*. Stanford, CA: Stanford University Press.

Hsiung, Ping-chen. 2005. *A Tender Voyage: Children and Childhood in Late Imperial China*. Stanford, CA: Stanford University Press.

Hsu, Carolyn. 2007. *Creating Market Socialism: How Ordinary People Are Shaping Class and Status in China*. Durham, NC: Duke University Press.

Hu, Kelly. 2008. "Discovering Japanese TV Drama through Online Chinese Fans: Narrative Reflexivity, Implicit Therapy and the Question of the Social Imaginary." In *Media Consumption and Everyday Life in Asia*, edited by Youna Kim, 114–26. New York: Routledge.

Huang Quanyu. 1999. *Suzhi jiaoyu zai Meiguo* [Education for quality in America]. Guangzhou: Guangdong Jiaoyu Chubanshe.

———. 2001. *Jiating jiaoyu zai Meiguo* [Family education in America]. Guangzhou: Guangdong Jiaoyu Chubanshe.

Hung, Eva P. W., and Stephen W. K. Chiu. 2003. "The Lost Generation: Life Course Dynamics and *Xiagang* in China." *Modern China* 29 (2): 204–36.

Im, Manyul. 1999. "Emotional Control and Virtue in the Mencius." *Philosophy East and West* 49 (1): 1–27.

Iser, Wolfgang. 1978. *The Act of Reading: A Theory of Aesthetic Response*. Baltimore: John Hopkins University Press.

Jackson, Michael. 1989. *Paths toward a Clearing: Radical Empiricism and Ethnographic Inquiry*. Bloomington: Indiana University Press.

———. 1996. *Things as They Are: New Directions in Phenomenological Anthropology*. Bloomington: Indiana University Press.

———. 1998. *Minima Ethnographica: Intersubjectivity and the Anthropological Project*. Chicago: University of Chicago Press.

Jiang Xuelan. 2006. *Poyi haizi de xinling mima* [Decoding the password to your child's heart-spirit]. Nanjing: Fenghuang chuban zhuanmei jituan, Jiangsu shaonian ertong chubanshe.

Jiang Zemin. 2001. "Guanyu jiaoyu wenti de tanhua" [A talk regarding the education problem]. In *Suzhi jiaoyu de huhuan: Shuo "jianfu," tan gaige* [The call for education for quality: Say "reduce," discuss reform], edited by Li Peng and Chen Li, 3–6. Beijing: Xinhua chubanshe.

Jones, Andrew. 2002. "The Child as History in Republican China: A Discourse on Development." *positions: east asia cultures critique* 10 (3): 695–727.

Jullien, François. [1991] 2004. *In Praise of Blandness: Proceedings from Chinese Thought and Aesthetics*. Translated by Paula M. Varsano. New York: Zone Books.

———. [1992] 1995. *The Propensity of Things: Toward a History of Efficacy in China*. Translated by Janet Lloyd. New York: Zone Books.

Keenan, Barry. 1977. "T'ao Hsing-chih and Educational Reform, 1922–1929." In *The Dewey Experiment in China: Educational Reform and Political Power in the Early Republic*, 81–110. Cambridge, MA: Council on East Asian Studies, Harvard University

Keller, Helen. 2004. *Jiaru gei wo san tian guangming* [If I could have three days of light]. Translated by Li Hanzhao. Beijing: Huawen chubanshe.

Kinney, Anne Behnke. 2004. *Representations of Childhood and Youth in Early China*. Stanford, CA: Stanford University Press.

Kipnis, Andrew. 2006. "*Suzhi*: A Keyword Approach." *China Quarterly* 186:295–313.

———. 2007. "Neoliberalism Reified: *Suzhi* Discourse and Tropes of Neoliberalism in the People's Republic of China." *Journal of the Royal Anthropological Institute* 13 (2): 383–400.

———. 2011. *Governing Educational Desire: Culture, Politics, and Schooling in China*. Chicago: Chicago University Press.

Kipnis, Andrew, and Shanfeng Li. 2010. "Is Chinese Education Underfunded?" *China Quarterly* 202:327–43.

Kleinman, Arthur, Yunxiang Yan, Jing Jun, Sing Lee, Everett Zhang, Pan Tianshu, Wu Fei, and Guo Jinhua. 2011. *Deep China: The Moral Life of the Person, What Anthropology and Psychiatry Tell Us about China Today*. Berkeley: University of California Press.

Kohrman, Matthew. 2005. "A Biomythography in the Making." In *Bodies of Difference: Experiences of Disability and Institutional Advocacy in the Making of Modern China*, 31–56. Berkeley: University of California Press.

Kong, Shuyu. 2005. *Consuming Literature: Best Sellers and the Commercialization of Literary Production in Contemporary China*. Stanford, CA: Stanford University Press.

Kremer-Sadlik, Tamar, and Kris Gutiérrez. 2013. "Homework and Recreation." In *Fast-Forward Family: Home, Work, and Relationships in Middle-Class America*, edited by Elinor Ochs and Tamar Kremer-Sadlik, 130–50. Berkeley: University of California Press.

Kuan, Hsin-Chi. 2013. "China under the New Leadership." *Maryland Series in Contemporary Asian Studies* 2013, no. 2, art. 1. http://digitalcommons.law.umaryland.edu/mscas/vol2013/iss2/1.

Kuan, Teresa. 2012. "The Horrific and the Exemplary: Public Stories and Education Reform in Late Socialist China." *positions: asia critique* 20 (4): 1095–1125.

Kusserow, Adrie. 2004. *American Individualisms: Child Rearing and Social Class in Three Neighborhoods*. New York: Palgrave Macmillan.

Lacan, Jacques. 1977. "The Function and Field of Speech and Language in Psychoanalysis." In *Écrits*, translated by Alan Sheridan, 30–113. New York: W. W. Norton.

Laidlaw, James. 2002. "For an Anthropology of Ethics and Freedom." *Journal of the Royal Anthropological Institute* 8 (2): 311–32.

———. 2010. "Agency and Responsibility: Perhaps You Can Have Too Much of a Good Thing." In *Ordinary Ethics: Anthropology, Language, and Action*, edited by Michael Lambek, 143–64. New York: Fordham University Press.

Lakoff, George, and Mark Johnson. 1980. *Metaphors We Live By*. Chicago: University of Chicago Press.

Lambek, Michael. 2010. Introduction to *Ordinary Ethics: Anthropology, Language, and Action*, edited by Michael Lambek, 1–36. New York: Fordham University Press.

Lareau, Annette. 2011. *Unequal Childhoods: Class, Race, and Family Life*. 2nd ed. Berkeley: University of California Press.

Latour, Bruno. 2005. *Reassembling the Social: An Introduction to Actor-Network Theory*. Oxford: Oxford University Press.

Lee, Haiyan. 2007. *Revolution of the Heart: A Genealogy of Love in China, 1900–1950*. Stanford, CA: Stanford University Press.

Leung, Lisa Yuk-ming. 2004. "Ganbaru and Its Transcultural Audience: Imaginary and Reality of Japanese TV Dramas in Hong Kong." In *Feeling Asian Modernities: Transnational Consumption of Japanese TV Dramas*, edited by Koichi Iwabuchi, 89–105. Hong Kong: Hong Kong University Press.

Levy, Robert I. 1984. "Emotion, Knowing, and Culture." In *Culture Theory: Essays on Mind, Self, and Emotion*, edited by Richard A. Shweder and Robert A. LeVine, 214–37. Cambridge: Cambridge University Press.

Li, Jin. 2001. "Chinese Conceptualization of Learning." *Ethos* 29 (2): 111–37.

Li Peng and Chen Li, eds. 2001. *Suzhi jiaoyu de huhuan: Shuo "jianfu," tan gaige* [The call for education for quality: Say "reduce," discuss reform]. Beijing: Xinhua chubanshe.

Li Yuanjun. 2003. "A Growing Children's Book Publishing Industry in China." In *The Publishing Industry in China*, edited by Robert E. Baensch, translated by Zhuoran Zhang, 85–99. New Brunswick, NJ: Transaction.

Lienhardt, Godfrey. [1962] 2008. "The Control of Experience: Symbolic Action." In *A Reader in the Anthropology of Religion*, 2nd ed., edited by Michael Lambek, 302–10. Malden, MA: Blackwell.

Link, Perry. 2000. *The Uses of Literature: Life in the Socialist Chinese Literary System*. Princeton, NJ: Princeton University Press.

Liu Weihua and Zhang Xinwu. [2000] 2004. *Hafo nühai Liu Yiting: Suzhi peiyang jishi* [Harvard girl Liu Yiting: A memoir of cultivating quality]. Beijing: Zuojia chubanshe.

Lock, Margaret. 1991. "Flawed Jewels and National Dis/Order: Narratives on Adolescent Dissent in Japan." *Journal of Psychohistory* 18 (4): 507–31.

———. 1993. *Encounters with Aging: Mythologies of Menopause in Japan and North America*. Berkeley: University of California Press.

Lu Qin. 2001. "Cong 'xinling chenbao' dao 'zhixin fengbao'" [From a "spiritual dust-storm" to an "intimate windstorm"]. In *Suzhi jiaoyu de huhuan: Shuo "jianfu," tan gaige* [The call for education for quality: Say "reduce," discuss reform], edited by Li Peng and Chen Li, 221–42. Beijing: Xinhua chubanshe.

———. 2004. *Gaosu haizi, ni zhen bang!* [Tell your child, you're the best!]. Wuhan: Changjiang wenyi chubanshe.

Lukács, Gabriella. 2010. *Scripted Affects, Branded Selves: Television, Subjectivity, and Capitalism in 1990s Japan*. Durham, NC: Duke University Press.

Lutz, Catherine A. 1988. *Unnatural Emotions: Everyday Sentiments on a Micronesian Atoll and Their Challenge to Western Theory*. Chicago: University of Chicago Press.

Mahmood, Saba. 2005. *Politics of Piety: The Islamic Revival and the Feminist Subject*. Princeton, NJ: Princeton University Press.

Man Qimin. [1996] 1997. "Educational Disrepair and Quality Education Reform." Guest edited by Gregory P. Fairbrother. *Chinese Education and Society* 30 (6): 21–24.

Manning, Kimberley Ens. 2006. "Making a Great Leap Forward? The Politics of Women's Liberation in Maoist China." *Gender and History* 18 (3): 574–93.

Massumi, Brian. 2002. *Parables for the Virtual: Movement, Affect, Sensation*. Durham, NC: Duke University Press.

Mattingly, Cheryl. 1998a. *Healing Dramas and Clinical Plots: The Narrative Structure of Experience*. Cambridge: Cambridge University Press.

———. 1998b. "In Search of the Good: Narrative Reasoning in Clinical Practice." *Medical Anthropology Quarterly* 12 (3): 273–97.

———. 2006. "Hoping, Willing, and Narrative Re-envisioning." *Hedgehog Review* 8 (3): 21–35.

———. 2010. *The Paradox of Hope: Journeys through a Clinical Borderland.* Berkeley: University of California Press.

———. 2012. "Two Virtue Ethics and the Anthropology of Morality." *Anthropological Theory* 12 (2): 161–84.

———. 2014. *Moral Laboratories: Family Peril and the Struggle for a Good Life.* Berkeley: University of California Press.

Miller, Daniel. 2004. "How Infants Grow Mothers in North London." In *Consuming Motherhood,* edited by Janelle S. Taylor, 31–54. New Brunswick, NJ: Rutgers University Press.

Milwertz, Cecilia Nathansen. 1997. *Accepting Population Control: Urban Chinese Women and the One-Child Family Policy.* Nordic Institute of Asian Studies 74. Richmond, Surrey, UK: Curzon Press.

Ministry of Education [People's Republic of China]. 1999. "Guanyu jiaqiang zhongxiaoxue xinli jiankang jiaoyu de ruogan yijian" [Recommendations for strengthening psychological health education in primary and middle schools]. www.edu.cn/20010830/209821.shtml.

———. 2000. "Guanyu zai xiaoxue jianqing xuesheng guozhong fudan de jinji tongzhi" [Urgent notice regarding the reduction of students' excessive burden in primary schools]. http://moe.edu.cn/edoas/website18/05/info4705.htm.

———. 2002. "Zhongxiaoxue xinli jiankang jiaoyu zhidao gangyao" [Guiding outline for psychological health education in primary and middle schools]. http://news.xinhuanet.com/zhengfu/2002–09/26/content_575749.htm.

Munro, Donald J. 1977. *The Concept of Man in Contemporary China.* Ann Arbor: University of Michigan Press.

Murphy, Rachel. 2004. "Turning Peasants into Modern Chinese Citizens: 'Population Quality' Discourse, Demographic Transition and Primary Education." *China Quarterly* 177:1–20.

Naftali, Orna. 2009. "Empowering the Child: Children's Rights, Citizenship and the State in Contemporary China." *China Journal* 61:79–103.

———. 2010. "Recovering Childhood: Play, Pedagogy, and the Rise of Psychological Knowledge in Contemporary Urban China." *Modern China* 36 (6): 589–616.

Nagel, Thomas. 1979. "Moral Luck." In *Mortal Questions,* 24–28. Cambridge: Cambridge University Press.

National Women's Federation and Ministry of Education [People's Republic of China]. 2002. "Quanguo jiating jiaoyu gongzuo 'shiwu' jihua" [National plan for family education work in the tenth five-year period]. In *Gengxin jiating jiaoyu guannian* [Newer family education ideas], edited by Quanguo fulian ertong gongzuo bu, 207–13. Beijing: Zhongguo fazhi chubanshe.

————. 2004. "Guanyu quanguo jiazhang xuexiao gongzuo de zhidao yijian" [Regarding suggestions for the direction of national work on parent schools]. www.law-lib.com/law/law_view.asp?id=121397.

National Women's Federation and State Education Commission [People's Republic of China]. 1996. "Quanguo jiating jiaoyu gongzuo 'jiuwu' jihua" [National plan for family education work in the ninth five-year period]. www.women.org.cn/allnews/110302/39.html.

Nussbaum, Martha. [1986] 2001. *The Fragility of Goodness: Luck and Ethics in Greek Tragedy and Philosophy*. Cambridge: Cambridge University Press.

————. 1990. *Love's Knowledge: Essays on Philosophy and Literature*. New York: Oxford University Press.

————. [2001] 2006. *Upheavals of Thought: The Intelligence of Emotions*. Chicago: University of Chicago Press.

Nyíri, Pál. 2006. *Scenic Spots: Chinese Tourism, the State, and Cultural Authority*. Seattle: University of Washington Press.

Ochs, Elinor, and Tamar Kremer-Sadlik. 2013. "The Good Enough Family." In *Fast-Forward Family: Home, Work, and Relationships in Middle-Class America*, edited by Elinor Ochs and Tamar Kremer-Sadlik, 232–52. Berkeley: University of California Press.

Olberding, Amy. 2008. "Dreaming of the Duke of Zhou: Exemplarism and the *Analects*." *Journal of Chinese Philosophy* 35 (4): 625–39.

Ong, Aihwa, and Li Zhang. 2008. "Introduction: Powers of the Self, Socialism from Afar." In *Privatizing China: Socialism from Afar*, edited by Li Zhang and Aihwa Ong, 1–19. Ithaca, NY: Cornell University Press.

Ortner, Sherry. 2006. *Anthropology and Social Theory: Culture, Power, and the Acting Subject*. Durham, NC: Duke University Press.

Oxfeld, Ellen. 2010. *Drink Water, but Remember the Source: Moral Discourse in a Chinese Village*. Berkeley: University of California Press.

Plaks, Andrew H. 2006. "Xin 心 as the Seat of the Emotions in Confucian Self-Cultivation." In *Love, Hatred, and Other Passions: Questions and Themes on Emotions in Chinese Civilization*, edited by Paolo Santangelo and Donatella Guida, 113–25. Leiden: Brill.

Plumridge, Andrew, and Wim Meulenkamp. 1993. *Brickwork: Architecture and Design*. London: Studio Vista.

Pugh, Allison J. 2009. *Longing and Belonging: Parents, Children, and Consumer Culture*. Berkeley: University of California Press.

Rappaport, Roy. 1999. "Enactments of Meaning." In *Ritual and Religion in the Making of Humanity*, 107–38. Cambridge: Cambridge University Press.

Ricoeur, Paul. 1979. "The Metaphorical Process as Cognition, Imagination, and Feeling." In *On Metaphor*, edited by Sheldon Sacks, 141–57. Chicago: University of Chicago Press.

Robbins, Joel. 2004. *Becoming Sinners: Christianity and Moral Torment in a Papua New Guinea Society*. Berkeley: University of California Press.

————. 2012. *On Becoming Ethical Subjects: Freedom, Constraints, and the Anthropology of Morality.* Anthropology of This Century 5. http://aotcpress.com /articles/ethical-subjects-freedom-constraint-anthropology-morality/.

Rofel, Lisa. 1999. *Other Modernities: Gendered Yearnings in China after Socialism.* Berkeley: University of California Press.

————. 2007. *Desiring China: Experiments in Neoliberalism, Sexuality, and Public Culture.* Durham, NC: Duke University Press.

Rosaldo, Michelle Z. 1984. "Toward an Anthropology of Self and Feeling." In *Culture Theory: Essays on Mind, Self, and Emotion,* edited by Richard A. Shweder and Robert A. LeVine, 137–57. Cambridge: Cambridge University Press.

Rosaldo, Renato. 1986. "Ilongot Hunting as Story and Experience." In *The Anthropology of Experience,* edited by Victor Turner and Edward M. Bruner, 97–138. Urbana: University of Illinois Press.

Rose, Nikolas. 1990. *Governing the Soul: The Shaping of the Private Self.* New York: Routledge.

————. 1996. *Inventing Our Selves: Psychology, Power, and Personhood.* Cambridge: Cambridge University Press.

————. 1999. *Powers of Freedom: Reframing Political Thought.* Cambridge: Cambridge University Press.

Rosen, Stanley. 1999. "Editor's Introduction." *Chinese Education and Society* 32 (4): 5.

Rothman, Barbara Katz. [1989] 2004. "Motherhood under Capitalism." In *Consuming Motherhood,* edited by Janelle S. Taylor, 19–30. New Brunswick, NJ: Rutgers University Press.

————. 1994. "Beyond Mothers and Fathers: Ideology in a Patriarchal Society." In *Mothering: Ideology, Experience, and Agency,* edited by Evelyn Nakano Glenn, Grace Chang, and Linda Rennie Forcey, 139–57. New York: Routledge.

Sakamoto, Hiroko. 2004. "The Cult of 'Love and Eugenics' in May Fourth Movement Discourse." *positions: east asia cultures critique* 12 (2): 329–76.

Sausmikat, Nora. 2002. "Resisting Current Stereotypes: Private Narrative Strategies in the Autobiographies of Former Rusticated Women." In *China's Great Proletarian Cultural Revolution: Master Narratives and Post-Mao Counternarratives,* edited by Woei Lien Chong, 255–83. Lanham, MD: Rowman and Littlefield.

Schultz, Theodore W. 1981. *Investing in People: The Economics of Population Quality.* Berkeley: University of California Press.

Shouse, Eric. 2005. "Feeling, Emotion, Affect." M/C Journal 8 (6). http://journal. media-culture.org.au/0512/03-shouse.php.

✳ Shweder, Richard A. 2003. *Why Do Men Barbecue: Recipes for Cultural Psychology.* Cambridge, MA: Harvard University Press.

Sigley, Gary. 2006. "Chinese Governmentalities: Government, Governance and the Socialist Market Economy." *Economy and Society* 35 (4): 487–508.

Soper, Kate. 1986. *Humanism and Anti-humanism.* London: Hutchinson.

Stafford, Charles. 1995. *The Roads of Chinese Childhood: Learning and Identification in Angang.* Cambridge: Cambridge University Press.

————, ed. 2013. *Ordinary Ethics in China*. London: Bloomsbury Press.

State Council [People's Republic of China]. 1992. "Jiushi niandai zhongguo ertong fazhan guihua gangyao" [1990s program outline for the development of children in China]. In *Zhonghua renmin gongheguo jiaoyu falü fagui zonglan* [Education laws and regulations of the People's Republic of China: 1949–1999], 134–37. Beijing: Falü chubanshe.

————. 1993. "Zhongguo jiaoyu gaige he fazhan gangyao" [An outline for the reform and development of Chinese education]. www.hrbmzj.gov.cn/mzbk/04 /XZF/FLFG/JY/1018.htm.

————. 1999a. "Mianxiang 21 shiji jiaoyu zhenxing xingdong jihua" [Action plan for the vigorous development of twenty-first-century education]. In *2003–2007 nian jiaoyu zhenxing xingdong jihua* [Action plan for the vigorous development of education between 2003 and 2007], 22–39. Beijing: Zhongguo fazhi chubanshe.

————. 1999b. "Zhonggong zhongyang guowuyuan guanyu shenhua jiaoyu gaige, quanmian tuijin suzhi jiaoyu de jueding" [Central Committee of the Chinese Communist Party and the State Council, resolution for fully moving *suzhi jiaoyu* forward]. www.moe.edu.cn/edoas/website18/info33314.htm.

————. 2003. "Zhongguo ertong fazhan gangyao" [Outline for the development of children in China, 2001–2010]. http://nwccw.gov.cn.

————. 2004. "Guanyu jinyibu jiaqiang he gaijin weichengnianren sixiang daode jianshe de ruogan yijian" [Regarding suggestions for another step toward strengthening and improving the construction of young people's morals]. In *Guanyu jinyibu jiaqiang he gaijin weichengnianren sixiang daode jianshe de ruogan yijian* [Regarding suggestions for another step toward strengthening and improving the construction of young people's morals], 1–11. Beijing: Falü chubanshe.

Strassberg, Richard E. 1993. *Inscribed Landscapes: Travel Writing from Imperial China*. Berkeley: University of California Press.

Sun, Wanning. 2012. "Inequality and Culture: A New Pathway to Understanding Social Inequality." In *Unequal China: The Political Economy and Cultural Politics of Inequality*, edited by Wanning Sun and Yingjie Guo, 27–42. London: Routledge.

Sun Yunxiao. [2005] 2006. *Zenyang fudao haizi zuo zuoye* [How to help children with their homework]. Beijing: Beijing Chubanshe.

————. 2006. *Hao haizi, hao xiguan* [Good child, good habits]. Guilin: Lijiang chubanshe.

Sun Yunxiao and Bu Wei. 1997. *Ertong jiaoyu yousilu* [A collection of excellent thoughts regarding child education]. Shenyang: Liaoning remin chubanshe.

Taussig, Michael. 1993. *Mimesis and Alterity: A Particular History of the Sense*. New York: Routledge.

Throop, C. Jason. 2010. *Suffering and Sentiment: Exploring the Vicissitudes of Experience and Pain in Yap*. Berkeley: University of California Press.

Tu, Wei-ming. 1984. "Pain and Suffering in Confucian Self-Cultivation." *Philosophy East and West* 34 (4): 379–88.

———. 1985. *Confucian Thought: Selfhood as Creative Transformation*. Albany: State University of New York Press.

Turner, Victor. 1967. *The Forest of Symbols: Aspects of Ndembu Ritual*. Ithaca, NY: Cornell University Press.

Tylor, Edward Burnett. [1873] 2010. "The Science of Culture." In *Readings for a History of Anthropological Theory*, edited by Paul A. Erickson and Liam D. Murphy, 3rd ed., 30–42. Toronto: University of Toronto Press.

Wan Junren. 2004. "Contrasting Confucian Virtue Ethics and MacIntyre's Aristotelian Virtue Theory." In *Chinese Philosophy in an Era of Globalization*, edited by Robin Wang, translated by Edward Slingerland, 151–62. Albany, NY: State University of New York Press.

Wang, Huaiyu. 2007. "On *Ge Wu*: Recovering the Way of the *Great Learning*." *Philosophy East and West* 57 (2): 204–26.

Wang Lingling. 2004. *Shuli shichang jingji de jiating jiaoyu guan* [Establishing parenting values fit for a market economy]. Kunming: Kunming shi jiating jiaoyu yanjiu hui.

Wang Weiguo. 2001. "Shei zai neixin yu haizi jiaoliang: Tantao xinli jiaoyu wenti" [Who is troubled by their children: Probing the problem of psychological education]. In *Suzhi jiaoyu de huhuan: Shuo "jianfu," tan gaige* [The call for education for quality: Say "reduce," discuss reform], edited by Li Peng and Chen Li, 130–41. Beijing: Xinhua chubanshe.

Wang Xiaochun. 2000. *Zoujin haizi de xinling* [Walk into the hearts of children]. Beijing: Renmin weisheng chubanshe.

Wang, Xiaoyan, and Jian Liu. 2011. "China's Higher Education Expansion and the Task of Economic Revitalization." *Higher Education* 62:213–29.

Wang, Yunping. [2007] 2008. "Confucian Ethics and Emotions." *Frontiers of Philosophy in China* 3 (3): 352–65.

Watson, James, ed. 2006. *Golden Arches East: McDonald's in East Asia*. 2nd ed. Berkeley: University of California Press.

Weter, Karl. [2003] 2004. *Ka'er Weite de jiaoyu*. [The education of Karl Weter]. Edited and translated by Liu Hengxin. Beijing: Jinghua chubanshe.

White, Merry Isaacs. 2002. *Perfectly Japanese: Making Families in an Era of Upheaval*. Berkeley: University of California Press.

Wikan, Unni. 1990. *Managing Turbulent Hearts: A Balinese Formula for Living*. Chicago: University of Chicago Press.

Williams, Bernard. 1981. "Moral Luck." In *Moral Luck: Philosophical Papers, 1973–1980*, 20–39. Cambridge: Cambridge University Press.

Wissinger, Elizabeth. 2007. "Always on Display: Affective Production in the Modeling Industry." In *The Affective Turn: Theorizing the Social*, edited by Patricia Ticineto Clough with Jean Halley, 231–60. Durham, NC: Duke University Press.

Woo, Terry. 2002. "The *Nü-hsiao Ching*: A Handbook on Self-Cultivation for Women." *Studies in Religion* 31 (2): 131–43.

———. 2009. "Emotions and Self-Cultivation in *Nü Lunyu* 《女論語》 (Woman's Analects)." *Journal of Chinese Philosophy* 36 (2): 334–47.

Working Committee on Education, Science, Culture and Hygiene of the Standing Committee of the People's Congress of Yunnan Province [Yunnan sheng renda changweihui jiao ke wen wei] [People's Republic of China]. 2005. "Guanyu Kunming shi chuzhong, xiaoxuesheng zexiao he wailai wugong renyuan zinü jiuxue wenti de diaocha baogao" [An investigative report regarding Kunming's school selecting junior middle and primary school students and the issue of school attendance amongst children of industrial workers from outside]. www.yn.gov. cn/yunnan,china/72628257770504192/20060829/1096859.html.

Woronov, Terry. 2003. "Transforming the Future: 'Quality' Children and the Chinese Nation." PhD diss., University of Chicago.

———. 2007. "Chinese Children, American Education: Globalizing Child Rearing in Contemporary China." In *Generations and Globalization: Youth, Age, and Family in the New World Economy*, edited by Jennifer Cole and Deborah Durham, 29–51. Bloomington: Indiana University Press.

———. 2009. "Governing China's Children: Governmentality and 'Education for Quality.'" *positions: east asia cultures critique* 17 (3): 567–89.

Wu Jinyi. 1991. *Zhongguo renkou suzhi* [China's population quality]. Beijing: Zhonggong zhongyang dangxiao chubanshe.

Yan, Hairong. 2003. "Neoliberal Governmentality and Neohumanism: Organizing Suzhi/Value Flow through Labor Recruitment Networks." *Cultural Anthropology* 18(4): 493–523.

Yan, Yunxiang. 2003. *Private Life under Socialism*. Stanford, CA: Stanford University Press.

———. 2011. "The Changing Moral Landscape." In *Deep China: The Moral Life of the Person, What Anthropology and Psychiatry Tell Us about China Today*, edited by Arthur Kleinman, Yunxiang Yan, Jing Jun, Sing Lee, Everett Zhang, Pan Tianshu, Wu Fei, and Guo Jinhua, 36–77. Berkeley: University of California Press.

———. 2013. "The Drive for Success and the Ethics of the Striving Individual." In *Ordinary Ethics in China*, edited by Charles Stafford. London: Bloomsbury Press.

Yang Dongping. [2004] 2006. "An Analysis of Commidification [*sic*] of Education." *Chinese Education and Society* 39 (5): 55–62.

———. 2006. "Pursuing Harmony and Fairness in Education." *Chinese Education and Society* 39 (6): 3–44.

Yang, Jie. 2012. "*Song wennuan*, 'Sending Warmth': Unemployment, New Urban Poverty, and the Affective State in China." *Ethnography* 14 (1): 104–25.

———. 2014. "The Happiness of the Marginalized: Affect, Counseling and Self-Reflexivity in China." In *The Political Economy of Affect and Emotion in East Asia*, edited by Jie Yang, 45–61. London: Routledge.

Yao, Yusheng. 2002a. "The Making of a National Hero: Tao Xingzhi's Legacies in the People's Republic of China." *Review of Education, Pedagogy, and Cultural Studies* 24:251–81.

———. 2002b. "Rediscovering Tao Xingzhi as an Educational and Social Revolutionary." *Twentieth-Century China* 27 (2): 79–120.

Yeh, Michelle. 1987. "Metaphor and *Bi*: Western and Chinese Poetics." *Comparative Literature* 39 (3): 237–54.

Zhang, Li. 2001. *Strangers in the City: Reconfigurations of Space, Power, and Social Networks within China's Floating Population.* Stanford, CA: Stanford University Press.

———. 2010. *In Search of Paradise: Middle-Class Living in a Chinese Metropolis.* Ithaca, NY: Cornell University Press.

Zhang, Tongdao. 2009. "Chinese Television Audience Research." In *TV China,* edited by Ying Zhu and Chris Berry, 168–79. Bloomington: Indiana University Press.

Zhou Hong. 2003. *Shangshi ni de haizi: Yige fuqin dui suzhi jiaoyu de ganwu* [Appreciate your child: A father's understanding of education for quality]. Guangzhou: Guangdong keji chubanshe.

Zhou Ping and Xiong Yan. 2003. *Guangming de qiyuan: Dangdai xiaoxuesheng jianxin shenghuo jiaoyu zhinan* [A bright start: A contemporary compass for the education of primary students' sound mind and healthy life]. Edited by Kunmingshi kexue jishu xiehui [Kunming Science and Technology Association]. Kunming: Yunnan daxue chubanshe.

Zhu Muju, ed. 2002. *Zoujin xin kecheng: Yu kecheng shishizhe duihua* [Understanding the new curriculum: A dialogue with curriculum practitioners]. Beijing: Beijing shifan daxue chubanshe.

Zigon, Jarrett. 2008. *Morality: An Anthropological Perspective.* Oxford: Berg.

Žižek, Slavoj. 1989. *The Sublime Object of Ideology.* London: Verso.

INDEX

"Accord with propensity and all will go well" proverb, 21, 137
"Action Plan for the Vigorous Development of Twenty-First-Century Education" (State Council), 39
adult diseases, 210
advice for parents: in *Appreciate Your Child*, 74–75, 78–81, 92, 105, 218n12; child-centered, vs. practical wisdom of parents, 61; dissemination of, 6, 42–45, 216n12; positive vs. negative models, 65 (*see also* exemplary models; horror stories); on psychological health of children, 9; on words' capacity to hurt, 145; *yousheng youyu*, 10, 34–35. See also *suzhi jiaoyu gaige; Who Shall Decide My Youth?*
aesthetic development, 217n16
affectivity, 186–207; and accumulation, 196–97; active vs. passive side of, 115; affective economy, 195–96, 201; affective subject, defined, 189; affective turn in social theory, 214n7; banking in affects (*qinggan yinhang*), 186–87, 193–97, 201, 205; via Beijing field trip, 192–97, 199, 202–4, 226n5; and celebrity (*mingliu*), 204, 226n11; of Chinese culture, 199–200; conceptions of, 189–92, 225n1; cultivated in children, 187–89, 196–99, 206–7; and Daoism, 9, 102, 214n7; definition of, 9; and disposition, 62–63, 187, 196; and the economic metaphor, 186; effecting the affective subject,

45–52; and ethics, 187–88, 200, 207; heart as seat of, 102; and heart-spirit (*xinling*), 204, 226nn11,12; and influence, 9, 63, 214n7; of Kunming Lake, 193–94, 197, 199–201, 205–7; of material environment for human ends, 205; overview of, 187; *qinggan*, defined, 186–87, 189, 198; of the Roman Coliseum, 201; of the Summer Palace, 193–94, 199–200; and surplus value of life, 201, 226n10; tactility, 190–91
agency, 8–9, 213n6; agent-regret, 17, 24, 118–19, 221n5; as doing, making, affecting, and assembling, 115, 139; as influence vs. action, 156; moral, 7, 15, 17–18, 139, 151, 207; natural course of action, 23–24; nonhuman, 9, 108, 187, 198; participatory, 215n23; power to affect, 108, 115, 214n7; as separation, 149. *See also* affectivity
Alcoholics Anonymous, 211
Allison, Anne, 13–14, 214n11
Althusser, Louis, 13, 60, 214n12
Anagnost, Ann, 14, 34, 163, 214n14, 218n6, 224n3
Analects, 63–64
Anderson, Marston, 71–72
anger, 98, 101–7, 219n7, 220nn15,17
ANT (actor-network-theory), 213n6
anthropology: context and variability in, 28–29; humanist vs. antihumanist, 8, 20; on the middle class, 227n5; on power vs. agency, 8; on reason vs. emotions, 101; research methodology, 26–29, 201

antihumanism, 8, 20, 115, 128–29, 139, 211
Appreciate Your Child (Zhou Hong),
    74–75, 78–81, 92, 105, 218n12
Arendt, Hannah, 113–14, 117
Aristotle, 103, 222n8, 225n11
Asian financial crisis (late 1990s), 11
Azande witchcraft, 117

Bakken, Børge, 41, 81, 135–36
baldness, stress-related, 210
Bateson, Gregory, 139, 211, 213n6
Beijing, 143, 222n20, 223n3. *See also under*
    affectivity
birth control, 35
birthday parties, 168–69
Book of Changes, 50
Book of Rites, 216n12
"Borrowing Arrows with Straw Boats"
    (*Romance of the Three Kingdoms*), 23
Bourdieu, Pierre, 149, 217n23
breast milk problems, 220n8
Bruner, Jerome, 222n8
Bruya, Brian J., 9
Burke, Kenneth, 69, 183
Bu Wei, 9, 223n3

Cai Chang, 90
Cai Yuanpei, 217n16
The Call of Education for Quality, 66, 69
campus culture, 136
Cao Yu, 96–97
capital, 178. *See also* cultural capital; human
    capital
capitalism, 13, 147, 162, 179–80, 210
care for others/filiality, 104, 181–82
CCTV, 43–44
celebrity (*mingliu*), 204, 226n11
CELF study (UCLA Sloan Center on
    Everyday Lives of Families), 91, 208–9,
    219n6
Champagne, Susan, 35
Chen Heqin: *Family Education,* 34, 43–44
Chen Jialing (case study), 1–7, 17–19, 24,
    26–27
Chen Zhili, 196
Child Psychology, 43–44
children: affectivity cultivated in, 187–89,
    196–99, 206–7; as delicate flowers,

221n19; economic value of, 181–82;
    heart-spirit of (*xinling*), 104–5; Japa-
    nese, 4, 210; naughtiness in, 127–28;
    North American vs. Chinese, 18,
    214n19; parental research into potential
    of, 48–51. *See also* politics of childhood
China (imperial period): Han dynasty, 45,
    111–12, 220n8; humiliation following
    the Opium War, 32–33; Ming dynasty,
    220n8; Qin dynasty, 216n12; Qing
    dynasty, 33–34; Tang dynasty, 55, 100,
    206, 220n11, 221n3; Western influence
    on, 33. *See also* PRC
China (Maoist period), 89–90, 218n2
    (ch 3)
China (post-Maoist period): exemplary
    models in, 81; gender difference in, 89;
    governmentality in, 98–99; moderniza-
    tion during, 7, 10, 41, 99; population
    project during, 10–11 (*see also* one-child
    policy); self-cultivation during, 80;
    socialist construction in, 41–42; social-
    ist market economy of, 39, 46; subject
    making in, 10; technocrats of, 41. *See
    also* PRC
China Tao Xingzhi Research Association,
    98
China Working Committee for Caring
    about the Next Generation, 98, 220n10
Ci Xi, Empress Dowager, 193–94, 200
Clough, Patricia, 192
CNP (Comprehensive National Power), 12
college entrance exam (*gaokao*), 54–55
color perception, 190
communication, intergenerational, 141,
    145–46, 223n13
competition: and disposition (*tiaojian*),
    114–18, 124, 139; and human capital,
    168, 171–77; job-market, 58–59, 116, 182,
    217n20; regime of, 210
Comprehensive National Power (CNP), 12
Compulsory Education Law, 54–55
Confucianism, 80, 100, 101, 102, 214n13,
    220nn11,13
conserving life energies, 172–75, 178–79
contradictoriness (*maodun*), 86, 93, 100,
    102–3
courage, 22, 221

cultural capital, 13, 116, 170, 195, 217n23, 224n6
cultural relativism, 16
Cultural Revolution, 224n4
cybernetic theory of self (Bateson), 213n6

Daoism, 9, 102, 214n7
Davies, Gloria, 220n13
Decoding the Password to Your Child's Heart-Spirit (Jiang Xuelan), 87–88, 90, 100
De Landa, Manuel, 189–90
Deleuze, Gilles/Deleuzian philosophy, 187, 189
Deng, Mr. (case study; Siwen's father), 171–81, 184–85
Deng Pufang, 78
Deng Siwen (case study), 119–22, 175–77, 203–4
Deng Xiaoping, 10, 36, 47
Desperate Housewives (television series), 160
developmental child psychology, 34
dime-plucking gangs (*bamaodui;* gangs that bully for money), 121, 123, 222n6
disposition (*tiaojian*), 110–39; and affectivity, 62–63, 187, 196; and Arendt's philosophy, 113–14, 117; art of, as modality of power, 137–38; "to be with time" concept (*déshí*), 138–39; and competition, 114–18, 124, 139; conditioning power of, 113–14; creating/providing, 113–16, 125–26, 130, 136–39; and educational discrimination, 124–28; forms/meanings of, 110–13; managing tendency, 21, 23–24, 108–9, 114, 118, 138–39, 150, 156, 170–71; moral responsibility for, 115–17; opportunities, taking advantage of, 24; overview of, 20–22, 26–27, 211; as power, 137–38; and power exercised at different scales, 25; as a practical activity, 23–24; and regret/blame, 115–19, 122, 129–31, 221n5; schemes of, 21–26; *shì* (potential born of disposition), 21, 61, 108, 114, 138; story of two monks and a well, 60; storytelling as expressing art of, 62; subjectivity vs. circumstance, 22–23, 26; and teachers' negative impression of students, 124,

133–34, 136–37; waywardness stories, 123–26; Yang family (case study), 126–30, 136–39; Zhang Xin (case study), 119–26; Zhou Huawei (case study), 130–35. See also *tiaojian; Who Shall Decide My Youth?*
Douglas, Mary, 162
Durkheim, Émile, 16

economy of dignity (Pugh), 51, 164–65, 184
education: academic inflation, 59; American vs. Chinese, 18, 47, 214n19; college-degree depreciation, 11–12; conduct texts for educators, 45, 216n12; cram classes, 57–60; creativity taught via subjectivity, 30–32; desire for achievement in, 5; English classes, 52–53; exam-centric, 11–12, 34, 47, 52–59, 105–6, 174; expansion of higher education (late 1990s), 12–13, 58–59, 222n9; fetal, 35, 216n12, 220n8; free, 54–55; gymnastics, 34; homework, decrease in, 208–9; *jianfu* (reducing the burden) movement, 70–71, 218n5; key schools, 106, 217n18; "985" institutions, 217n20; overproduction of college graduates, 137, 222n9; private funding for, 20; reform of, 33–34, 38–39, 46, 106 (see also *suzhi jiaoyu gaige*); rote learning, 32–34, 55; school selection and fees, 56–58, 106, 110, 130, 163; of sensory emotions (*qinggan*), 188 (*see also* affectivity); special-talent, 50–53; suspension of, 224n4; in traditional art, 30–32; "211" institutions, 54, 59, 217n20; vocational, 47, 54, 140, 216n14
educational discrimination, 124–28, 170–71
Education for Quality in America (Huang Quanyu), 30–32, 43, 46, 61
education mama (*kyōiku mama*), 89
The Education of Karl Weter, 78
emotion work, 85–109, 220n15; anger and ambivalence, 101–7, 220nn15,17; color experiments, 107–8; contradictoriness (*maodun*), 86, 93, 100, 102–4; definition of, 86; in a durable context, 107–8; emotion as discernment, 101–3, 108–9;

emotion work *(continued)*
emotion vs. situation, 102–4; gendered, and responsibility, 87–91, 100, 218n2 (ch 3), 219nn5,6; imaginative horizons of parents, 104–6; overview of, 85–87; reason vs. emotions, 101; rule of emotional management, 97–101, 219–20nn7,8; self-cultivation, 100–103, 220nn11,13; and the virtual vs. the actual, 108; Wang Yan (case study), 85–86, 91–94, 99–101, 104, 119, 182; Wen Hui (case study), 93–95, 99–100, 103–4, 119; Zhou Huawei (case study), 95–100, 104–5, 130–36, 139, 158–59

enumeration, 105–6

environmentalism, 135–36, 193–94

ethics: and affectivity, 187–88, 200, 207; Confucian, 80, 101; Durkheim on, 16; and property, 183; of trying, 18–19, 24, 156–59, 164. *See also* moral experience

eugenics, 34–35, 215n2

Evans, Harriet, 214n12, 218n2 (ch 3)

Evolution and Ethics (Huxley), 33

examination regime, 52–59

exemplary models, 74–84, 98; ambivalence about, 81–84; *Analects,* 63–64; battling fate in, 75–78; disability inversion, 74–81; incongruity in, 75, 77; naturalizing potential, 78–81; overview of, 62–65; studying for success (*chenggonxue*), 77; tales of famous men, 78; Zhou Tingting case, 64–65, 74–75, 77–78

existential control (Jackson), 110, 163, 185

Family Education (Chen Heqin), 34, 43–44

Family Education Digest, 44

Family Education in America (Huang Quanyu), 30, 37, 43, 47

family education work (*jiating jiaoyu gongzuo*), 40, 44–45, 216n11

family violence (*jiating baoli*), 96–97

Farquhar, Judith, 25, 101

fast food, Western, 169

fate (*yaohao*), 105–6, 221n20

fetal education, 35, 216n12, 220n8

fetishism, 14, 162–63, 214n14, 224n3

feudalism, 22

Field, Norma, 210

five-year plans, generally, 40–41

flow, 214n7

Fong, Vanessa, 104, 220n17

Fordism, 49

Foucault, Michel, 16, 20–23, 137–38

Frames of Mind: The Theory of Multiple Intelligences (Gardner), 216n15

Fu Kejun, 105

Furth, Charlotte, 220n8

gakureki shakai (academic-record society), 13

gambling, 121, 123

gaokao (college entrance exam), 54–55

Gao Xuan, 141

garden technology, 200

Gardner, Howard, 48, 165; *Frames of Mind: The Theory of Multiple Intelligences,* 216n15

Gates, Bill, 77

Geertz, Clifford, 15, 160

gender and responsibility, 87–91, 100, 218n2 (ch 3), 219nn5,6

gift giving to teachers, 171

Golden Arches East, 169

Good, Byron, 222n8

government, 21–22, 137–38. *See also* disposition

grandparents, 27–28, 215n24

Great Learning, 80

Greenhalgh, Susan, 12–13, 19, 216n8

Guattari, Félix, 189

"Guiding Outline for Psychological Health Education in Primary and Middle Schools" (Ministry of Education), 39

Han dynasty, 45, 111–12, 220n8

Harvard Girl Liu Yiting (Liu and Zhang), 35–36, 78, 215n4

HDI (Human Development Index), 12

heart-spirit (*xinling*), 104–5, 204, 226nn11,12

hero (Greek tradition) vs. good strategist (Chinese tradition), 150

high blood pressure, 210

"high-quality child" subject position, 7–8, 13, 162, 182

history, action/reaction dialectic governing, 23, 215n22
Hochschild, Arlie Russell, 86
hope, ethics of, 18
horror stories, 62–74, 98; disproportion in, 68, 70; incongruity in, 68–74; monstrosity in, 68–70; normative guidelines derived from, 64; overview of, 62, 64–65; of school shootings, 218n4; Shōnen A case, 218n4; of teachers' negative impression of students, 124, 133–34; Xu Li case, 64–75, 78, 82, 95, 116
"How Are We to Be Fathers Now?" (Lu Xun), 34
"How to Be a Parent That Conforms to Current Trends" (Zhang Zonglin), 34
Hsu, Carolyn, 12
Huang Quanyu: *Education for Quality in America,* 30–32, 43, 46, 61; *Family Education in America,* 30, 37, 43, 47; on *suzhi jiaoyu,* 46, 48
human capital, 162–85, 210; and commercialization of childhood/education, 162–63; and competition, 168, 171–77; and conserving life energies, 172–75, 178–79; vs. cultural capital, 170, 224n6; and developing a child's social virtues, 171, 224n7; economic value of children, 181–82; and the economy, 38, 58, 166–67, 170; and education, 13, 58; and educational discrimination, 170–71; and an ethics of trying, 164; family as production unit, 165–71, 179; and gendered division of labor, 91; and managing uncertainty, 163–64, 170, 177–81; and the Marxist conception of ideology, 162; Marxist formulation of, 162–63; measures of, 12; as metaphor, 164, 177–81, 186, 225n10; overview of, 162–65; and overwork, 173, 179; and rules of life, 182–85; Schultz on, 167, ,179; *Snail House* on, 183–84; and social spending, 168–69; *suzhi* as, 163; theory of, 59; and *tiaojian* creation, 163, 166, 171, 182–83
Human Development Index (HDI), 12
humanism, 211. *See also* antihumanism

human technology, 41
Hu Qiuli (case study), 85, 101, 202–3
Hu Shi, 219n5
Huxley, Thomas: *Evolution and Ethics,* 33

ideology: Marxist conception of, 162; mystification argument, 13–14; vs. subjectification, 14, 214n11
Illongot hunting stories, 71
imperceptible change (*qianyi mohua*), 206
imperial civil service examination system (*keju*), 55, 174
incongruity, 68–74, 75, 77
individualism, 148–49, 160–61
inferiority complex, 169
intellectual development, 217n16
Internet use in China, 142, 223n3
Intimate Sister. *See* Lu Qin

James, William, 69, 221n22
Japan, 4, 210
jianfu (reducing the burden) movement, 70–71, 218n5
Jiang Xuelan: *Decoding the Password to Your Child's Heart-Spirit,* 87–88, 90, 100
Jiang Zemin, 47, 71, 98, 191
jieceng (socioeconomic differences), 110–11, 221n1
job-market competition, 58–59, 116, 182, 217n20
Jullien, François, 21–24, 62, 118, 138, 149–51
junior middle school, 54–55, 59–60

keju (imperial civil service examination system), 55, 174
Keller, Helen, 78, 197–99
Kinney, Anne Behnke, 216n12
Kipnis, Andrew, 12, 216n14, 219n5
Kleinman, Arthur, 20
Kuang Heng story, 111, 221n3
Kunming (Yunnan Province), 4–5; information access in, 112; parenting advice disseminated in, 43–44; training classes in, 44, 216n10; urban character of, 3
Kunming Lake (Summer Palace, Beijing), 193–94, 197, 199–201, 205–7
Kusserow, Adrie, 148–49, 159–61, 213n4, 221n19

labor as metaphor, 178–79
Lambek, Michael, 15
land reform era, 76
Lang Lang, 96–97
laosanjie generation, 77
La Perrière, Guillaume de, 21
Lareau, Annette, 51, 208
Lee, Haiyan, 220n13
Lei Feng, 153
Liang Qichao, 32–34
life energies, conserving, 172–75, 178–79
Link, Perry, 68
linmo (copying in the close presence of
    great work), 32
Li Shengchun (*case study*), 94–95, 103
literature: neoliberal self-making fables, 77,
    218n10; socialist realism in, 72, 218n6;
    social reform via, 71–72; Western
    realism in, 71. *See also* narrative
Liu Haiyang, 224n5
Liu Liu, 183
Liu Xiang, 220n8; *Traditions of Exemplary
    Women,* 216n12
Liu Yiting, 35–36, 215n4
Lock, Margaret, 4
Lu Qin (Intimate Sister; *Zhixin Jiejie*),
    66–70, 72–74, 98; *Tell Your Child,
    You're the Best!,* 95, 105
Lu Xun: "How Are We to Be Fathers
    Now?" 34; "Shanghai Children," 34

Mahmood, Saba, 215n23
Ma Jiajue incident (Yunnan University,
    2004), 169, 187–88, 224n5
Malinowski, Bronislaw, 28
Managing Turbulent Hearts (Wikan), 15,
    214n16
Mao Zedong, 224n4; "Talks at the Yan'an
    Forum," 72
Massumi, Brian, 107–8, 190–91, 196, 226n10
Mattingly, Cheryl, 18, 71, 73
medicalization of childhood, 4–5
men: fathers as preferred parent, 91, 100;
    fathers' attitude toward child's educa-
    tion, 52, 171; fathers' responsibility,
    90–91, 219n6; housework by husbands,
    90; Mr. Deng (*case study*), 171–77; as
    represented in a television series, 222n2

Mencius, 63, 102
Mengqiu, 221n3
meritocracy/academic degrees vs. skills
    /abilities, 172
metaphor: *bi,* 180; human capital as, 164,
    177–81, 186, 225n10; ontological, 178–
    79; poetic, 180; pragmatic value of,
    179–81; theories of, 178, 180, 225nn11,12
middle class: American vs. Chinese, 137;
    anthropological studies of, 227n5;
    anxiety of, 58; concerted cultivation
    practiced by, 51; determination of, 27;
    Kusserow on, 159–60; mindlessness of,
    putative, 210, 227n5; *tiaojian* fever
    among, 136 (*see also* disposition). *See
    also* emotion work
Ming dynasty, 200, 220n8
Ministry of Education (PRC), 36; "Guiding
    Outline for Psychological Health
    Education in Primary and Middle
    Schools," 39; on the higher-education
    expansion, 58; "Recommendations for
    Strengthening Psychological Health
    Education in Primary and Middle
    Schools", 39
modeling/exemplars, 62–63, 217n1. *See also*
    exemplary models; horror stories
modernization: economic and subjective, 7,
    209; and the one-child policy, 7; and
    politics of childhood, 37, 42; post-
    Maoist, 7, 10, 41, 99
money vs. wealth, 162
moral coding/diagnosing in narrative, 71–74
moral constancy (Jullien), 23
moral development, 217n16
moral experience: anthropology of moral-
    ity, 15–16, 214n18; of the Balinese, 15;
    definition of, 15; ethical work of Chi-
    nese mothers, 17–18; ethics of trying,
    18–19, 24, 156–59, 164; ethnographic
    literature on, 15; heroin overdose exam-
    ple (*case study*), 17; and judgment, 16,
    214n18; locating, 13–19; at the macro
    level, 19–20; in modern secular socie-
    ties, 16–17; moral development in utero,
    216n12; regret/blame, 115–19, 122,
    129–31, 221n5; and social order, 14–15;
    vigilance vs. being easygoing, 19

moral luck, 16–17, 118–19
mothers: ambivalence of, 104; child-rearing experts on, 87; devotion of, 219n5; vs. fathers, parental intensity of, 225n9; "good mother" subject position, 7–8, 13–14, 162; and grandparents, 28, 215n24; in Japan, 13; proletarianization of, 13; responsibility for fetal education, 220n8. *See also* emotion work
multiple intelligences (Gardner), 48, 165, 216n15
Must-Read for Parents, 43–44

Naftali, Orna, 220n15
narrative: lifting of symptoms in, 73; power of, 71; "rags to riches" stories, 77; "speaking bitterness" genre, 76; subjunctivity of, 222n8; success stories, 77–78, 218n10; waywardness stories, 123–26. *See also* exemplary models; horror stories
"National Plan for Family Education Work in the Ninth Five-Year Period," 44–45
national revitalization, 9–13, 200, 209
National Women's Federation (PRC), 40, 44
neoliberal self-making fables (Anagnost), 77, 218n10
New Culture Movement (1915–21), 34
"1990s Program Outline for the Development of Children in China" (State Council), 39–40, 44, 216n11
the nouveau riche, 122–23
Nussbaum, Martha, 101–2

Olberding, Amy, 63
one-child policy, 6–7, 10, 19–20, 33, 37, 42, 70, 181
Opium War (1840), 10, 33
opportunities, 24, 215n24
"Outline for Reform and Development of Chinese Education" (State Council), 39–40
"Outline for the Development of Children in China, 2001–2010," 39
Oxfeld, Ellen, 214n18

pathway consumption (Pugh), 58
People's Republic of China. *See* PRC

physical development, 217n16
"Pierce a hole for some light" (*chuanbi yinguang*) proverb, 111
plurality, human condition of, 114
poetry, classical, 220n13
politics of childhood, 30–61; American vs. Chinese education, 30–32; blueprints for construction of childhood, 37–52; and developmental child psychology, 34; disseminating child-rearing knowledge, 42–45, 216n12; effecting the affective subject, 45–52; and eugenics, 34–35, 215n2; examination regime, 52–59; excellent births campaign (*yousheng youyu*), 11, 34–37; family education work, 40, 44–45, 216n11; *Harvard Girl Liu Yiting*, 35–36, 78, 215n4; intelligence education, 35–36; media attention to child rearing, 43–44; modern Chinese childhood, 33–37; and modernization, 37, 42; in the New Culture Movement, 34; overview of, 30–33; parenting advice, 42–44; post-Maoist, 34; and potentiality, 48–51; and reproductive health, 34–35; and state legitimacy, 38–39; state plans for raising high-quality children (see *suzhi jiaoyu gaige*); and traditional art education, 30–32; verbs in PRC government policies, 41–42, 216n8; well-rounded development of children, 45, 50–51, 217n16
pop stars, 168–69
Population and Family, 44
population size/quality, 10–11, 12–13. *See also* one-child policy
potential: born of effort, 142, 151–52; naturalizing, 78–81; parental research into, 48–51; responsibility of educators to liberate, 196; *shi*, 21, 61, 108, 114, 138
power: "to be with time" concept (*déshi*), 138–39; force relations, 21, 23, 113–14; of narrative, 71; scalar correspondence of, 25; via texts for guiding conduct, 45, 216n12; *tiaojian* creation as modality of, 137–38; *yangsheng* (cultivating-life) practices, 25. *See also* sovereignty

PRC (People's Republic of China): active verbs in policies of, 41–42; economic reforms in, 33; formation of, 40–41; imbalances/malaise in, 8; mothers vs. fathers in, 90–91; policy-making directives/guidelines of, generally, 40–41; population management by, 12–13, 19–20 (*see also* one-child policy); stigma in, 20. *See also* China (imperial period); China (Maoist period); China (post-Maoist period)

Precious (case study), 1–4, 7, 17–19, 24, 26, 27–28, 214n19

propensity, logic of, 114, 119, 128–29, 138, 156. See also *shi*

psy (Rose), 10, 98

psychological child: emergence of, 6; and fetishism, 14, 214n14; inner life, turn toward, 9–10; vs. psychological soft individualism, 213n4; and social order, 14–15

psychological health: Chinese concern with, 4–5; as an educational issue, 5; and enumeration, 105–6; and heart-spirit (*xinling*), 104–5; Lacanian psychoanalysis, 73; medicalization of, 5, 213n3; via naturalizing potential, 78–81; official policy on, 5; and self-cultivation of parents, 100, 220n11; in the Xu Li case, 73, 78

psychology, popularity of, 43

Pugh, Allison, 51, 58, 164–65

qi (circulatory energy), 9

Qian Xuesen, 41

Qin dynasty, 216n12

Qing dynasty, 33–34

qinggan (sensory emotions). *See* affectivity

"rags to riches" stories, 77

reason vs. emotions, 101

reciprocity, 20, 181–82

"Recommendations for Strengthening Psychological Health Education in Primary and Middle Schools" (Ministry of Education), 39

"Regarding Suggestions for Another Step toward Strengthening and Improving

the Construction of Young People's Morals" (State Council), 188

regret: agent-regret, 17, 24, 118–19, 221n5; general, 118, 221n5. *See also under* disposition

relational sensitivity in children, 6

Ren Baoru, 141

ren shang ren (person above other persons), 12

"Resolution for Fully Moving *Suzhi Jiaoyu* Forward" (1999), 36, 38, 112

respect for children, 4, 6

ritual, 68–69

Robbins, Joel, 14

Rofel, Lisa, 218n2 (ch 3)

Romance of the Three Kingdoms, 23

Rose, Nikolas, 9–10, 98

Rothman, Barbara Katz, 13

rusticated youth (lost generation), 165, 224n4

school refusal syndrome/*yanxue* (sick of learning), 4, 129

Schultz, Theodore, 167, 179

screening theory, 59

self-confidence, 169–70, 179, 210

self-cultivation (*xiushen*), 80, 100–103, 200, 207, 220nn11,13

selfishness, 181

self-realization vs. social recognition, 147–52

self-respect, 169

senior middle school entrance exam (*zhongkao*), 54–56, 59–60

sensory emotions (*qinggan*). *See* affectivity

Serenity Prayer, 211

"Shanghai Children" (Lu Xun), 34

Shanghai Film Company, 144

Shangjunshu, 22

"She who discerns timing and situations wisely is a hero" proverb, 21, 137

shi (potential born of disposition), 21, 61, 108, 114, 138

Shweder, Richard, 87, 107

Sino-Japanese War (1895), 33

Snail House (television series), 183–84

soap operas, 141, 222n1. See also *Who Shall Decide My Youth?*

social/economic realms, interdependence of, 149, 223n18

social engineering, 40–41. See also specific programs, e.g., *suzhi jiaoyu gaige*

social harmony, 5

socialism: capitalism's hybridization with, 147; construction under, 41–42; market economy under, 39, 46; planned economy under, 166–67, 170, 179; realism of, 72, 218n6

social recognition vs. self-realization, 147–52

Song Hua (case study), 83–84

soul (*xinling*), 104, 221n18

Southern Tour (Deng Xiaoping's, 1992), 10, 36

sovereignty, 21, 25

Spencer, Herbert, 217n16

Spinoza, Baruch, 189

spontaneity, 32, 45, 62, 138, 195–96

Spring and Autumn Annals, 25

State Council (PRC), 30; "Action Plan for the Vigorous Development of Twenty-First-Century Education," 39; "1990s Program Outline for the Development of Children in China," 39–40, 44, 216n11; "Outline for Reform and Development of Chinese Education," 39–40; "Regarding Suggestions for Another Step toward Strengthening and Improving the Construction of Young People's Morals," 188

status (class) differentiation, 158–59, 184

Struggle (Fendou; television series), 143

study abroad, 227n3

studying for success (*chenggonxue*), 77

subjectivity: vs. art of disposition, 26; as constructed, 20; and historical circumstance, 22–23; and the political vs. the personal, 9–10. See also Yang family

Sullivan, Annie, 78, 198

Summer Palace, 193–94, 199–200

Sun Yunxiao, 9, 49–50, 98–100, 105

Sunzi (Art of War), 22, 138, 151–52, 156

suzhi (quality): and affectivity, 195; as cultural capital, 116; discourse on, 36–37, 136; and family education work, 40; good parenting's attention to, 9;

hierarchies of, 37; and holistic development of students, 40; as human capital, 163, 167, 169; of laborers, 30, 39; in policy documents, 42; population improvement via raising, 37; psychological, 217n16; school-based efforts to raise, 24, 37–38; and teachers' attitude toward children, 124; in wealthy peasants, 122–23

suzhi jiaoyu gaige (education for quality reforms): and affectivity, 191; ambiguity/contradictions in, 38, 42, 45–52, 214n9; books on, 43; and debate over photocopying (*fuying*), 32; emergence/establishment of, 36, 39–40, 42, 65; vs. excellent births campaign, 36; exercise, 38; Fu Kejun on, 105; goals of, 30–31; historical context of, 36; and holistic development of students, 39–40; Huang Quanyu on, 46, 48; humanism of, 41; and "joys of the literati," 217n16; and junk food, 38; Lu Qin on, 66; morality class, 38; and natural attitude, 11; popular advice on, 10–11; "Resolution for Fully Moving *Suzhi Jiaoyu* Forward," 36, 38, 112; storytelling's role in, 62–64 (*see also* exemplary models; horror stories); on success, 47–48; and symptoms of bad parenting, 73–74; Zhou Ting influenced by, 188–89

symptoms, 73

systemic family therapy, 3, 213n1

tactility, 190–91

"Talks at the Yan'an Forum" (Mao Zedong), 72

Tang dynasty, 55, 100, 206, 220n11, 221n3

technology, 13, 41–42, 200

television, 141–43, 222n1. See also *Who Shall Decide My Youth?*

Tell Your Child, You're the Best! (Lu Qin), 95, 105

ten-year plans, generally, 40–41

theory development, theory of, 63

Tiananmen crisis, 142

tiaojian (conditions; circumstances): biological/physical, 113; definition of, 110–11; of good schools, 112; historical,

tiaojian (continued)
112–13; of human geography, 112; and independence in children, 111; Kuang Heng story, 111, 221n3; of market economy, 112–13; policy documents on creating, 112; social, 112–13. *See also* disposition
time as metaphor, 178–79
Tokyo Love Story (television series), 143
Toyotism, 49
Traditions of Exemplary Women (Liu Xiang), 216n12
travel and affectivity, 199–200
Turner, Victor, 68–69

uncertainty, managing, 163–64, 170, 177–81
United Nations charter on children's rights, 216n11

victory, Chinese vs. ancient Greek view of, 150
virtue: Confucian virtue ethics, 63, 80, 101; cultivated in children, 167, 171, 182; inspirational force of, 62. *See also* exemplary models
vocational education, 47, 54, 140, 216n14

Wang Fuzhi, 22–23, 114
Wang Lingling, 48–49, 112, 164–72, 176–80, 184, 202–3, 206, 224n7
Wang Yan (case study), 85–86, 91–94, 99–101, 104, 119, 182
Watson, John B., 89
waywardness stories, 123–26
wealthy peasants, 122–23
Wen, King, 102
Wen Hui (case study), 93–95, 99–100, 103–4, 119
Western realism, 71
Weter, Karl, 78
Where Are We Going, Dad? (*Baba qu na'er?;* television series), 160
Who Shall Decide My Youth? (television series), 140–61; American influence on, 148–49; aspiration inspired by, 142–44, 147; audience for, 141; on child's autonomy vs. maternal control, 141–42,
147–48, 157; on communication, intergenerational, 141, 145–46, 223n13; as a cultural text, 160; denial of necessity in, 159–61; ethics of trying in, 156–59; on family harmony, 141; goals of, 141, 144, 147; logic of propensity in, 156; male characters in, 222n2; media coverage of, 146; as motivational drama, 141, 143; Pili story line, 147–51, 154, 157; popularity of, 140; on potential born of effort, 142; realism of, 144, 146, 158; on reality as crushing, 153–55; reforming parents via, 144–47; on self-worth, 150; setting/themes, 140–41, 143, 154; on social recognition vs. self-realization, 147–52; on *tiaojian* creation, 150–51, 154, 159–60; viewer responses to, 142–44, 146–47, 154, 157–58; Xiaoyang story line, 152–57
Wikan, Unni: *Managing Turbulent Hearts*, 15, 214n16
Williams, Bernard, 16–17, 118, 221n5
wisdom, 211
Wissinger, Elizabeth, 195, 200
women: emotionalism of, 87, 89–90 (*see also* emotion work); entry into the workforce by, 89; female subjectivity, 214n12. *See also* mothers
working class, 160–61
Woronov, Terry, 36–38
Wu Linlin (case study), 60, 85–86, 92–94, 100, 202

xing (being okay with everything), 79, 218n12
Xue Yi (television series), 76
Xu Li case, 64–75, 78, 82, 95, 116

Yan, Yunxiang, 5, 12
yanfu cimu (strict father and compassionate mother), 83, 90
Yang family (case study), 126–30, 136–42, 159
yangsheng (cultivating-life) practices, 25
Yearnings (television series), 142
Yeh, Michelle, 180
"You don't want to lose at the starting line" saying, 12, 209

yousheng youyu (excellent births, excellent rearing) campaign, 10–11, 34–37
Youth League, 38
Youth Research Center, 98
Yunnan Province, 112. *See also* Kunming
Yunnan University, 54, 217n20

Zhang, Qicheng, 25, 101
Zhang Haidi, 78
Zhang Xin (case study), 50, 119–26, 176–77
Zhang Zonglin: "How to Be a Parent That Conforms to Current Trends," 34
Zhao Baogang, 140, 143, 157, 222n2. See also *Who Shall Decide My Youth?*
Zhao Haihua (case study), 52–53

Zhao Jiajia (case study), 130–35, 158–59
zhongkao (senior middle school entrance exam), 54–56, 59–60
Zhou Hong, 64–65, 76–77, 94–95, 98, 100; *Appreciate Your Child,* 74–75, 78–81, 92, 105, 218n12
Zhou Huawei (case study), 95–100, 104–5, 130–36, 139, 158–59
Zhou Ting, 186–89, 191–94, 196–206, 225–26nn2,3, 226nn11,12
Zhou Tingting case, 64–65, 74–75, 77–78
Zhou Zuoren, 34
Zhuangzi, 23–24
Žižek, Slavoj, 73, 162